The Classical Drama
of India

The Classical Drama of India

Studies in its Values for the Literature and Theatre of the World

HENRY W. WELLS

Issued under the auspices of

THE LITERARY HALF-YEARLY

GREENWOOD PRESS, PUBLISHERS
WESTPORT, CONNECTICUT

Library of Congress Cataloging in Publication Data

Wells, Henry Willis, 1895-
  The classical drama of India.

  Reprint of the ed. published by Asia Pub. House,
Bombay, New York, which was issued under the auspices
of the Literary half-yearly.
  Includes index.
  1. Sanskrit drama--History and criticism. I. Ti-
tle.
[PK2931.W4 1975]   891'.2'2009   74-27429
ISBN 0-8371-7898-3

Originally published in 1963 by Asia House, Bombay, New York

Reprinted with the permission of Asia Publishing House, Inc.

Reprinted in 1975 by Greenwood Press,
a division of Williamhouse-Regency Inc.

Library of Congress Catalog Card Number 74-27429

ISBN 0-8371-7898-3

Printed in the United States of America

To

KAPILA VATSYAYANA

Contents

I / Introduction

THE SOMEWHAT unusual form of this book, which is determined by the character of its subject, warrants a short prefatory explanation. If the truly remarkable Sanskrit drama were more familiar or readily accessible than is in fact the case, a descriptive method would be rightly preferred. But in fact no account that is not concentrated upon fundamentals can be seriously rewarding. The book is, accordingly, a sequence of reflective essays built around a central idea, developing a single thesis from various angles, considering first the features of the Indian drama the nearest to that of the West, and so coming by deliberate degrees to the unique problem posed by a theatre at once spiritually contemplative and theatrically successful. The reader should not, then, anticipate an historical survey or a comprehensive description. The earlier chapters define the aims which this drama serves, the later chapters, the means which the playwrights employ through their manipulation of form and detail.

Few books have thus far appeared in English and surprisingly few in the Western languages as a whole dealing with the Sanskrit theatre in any general terms whatsoever. Studies in India itself have been in almost every sense of the word dispersed, issuing from many hands, appearing in widely different parts of the country, and as a rule treating some highly specialized topics. Feeling, perhaps, that an insuperable wall has been created by the outside world against a current interest in the Sanskrit theatre, the Indian scholars themselves have shown scant interest in interpreting to others the splendors of their dramatic literature. In short, they have written relatively little from the point of view of comparative literature. Meanwhile the attention of the West has been primarily occupied with its own rich accumulations of drama and has, fortunately, made some fruitful excursions into the theatre of the Far East, especially of China and Japan. Even that eminently going concern, the dance-theatre of Bali, has attracted popular attention in the West and recent Hindu dancers, as Shan Kar, whose art dispenses with language, have seemed better carriers of the spirit of India than the great dramatists who wrote some fifteen hundred years ago in a language now almost exclusively academic.

A further obstruction to fresh study by English scholars has been the oblique blessing of an undoubted masterpiece in exposition of literary and dramatic history, A. B. Keith's *Sanskrit Drama*, published over a generation ago. Few Indians have thus far written with equal authority. So thorough a survey, generous in its extent, meticulous in its documentation, and mature in its judgments, apparently has had for several decades the dubious good fortune of discouraging fresh inquiry. Yet his unquestionable erudition notwithstanding, it has gradually become clear that Keith wrote from a number of prepossessions ill adapted to favoring a broadminded or sympathetic view. His defect is partly owing to a commitment to British morality but much more to a conservative view in aesthetics leading him to discover the norm for serious drama in Greek tragedy and the ultimate wisdom in theatrical opinion in the theories of Aristotle. Thus classical prejudices are superimposed upon British principles, the British principles themselves leaning considerably more upon the precepts of Matthew Arnold than upon the practices of Shakespeare. Keith approached Indian drama and poetry with an analytical mind but a cold heart. Within the last forty years, a warmer and more sympathetic understanding has developed. Imagination in the theatre—or out of it—is very different today from what it was in the times of Pinero. The change in the times encourages a new outlook.

Because its method is primarily speculative, this book is organized on lines totally different from those of an orthodox history of dramatic literature. The evolution of the drama from the historical viewpoint is barely mentioned; none of the singularly vexed chronological puzzles are debated ; no author is studied intensively ; no apparatus for scholarly research is proposed and no textual exegesis offered. No philological problems are discussed and analysis is presented more with the English-speaking reader or even stage-producer or man of the theatre in mind than the professional

2

Sanskrit scholar. The writer himself is not of that fraternity but author of several books dealing with poetry, drama, and comparative literature. It is from the standpoint of world drama and world literature that the Indian plays are reviewed, with confident belief that from this perspective they will be found worthy of high place among plays in a harvest comprehending all times and lands.

The first chapter defines both the likeness and difference between English poetic drama, especially the Shakespearean and Elizabethan, on the one hand and the Sanskrit on the other, interpreting the theatre presumably the less well known, at least in England and America or even in such a country as Japan, with reference to that more readily accessible to the modern mind wherever it exists. Comparisons are made not to the advantage of one and detriment of the other but simply to clarify what their respective aims are, where these are alike and where they diverge. The second chapter, more judicial, more pragmatic, and less specialized, discusses the simpler question, why certain plays, unlike others, still have validity not so much for audiences in India itself (though that question is by no means disregarded) as for audiences today throughout the world. A succeeding section examines the imaginative modern plays closest to the Sanskrit in spirit and in form.

Since Indian drama is deeply grounded in Indian thinking, both philosophical and religious, the fourth chapter offers an exposition of the spirit of the drama in relation to that of serious and reflective Indian literature in general. The architecture of the successful native theatre was strictly determined by the spiritual terrain on which it was built, even though no other literary or artistic expression of Indian culture in its final form closely approached that of the stage—no more, for example, than Shakespeare's plays are "representative" of Elizabethan literature as a whole.

The fifth and most crucial chapter expounds the book's main thesis, an exposition of spiritual equilibrium as the goal to which the plays aspire.

Most of them are homogeneous expressions of a highly sophisticated court culture and many, as the masterpiece of romantic comedy, *The Little Clay Cart*, even reflect a well developed urban life. But throughout all the plays the current of religious sentiment runs strong. In a few dramas, the best of which, interestingly enough, lie outside the general pale of Sanskrit, religious feeling and folk-culture actually predominate. A chapter on the sacred drama is

3

primarily concerned with two such works, the famous Tamil play, *Arichandra*, from southern India, and the Tibetan traditional drama, *Tchrimekundan*. Analysis of these should illuminate even the main stream of Sanskrit drama, since they are unsurpassed distillations of religious conceptions in dramatic form.

The Indian drama, it should be confessed, must reveal certain inveterate delinquencies, especially in Western eyes. If as dramatic art it has certain great virtues, so it has also palpable defects. Often both these qualities, ironically enough, arise from the same core of experience and mutually interpret each other. A short chapter, then, examines features which this writer, at least, can only regard as deficiencies in the literature, in the theatre, or in both. There are also qualities that tend to limit the appeal of inferior plays to the land of their origin. Chapter Seven is thus the antithesis of Chapter Two. One deals with plays falling short of universal currency, the other, with those sharing in it.

Three chapters follow offering a general view of the technique of the plays. One is concentrated on a single convention, the use of swooning, from a close study of which much of the aesthetics of the Sanskrit drama can be deduced. There follows a more excursive statement of the style in which the plays were presumably first presented and which must, at least to some extent, be used whenever they are successfully performed. Thereafter is an analysis of the technique of the plays considered primarily as dramatic literature.

Finally, lest the argument remain too abstract, too negative, or too doctrinaire, two major plays representative of the two most important types of drama known to the Hindus are studied with considerably closer attention to detail. The words comedy and tragedy do not apply here though they do give a rough and approximate analogy. *The Little Clay Cart* is surveyed as an example of the *prakarana*, *Rāma's Later History*, of the *nātaka*. The flight of the central chapters into the abstract will, then, be terminated by a landing on the firm surface of specific, material achievement, where the spirit and doctrine are made flesh and thus manifested in the art of a supremely poetic theatre.

Such is the program. Descriptions of scenes are occasionally repeated so that they may be viewed afresh from new angles and ground retraced to facilitate further advances. The succession of chapters each in a sense an essay in itself will, it is hoped, be found appropriate in introducing a subject so full of controversy, of theory, and, for some readers, perhaps, of news. Although the book as a whole aims at critical unity, the ideas constitute a system of component parts which in turn result in chapters measurably self-sufficient. Furthermore, if progress on little-travelled paths should offer some difficulties, these may be eased by the presence, as it were, of landing-places between the stairs.

2 / Poetic Drama in England and India

THE VALUES of comparative literature are unusually apparent as thought turns to the relations, both positive and negative, between Shakespeare's plays and certain masterpieces of ancient drama not far from them in power, the chief works of the Sanskrit stage. There can be none of the routine questions of borrowings, great or small, nor of any direct indebtedness whatsoever. A questioner is induced to face major issues and above all to examine assumptions which any culture at first blandly makes regarding itself and later allows to pass virtually unchallenged. The likenesses between the two theatres define the essentials of all good drama; the differences describe outstanding distinctions between East and West and so delineate the peculiarities of each.

A fair amount of writing already glances at these matters but must be acknowledged as more often than not distinctly superficial. To Englishmen, for example, Kālidāsa is "the Indian Shakespeare;" to Indians Shakespeare appears as "the English Kālidāsa." Such observations are not so much thoughtful comment as an international exchange of courtesy, as if writers from countries substantially removed from each other should lift their hats with reciprocal bows. A certain amount of imperceptive criticism in the West has simply regretted that the Indian classics fail at many points to resemble the classics of the Hellenic world. Since the Indian plays have many more points of resemblance to Shakespeare than to Sophocles, it may be regretted that they have so often been viewed negatively in relation to the Greeks and so seldom positively in relation to the Elizabethans.

It is clear that the Sanskrit playwrights shun tragedy, satire, naturalism, and the particular seriousness and involvement with

6

life that leads to the most convincing character-delineation and to a conviction that some particular problem in life is plumbed deeply. Indian idealism, founded on conceptions of felicity, not of logic, has frequently appeared to Westerners a specious gloss on experience. Shakespeare, Ibsen, Strindberg, Pirandello, even O'Neill and Brecht, generally seem to Westerners to touch life more to the quick than the Sanskrit playwrights. The latter, lacking a profound conviction of evil and consequently a high intensity of moral earnestness, appear to want substance. Westerners, in short, are likely at first to find Sanskrit drama enervating whereas their own drama seems to them invigorating. For a few readers Sanskrit works have created somewhat the stifling sensation that Neitzsche, who professed no religion save that of his own concoction, declared himself to feel on entering a church. There is no violent purgation, as achieved by Greek tragedy. There are none of the flashes of psychological insight or political wisdom which may occasionally be found in the great Scandinavians. Yet, as will shortly be observed, many of the qualities which we do actually value most highly in all western theatrical masterpieces are found in the Sanskrit works together with some which are at once almost unique achievements and still valuable for our modern world. Though lacking the social criticism of Ibsen or Shaw, or, for that matter, of Molière, Indian drama has great aesthetic attraction and many spiritual values commonly forgotten in the present-day world but found, perhaps, in Calderón, though still more abundantly on the medieval stage, so often dedicated to the theme of man's redemption.

As initial comment it must be admitted that our view of the European stage as it has existed for long periods of time is much more comprehensive than any available view of the great Indian theatre which flourished for approximately the first thousand years of the Christian era. To be sure, our record for the European "dark ages" is dim so far as the stage is concerned but for other and more fruitful periods extensive documentation, of course, exists. Very little now is known of the Indian stage before Christ and so far as we know there is little worth cherishing in the long period from 1000 A.D. to the beginning of the present century. More important from the critical standpoint, the Hindus distinguished sharply and no doubt rightly between their serious and their frivolous theatre, their poetic drama and their theatrical entertainment.

The extreme fluidity of Indian thinking notwithstanding, the

7

drama shows no consciously opposed philosophies of life, as these are projected, for example, in that supreme spectacle of dramatized philosophical debate, Goethe's *Faust*. Especially in the field of comedy, Gupta sophistication notwithstanding, there are no formulations of specifically comic attitudes, as Aristophanes' sensualism, Cervantes' romantic dualism, Molière's urbane materialism, or Machiavelli's calculated satire. Comedy in the European sense is almost as far removed from the Indian consciousness as tragedy. Farce and broad erotic humor were indeed popular but, as may readily be supposed, failed to produce memorable dramatic literature. To all intents and purposes Indian classical drama means the serious plays all very broadly speaking in the vein of European "tragicomedy," commencing with Bhāsa and concluding several centuries later with Bhavabhūti. The religious and philosophical outlook and the aesthetic forms associated with this tradition remain to a remarkable degree constant. At least for critical purposes Indian drama is, then, more of a piece than the European. Not only does it represent a considerably less extended geographical and temporal realm than Western drama; it represents a much less diversified terrain critically considered. Dramatic thought in the West tends to be divisive, throwing off ever new forms, experimenting restlessly, reflecting the intellectual and spiritual conflicts within Europe itself. It is the same with drama as with religion. The West lives in more violent strife. Whereas Westerners are loath to permit affiliation with more than a single religion or school of philosophy, tending toward combative fanaticism and a logical consistency that society itself finds it difficult to maintain, Easterners readily allow the individual to espouse more than one religious cult or philosophical system.

Indians are by no means greatly concerned with logic or with the individual's private problem of spiritual unity or harmony, in the manner of Strindberg or O'Neill; their desire is for a religiously conceived and universal goal of spiritual equilibrium. Though highly conscious of the individual mind, the Eastern thinker is reluctant to see each person as a private or clinical case, preferring to view every man in terms of his access to the universal. A picturesque analogy comes to mind in the instance of nudity and costume. A tropical land at least permits the simplicity of nudity where, rather roughly speaking, all persons are alike. Northern lands, on the contrary, requiring costume for the sake, not of decoration, but of warmth, invite all the infinite variety of which dress is capable. By and large, Western drama deals with struggle to attain unity or, in other words, with images of forces competing for dominance; Eastern drama celebrates the imagined attainment of unity. What appears stimulating to one culture seems dissonant to the other; what seems harmonious to one, seems insipid to the other. The aims of the two civilizations are different and so are the images in which each finds satisfaction.

That the problems of life are essentially beyond solution also may be the grim conclusion of serious tragic drama in the West. That the contradictions in experience are themselves amusing, keeping life in brisk motion, may be the diverting conclusion of serious, witty comedy in the West. The East attaches little importance to contradictions except insofar as opposites fall naturally into and equilibrium resembling the patterns of a balanced dance.

Of all forms of expression in the West the drama has most fully realized the force of irony. Western tragedy presents an ironical impasse at which the soul grieves; Western comedy, an ironical angularity at which the mind smiles. The theory of irony encompasses the greater part of both comedy and tragedy; tragic irony is of the essence of Aeschylus, Sophocles and Euripides; comic irony, or the saltiness in the spectacle of one or more persons acting inconsistently, also begins with the Greeks but grows more conspicuous as time advances. The paradoxes inveterate in Christianity, with ideals so far beyond earthly realization, provide the core of medieval comedy, belatedly to fructify and culminate in such supreme humorous works as *Don Quixote, Orlando Furioso, Gargantua,* and Shakespeare's comedy, reaching its apogee in the Falstaff episodes. The Hindus are as broad-minded as the Christians, possibly going to even greater extremes and experiencing life in even greater diversity or contradiction. No culture, at least, has been either more ascetic or more sensual. That man is basically both angel and beast troubles the West ; on the contrary, our divided human nature enables the East to experience aesthetic pleasure in discovering life arranged so symmetrically. The stage in the West records humanity in its striving, that of the East, in its repose. Objectively considered, theatres of both regions arrive at much the same report on the facts of human nature but subject these facts to radically different interpretations. The Eastern thinker marvels that the West can be so troubled by the storms on life's surface; the Western thinker marvels that the East can remain so blandly submerged in contemplation. The Western dramatist is a general deploying life's forces into a battle, the Eastern dramatist, a choreographer arranging them in a dance. One drama exploits free will, the other, destiny; one exploits tension, the other conspires to eliminate it.

Lacking in the background of their thinking a clearly established view of the Sanskrit stage, most European or American critics of their native drama lose sight of the primary importance of this tension as the goal to which their dramatists aspire. For the present investigation Shakespeare holds a sufficiently central place and provides the most conspicuous examples. In comedy and at times even in tragedy there is, for instance, a persistent development of the classical irony, *odi et amor*.

> I hate and love—ask why—I can't explain;
> I feel it's so, and feel it racking pain.

Othello might have used the very words of Catullus and so might Beatrice or Benedick, Claudia or Isabella, Katharine or Petruccio, Antonio or Viola-Sebastian, and all those many characters engaged in one form or another of lovers' quarrels. Hamlet loves and hates his mother, Brutus loves and hates Caesar, Coriolanus loves and hates Rome, Henry IV loves and all but despises his son and heir, King Lear helplessly vacillates between love and hatred of his youngest daughter, once his favorite child. Of course there is always some form of spiritual relief when the play reaches its end but the play itself is propelled by these tensions. So the feud between the Montagues and the Capulets is a tragic force alive in the air breathed by all persons in *Romeo and Juliet*. There may even be a profoundly skeptical element congenial to forceful Western drama, as in *Troilus and Cressida*, where the play calls sharply in question the values of both romantic love and military grandeur. Rival claims of the worship of pleasure and political power are the coordinates on which are suspended the tragic tales of Antony and Octavius, Richard II and Bolingbroke. Similarly, the Christian world-view of human life upon earth as a struggle between the evil and the good, body and soul, dominant in such melodramas as *Richard the Third* and *Macbeth*, produces a very different type of play from a philosophy that integrates universal forces, manifest alike in plant, animal and man, with the dramatic conflicts better symbolized by the rotation of the seasons, wet or dry, hot or cold, than by essentially moral conflicts. The spirit of Western drama manifested itself synchronously with the ritual of competitive sport as practised in ancient Greece. In its origins all drama may well be indebted to dancing but European dramatic tradition was cross-fertilized from several other sources, among them being a particularly strong conviction of contention or strife as lying at the root of human experience. Competitive evolution or progress takes the place of harmonious rotation. European drama moves further from the abstractions of dancing than does that of Asia and places a greater emphasis on the excitement of its narrative, on the hostility of rival forces ; Eastern drama remains more abstract, closer also to the spirit of music, and places far stronger emphasis on the repose experienced through the contained work of art. European drama is work in progress, Indian drama, work in fulfilment.

The relative repose expressed by the Sanskrit stage can scarcely be conceived by the Western mind without special imaginative exertion or, to state the case differently, without a studied resignation to the spell of the Asiatic work. The Westerner must approach this exotic flowering with an active mind and a receptive heart. Although Sanskrit poetic drama observes a certain decorum, avoids tragedy, and shuns indignity, it cannot be strictly described as optimistic. The play must, to be sure, have an happy ending and even at its most serious be tragicomedy. Yet it is much more revealing to observe not that the ending is fortunate but that the entire work is of a piece and connotes spiritual composure. The Sanskrit drama begins and ends with prayer, a petition for human welfare. Yet the most illustrious of the plays, *Shakuntalā*, ends with the petition that the speaker, who comprehensively personifies the dramatis personae, the actors as individuals, and the entire audience, shall not be born again on earth. This petition expresses, at least from the Western point of view, an outlook far from optimistic. Emphasis falls not on optimism but on composure. This is the mode of Karna in Bhāsa's great play, *Karna's Task*, where Karna is depicted as the hero, following strictly in the steps of the *Bhagvad-Gītā*, walking serenely to his doom. Death impends but with it neither tragedy nor transfiguration, neither calamity nor apotheosis. Tragedy signifies purgation achieved through images of strong suffering having a more or less violent impact on the audience. Tragicomedy as commonly practised and understood in Europe implies an optimistic ending. Indian drama embraces neither conception. It is all of a piece, from beginning to end, circular as a flower is circular, and connotes spiritual peace. Its serenity is religious and austere, not sentimental or romantic.

The violence of *Hamlet* is in keeping with the tragic conception in Aeschylus, the agony in *King Lear*, with the bleakness occasionally encountered in Euripides and his imitator, Seneca. No play can be less like a Sanskrit drama than *King Lear*, so far as the view of life is concerned. *Shakuntalā* is the serenest daylight, *King Lear*, a midnight storm. True, the evil suffer in *King Lear*, but the good suffer most in the comprehensive misery ; the mad king bearing the most loving of daughters dead in his arms stands in the final tableau at the antipodes from Dushyanta clasping his son for the first time to his breast. One play is disillusion, the other, illusion ; one depicts how desperate star-crossed men and women can be, the other, not life as actually serene but serenity as its jewel, the hard-won gem found in the foreheads of those blessed by the god, the ultimate· spell controlling the ills of life. No Hindu supposed the actual course of human events to be reflected on the stage. There was no romantic misreading of existence. The stage, on the contrary, was a ritual to frustrate the malignity of events, no literal report or mere commentary on this malignity. The theatre was one of the disciplines of contemplation by which peace was established within the soul. As previously urged, the two philosophies by no means differ in their interpretation of the basic human condition. They differ only in the manner of confronting it. One implies the value of the intelligence and the will to ameliorate the forces of evil ; the other implies the power of the spirit to transcend them.

Vast as are the differences between the spirit or inner meaning of the two dramatic literatures, the common ground between Shakespeare on the one hand and Bhāsa, Kālidāsa and Bhavabhūti on the other is even more striking. The differences are for the most part spiritual, philosophical and moral, the similarities, for the most part distinctly aesthetic. Many of the precepts in Indian criticism suggest a ready means to appraise this relation. Sāgaranandin, for example, quotes ancient authority to support the view that the entire play develops from a single seed and is, in other words, an organism. He also quotes authority for the established view that the best play harmonizes the greatest number of disparate parts. These two propositions fully accord with Shakespeare's practice. The containment in a single play, for example, of verse and prose, of characters and speech from all levels of society, of free movement for the imagination, of pantomime and poetry in that marvelous wedlock of the Elizabethan poetic stage, all witness a common ground between the two great traditions. Shakespeare and Sūdraka are both of imagination all compact. *The Little Clay Cart*, in fact, seems even to enlarge upon the spacious freedom enjoyed by the Elizabethan stage.

A Midsummer-Night's Dream has been the mòst popular of Shakespeare's plays in India. For this there need be small wonder, since it is a festival drama, highly fantastic, with little that can be regarded as serious action, with fate vastly more important than will, and a synthesis of gods and mortals, princes and poor tradesmen, fairies from folklore and deities from ancient mythology, dance and pantomime, philosophy and nonsense, naturalism and supernaturalism, colloquial prose and lyric verse, easy dialogue and the most artificial poetry. As witnessed here, Elizabethan practice actually stands much closer to the Sanskrit of Sūdraka or Bhavabhūti than to the Greek of Sophocles or the French of Racine.

Many theatrical conventions familiar to Shakespeare are equally familiar to Indian playwrights. Like the great Elizabethan, they enjoy conventions of invisibility, soliloquy, asides, plays within plays, off-stage voices, elaborate pantomime, song and dance, background music, poetry that paints scenery for the mind's eye only, highly prominent stage properties, overheard conversations, a stage divided into two parts, and time and space represented symbolically and with the utmost freedom. On both stages costume is treated symbolically and color symbolism is conspicuous.

The structure of the act as a unit and the alternation of minor with major groups of characters are often surprisingly similar on the two stages. Few instances illustrate this better than the Shakespearean play farthest from Sanskrit drama in its philosophical content, *King Lear*. Sanskrit practice provides that as prologue to each act, or *viskambhaka*, minor characters shall exercise a choral function, describing what has occurred or what is occurring off-stage and introducing the more important episodes to follow. This is precisely the method employed by Shakespeare. The first act of

King Lear begins with seemingly casual talk by Gloucester, Kent and Edmund, though the very first words, reporting a surprising change of mind on the king's part, subtly lead the way to the ensuing episode. Act Two commences with more prose, a talk between Edmund, Curan, Edgar and Gloucester. Much is learned here of importance for the action but little or nothing takes place. Act Three begins with a conversation between an unnamed gentleman and Kent regarding the storm, again preparing the way for Lear's entrance. The prologue to Act Four again paints the physical scene, this time shifting the picture to a point near Dover. Speakers are an old man, Gloucester and Edgar. Act Five also begins slowly and at a relatively low pitch. Speech is essentially colloquial. Edmund and Regan are talking. The act itself consists of over four-hundred lines. Lear enters only seventy lines before the play ends. Pressure steadily mounts from its point of least intensity to a climax. Indian drama is less concerned with climax and surprise than the melodramatic Elizabethan stage but the aesthetic consideration shaping the introduction of the acts reveals a common strategy in both the Sanskrit and the Elizabethan theatre.

Each school of playwriting represents court drama that never-theless has by no means lost touch with popular sentiment and with folklore. The lighter Indian plays much resemble the lighter Eliza-bethan. So the witty court comedy by Kālidāsa, *Mālavikāgnimitra*, shares very much the spirit of John Lyly's *Endimion* or Shakes-peare's *Love's Labour's Lost*. The same vein of eclecticism is in each. Courtly as Shakespeare's play is, it ends in a folk-dance allegorical of winter and summer and the similarly folkloristic elements in Kālidāsa's most sophisticated play are unmistakable, especially in the episode of the tree blossoming at the touch of the heroine's foot.

Shakespeare's most impressive scenes have the symbolic force of all great poetry, as do all major scenes in the Hindu masterpieces. Both the likeness and the difference that appear as a critical view places side by side on the one hand the roles of Prince Hal and Fal-staff and on the other the parts of the typical Indian hero-prince and his companion, the *Vidūsaka*, point in these directions. Prince Hal, at least in his later phase, represents true nobility ; his com-panion, the love of the flesh. Each of the four figures rises to symbolic stature. But the contrasts in the thought of the two playwrights remain equally sharp. Although the aesthetic principles governing form and execution are much the same in both literatures, a wide philosophical difference exists, a difference also governing much in the spirit and detail of the two works. Prince Hal and Falstaff are never really true or intimate friends and in the end break off all pretense to such a relationship, Hal chastizing his former companion from the standpoint of a severe and hostile judge. We learn that Falstaff dies with, if not precisely of, a broken heart. In cold blood the Prince, at last become king, declares that he has merely been using Falstaff to his own ends as an experiment in the exploration of evil. Flesh and soul in the end part company. Prince and *Vidūsaka* on the Indian stage in quite the contrary manner are at all times true and devoted friends. Flesh and spirit are not at war, nor are pleasure and philosophy. Falstaff is portrayed as a hypocrite, as one who pretends to virtue and practises vice. From several aspects he remains the quintessence of comic irony, a ridiculous butt for the humor of others. But the *Vidūsaka* is a Brahman, a priestly man, the antithesis, to be sure, of the true idealist or ascetic, but throughout fastidiously presented by the playwright with a friendly eye. Though no doubt absurd, he is in no sense evil ; he retains his gift for prophecy and truth-telling ; he is a sincere, loving and loyal friend ; much as he relishes his food, he has no ridiculous commerce with the opposite sex, nor does his warm friendship imply the burden of homosexuality. Both pairs are studied portraits in contradiction. But whereas the two portraits by the English poet add satire to humor, the kindlier humorous pictures by the Indian remain untouched by satire or Attic salt. The Indian dish may be too sweet for the Western palate but is at least consistent with all the rest of the Indian meal and with the purpose to which its far more ideal or spiritual banquet is designed.

The impression of serenity conveyed by major Sanskrit drama derives first of all from a phenomenal solicitude for form. This attention on the playwright's part is at least indicated in the almost unprecedented elaboration of the rules of composition laid down in critical writings surviving from several periods of Indian theatrical history. Like other rules or laws, these may not always have been observed but there seem to have been helpful rules or at least precepts for almost every conceivable dramatic occasion. As result of this Hindu scholasticism, an extreme decorum was certainly maintained. The formal disposition of events, as in the quartet constituting the unrivalled fourth act of *Rāma's Later History*, illustrates this extreme formality. The entire manner of composition suggests a rigorous choreography. Each theme or segment in the work balances another. Though the playwright's sophistication often tends to conceal his artistry from casual glances, deeper inspection always reveals the rigorous organization. These conditions are best illustrated in that most elaborated of dramas, the humorously named *The Little Clay Cart*. So intricate and yet firm is the structure here that an entire essay is required to cover merely the surface of the subject and in this review a bare reference must suffice. The formal beauty of such works as *The Vision of Vāsavadattā Nāgānanda, Mudrārāksasa*, or *Karna's Task* can scarcely be exaggerated. Much of the celebrity justly won by *Shakuntalā* derives from a flower-like perfection in the execution ; no line or phrase in the play is wasted. The dismemberment of this masterpiece committed in most modern productions in the interests of a time-schedule or other theatrical contingency has invariably resulted in serious disfiguration. The play's true value can only be seen when the whole is presented. No doubt an abridged version may please its audience but the audience at such a production is happily, perhaps, unaware of how much is missing.

Part of the serenity is due to the pervasive idealization. The worst of human nature is no more admitted to the Sanskrit stage than it is invited to enter the chancel of a church. Suffering is, of course, depicted freely, but never in its coarser or more material forms. Thus torture, disfigurement, purely physical discomfort, as developed to so extraordinary and shocking a degree in the great third act of *King Lear*, are unthinkable in the Indian theatre. Moral obliquity is also considerably circumvented and moral indignation as known to Juvenal in his *Satires*, to Terence in his plays, or to Shakespeare, Calderón, Racine, Ibsen, Schiller, or even Machiavelli, is conspicuously absent. Indian drama has neither the salt of Attic comedy nor the gall of Attic tragedy. Clearly, its province is not to present the uglier facts of life. Philoctetes' wound, Cassandra's madness, Hercules' torment, are all unknown. No hero envelops himself in a poison robe or is consumed in a raging fire. Not only does no hero die on the stage; none dies off the stage, as in Greek tragedy.

The villain in the Western understanding of the word is simply not to be found. True, Rāvana abducts a heroine but this Lord of Darkness has much more nobility than an Iago or a Richard Third, and is by no means condemned and executed as Shakespeare condemns and executes Macbeth. The suffering, which is profusely depicted but never distressingly realistic or physical, springs far more from the malignity of fate than from that of erring man. The leading characters are regarded as worthy of admiration and complete sympathy, not as either evil or stupid, for if evil, then we might have tragedy or melodrama, and if stupid, satire or the comedy of manners. Once Rāma declines to speak a harsh word on the ground that it is ignoble to speak ill of any man. His wicked stepmother is no doubt malign, if not quite sinister, an enemy of the forces of light. Yet even she is exonerated. By a slip of the tongue she condemns Rāma and Sītā to ten years of exile; she had intended to say, ten days ! This is no Lady Macbeth ! The grim ascetic whose curse against Shakuntalā is root of all the woe in Kālidāsa's masterpiece is really a good man and is even described as "a great saint," and that without a trace of irony. He is only irascible and short of temper. At the request of a pair of young ladies he greatly moderates his curse and it is surely not his fault that Shakuntalā loses her ring of recognition. Moreover, this unhappy ascetic is never seen on the stage ; we only hear a few of his words while he himself remains invisible. He is more talked about than heard. Shakuntalā's faults are extremely venial and at no time deliberate or even conscious. Grieving for her privation in the absence of her lover-king, she simply does not hear the loud-voiced ascetic calling to her for hospitality. The ring falls from her finger unperceived while she performs a pious act of ablution. Similarly, in Kālidāsa's *Vikramorvacī*, Urvacī strays into a forbidden area of the forest without being in the least aware of what she is doing. The ravisher in the first act of this play is neither seen nor heard. In *Nāgānanda*, Garuda's threats and cruelty seem utterly effaced by his complete repudiation of his evil practices and restitution of all the blessings that his evil conduct has once denied to man or beast. Garuda is no more to be morally condemned for what he has done than if he were an animal or, for that matter, the divine bird that he actually is. In the end his magnanimity is celebrated, not his vice condemned. The audience is to understand that in all that he has done he has only been fulfilling destiny. He is not a free agent ; he embodies or represents the forces within the universe that promote hostility. These are unpleasant truths or facts in the nature of things which the sage in meditation transcends, overriding them by the strength of his vision. The medieval Christian drama instructs its audience how sins are punished ; the nineteenth-century drama how evils may be ameliorated or even removed ; the Indian drama, following a far different course, largely rejects the conception of sin and underplays the potency though not the existence of evil. Its heart lies in the power of contemplation, which triumphs over all obstacles regardless of their virulence. A too casual Western reader may grossly mistake Hindu idealism for romantic sentimentality, for the belief that all's well with the world. The reader educated in the naturalistic tradition observes the conduct of a Sanskrit play and promptly declares it a deceitful flattery of life, a puerile evasion of the harsh facts of existence. But, as previously urged, the Indian playwright never proposes to report the facts of life. He proposes, as the author of the *Bhagvad-Gītā*, to show a discipline by which man as a contemplative being rises superior to the sordid realities of existence.

To some Western eyes the Sanskrit drama will be vitiated or even completely invalidated by its philosophical position. It will appear a weak evasion of reality. This essay is scarcely the place to advance a conclusive answer to the problem. But in the interests of art, if not of wisdom, it seems fair to suggest that the two attitudes, though certainly in a sense opposites, are not in practice mutually exclusive. Quite possibly the religious outlook of the East and the secular outlook of the West may coexist, side by side. The profoundly illogical though sagacious traditional outlook of the ductile East will certainly admit such a compromise and the experience of the West itself is by no means antagonistic to it. One outlook is like drawing the breath in, the other like releasing it ; one like tightening the muscles, the other like relaxing them. After all, the basic conceptions of moral goodness as represented in the two literatures are not as far apart as may at first appear. The Indian drama studiously celebrates goodness and rejects only the bolder confrontation of evil. Eastern thinking by no means denies the validity of ethics nor Western thinking the advantages of at least a Stoical contemplation. But the West dispenses with the tropical profusion of idealized images alike conspicuous in Hindu mythology, poetry, and drama.

Shakespeare and the Indian masters thus represent two sharply contrasted aspects of the same essential humanity. Although some imaginative effort is required for an Indian adequately to grasp the work of Shakespeare or for a Westerner to grasp a master-piece by Kālidāsa, Sūdraka, or Bhavabhūti, success is by no means impossible and moreover is highly rewarding. In their more abstract or specifically aesthetic properties they are most alike. This like-ness obviously has its encouraging aspects. In their more philo-sophical, religious and moral properties they diverge the most widely and yet the position maintained by each is so well grounded in basic human needs that it seems no vain prophecy to hold that future generations will witness a fuller and more rounded humanity because at last occasion becomes ripe for cordial conjunction between the religious or contemplative mind of the East and the ethical or pragmatic mind of the West. Shakespeare and Kālidāsa are sur-prisingly united in their art and complementary, not hostile, in spirit.

3 / *Sanskrit Drama and the World Stage*

ONE OF the most remarkable of dramatic literatures has for nearly a thousand years been wrapped in a cloud through which, it may fairly be said, only occasional beams of light have emerged. Such is the drama of ancient India, never adequately interpreted by criticism since the period of its flourishing shortly after the begin- ning of the Christian era to a little before the completion of the first Christian millennium. We know it as arising largely under the stimulus of the brilliant court cultures once distributed through- out India and as gradually becoming extinct as a creative force during years when the Islamic invasions materially altered the face of the Asian sub-continent. Many of the legends forming its plots survived all changes and do survive even to the present day. Its influences, as well-known, are still felt in the presentational arts—drama, puppetry, symbolic dance—extending even from as far as Tibet to Bali. But the languages in which the plays were written have become almost as divorced from world-currency as Anglo- Saxon from the average American or modern Englishman. More- over, it must be acknowledged that the acting styles are nearly as far removed as the original languages. Although Indian dramatic traditions are older and probably more important in a comparative view than those of the Far East, the Indian heritage has been less well preserved than that in Japan or even in China. Nor have the vicissitudes of this heritage in its native land been relieved by any consistent efforts abroad. Many surviving plays have, to be sure, been translated into the European languages, especially into English. It is well-known that they have at times been much praised as dramatic poetry and their original force as pieces for the theatre has been at least acknowledged by scholars. Most of the translations, however, were made from fifty to a hundred years ago ; many are either stylistically out of date or were originally intended merely as aids to linguistic study, not contributions to dramatic literature. But changes are now visible. Under the spell of an increasing national pride in India since the Second World War there have been a fair number of productions in Sanskrit, given as a rule under academic auspices, the learned character of the languages promoting such presentation. Elsewhere two of the plays, Kālidāsa's *Shakuntalā*, and Sūdraka's *The Little Clay Cart*, have been seen at widely spaced intervals, usually given by amateurs, and generally with a sentiment of esotericism, in versions greatly altered and abridged, colored by strong incursions of Western romantic sentiment.

The prospect that the unfavorable conditions will be materially relieved derives from the persistent view that the plays are of high intrinsic value and the fact that they are gradually becoming better understood and more effectively reinterpreted. In India itself the dramas seem destined to be increasingly performed both in the original languages and even in translations addressing a wider audience than these tongues can ever be expected to reach. Outside India the prospect brightens perceptibly. New and more useable translations are becoming available, while the restive departure of Western stages from nineteenth-century realism or naturalism encourages the cultivation of this supremely imaginative drama. Its myths have persistent value ; its poetry is much closer to the mind of the West than is the poetry of the Far East ; its sheer theatricality and continuity in pantomime elevate it far above a merely provincial theatre. To the greater part of the world, Sanskrit may be a "dead language," but both the poetry and theatricality of Kālidāsa, Bhavabhūti, Bhāsa, Sūdraka and others still prove eminently alive. Their plays must always have much to teach us regarding the arts of acting and playwriting as well as of poetry itself and offer inexhaustible treasures of psychological, religious, and spiritual insight. Ranging from the comparatively naive to the superlatively sophisticated, they serve many purposes and many different audiences.

A discussion of the problem calls for a brief introductory statement regarding its scope, though the circumstances are, naturally, well-known to scholars. The full extent of the early Indian dramatic literature cannot be computed. To begin with, the chronology presents insuperable difficulties. Fragments of early works exist and the tradition merely peters out around 1000 A.D. with a gradual decline in force that can neither be strictly dated nor defined. Plays that have survived are of many sorts and in several languages. Although their key-language is Sanskrit, scarcely a single important play is wholly in that tongue. Sanskrit is, of course, used in conjunction with one or more dialects, the former serving almost as a liturgical language, for the chief characters or scenes, and the popular dialects for the less exalted roles. The most important features of Sanskrit drama extend to the Tibetan stage and to drama entirely in other tongues, especially the Tamil of Southern India. It must be frankly acknowledged that many plays are of small value, indeed of almost no value whatsoever as surviving works for the modern theatre either in or outside India. Some of these inferior works are erotic trifles, others, wooden allegories, the one, too slight, the other, too rhetorical and pretentious to rise to imaginative or lasting power. Probably some fine pieces still remain to be unearthed. It will be remembered that less than fifty years ago thirteen plays, several of high worth, were discovered in a single manuscript collection ascribed to Bhāsa. From the total deposit at the present time at least fifteen representative plays lie within range of successful production in virtually any quarter of the civilized world. This chapter is in substance a defense of this statement.

The putting on of the plays calls for a strenuous though by no means an impossible exercise of thought, patience, imagination, and research. None is easy. But their production rests potentially within the grasp of any actors reasonably acquainted with poetic drama and stylized acting. Though large audiences cannot be expected for long runs, the plays are within the reach of good repertory companies. University theatres and groups with some training in dancing or in poetic speech enjoy an advantage. A few plays are metaphysical, a few appeal to children ; several are distinctly urbane and witty in the connotation of these words implying high sophistication. Almost all encourage spectacular presentation, researches in pantomime, the aesthetic use of costume and stage-properties, and artful elocution. Though no play is according to Western terms completely secular or religious, the range extends from works predominantly secular to those predominantly religious. Our view begins with consideration of the more secular as possibly, though by no means certainly, the more readily serviceable today.

It is regrettable that *Shakuntalā* has been more often read and seen abroad than *The Little Clay Cart*, for the former has leant itself to much sad dilution, to sentimental, romantic interpretation, leaving Kālidāsa's sterner and more religious conceptions unrealized. *The Little Clay Cart* is, on the contrary, theoretically at least more ingratiating and rewarding for contemporary actors. To be sure, it is very long. In fact, it is the length of two plays and was presumably compounded of two. But abridgment to proportions which seem reasonable to modern playgoers is at least possible and the separate acts, ten in number, may occasionally be given with far more success than implied merely in theatrical exercises. Sūdraka's words all but define an inspired stylized acting; pantomime is wedded to language with a firmness hardly duplicated in the entire scope of world drama. The detailed picture of customs and manners of a medieval Indian city-life notwithstanding, the play remains astonishingly fresh and universal. Both the pathos and the humor, the emotional depth and the intellectual acuteness, are wonderfully sustained and clearly intelligible. It is probably an easier work for an intelligent modern reader or actor to understand than any by Aristophanes or even by Plautus. Although Indian critics, as a rule devoted to a more metaphysical stage, do not regard it as their chief drama, it is potentially by far their best dramatic export. Both *Shakuntalā* and *The Little Clay Cart* have been sadly diluted but Sūdraka's play has never been dissipated and perverted as Kālidāsa's has been. A school of acting anywhere in the world can hardly find a work from which more can readily be learned. Especially for theatrical purposes, the best recent translation is that by Revilo Pendleton Oliver.

An erotic element is conspicuous in most Hindu dramas, as in most Hindu art. But there are a few outstanding exceptions in the theatre and, incidentally, where the relations of men and women are not in question, sex is seldom conspicuous, partly because where friendship is regarded as ethically quite as important as love between the sexes and second in ethical value only to family life, homosexuality has nothing remotely as conspicuous a place in Hindu thought as in that of Greece, Rome, or even modern Europe. The concept "plotting" suggested to the Hindu mind plots both of statecraft and of drama. Thus, the central figure in a few plays is a witty and idealized prime minister, utterly devoted to his sovereign and resorting to fantastic devices to achieve political ends. Two such statesmen are at times pitted against each other. These features govern the story of a notable play by Visākhadatta, *Mudrārākṣasa*. The conduct and quality of this work seem only superficially removed from us in time. It is a tense drama, clear, sustained, and consistent from beginning to end, artistically effective and realistically convincing. Though lacking the poetic and religious profundity of possibly more important and representative Sanskrit plays, it shares with them great driving force and is, in fact, one of the most concentrated of all in its effect. It could easily prove gratifying to a modern audience.

Less austere in sentiment and more lightened by humor and fantasy is Bhāsa's *The Minister's Vows*, which also centers attention on intriguing ministers. A love story is implied but not presented in action. Thus, two major figures in the plot, the king, Udayana, and his destined bride, Vāsavadattā, are both bypassed with extraordinary ingenuity. In almost every scene they are the chief subjects of discussion yet nowhere appear. Nevertheless action remains lively. By analogy, several elephants, all named, are important in the action yet they, too, are not represented on the stage. The scenes are animated and the story easy to follow. The action grips attention. Suspense is handled theatrically. The whole is a political fable, lacking deep poetic significance but with the bright sparkle of a truly ingratiating poetry. It has long been and will long continue to be notable dramatic entertainment. The audience fairly smacks its lips in gusto at the contention of the rival ministers.

These two plays, though of good quality, are in a distinct minority, political plays being less popular and amorous themes, whether in secular, mythological, or religious drama, taking the ascendency. Two amorous romances of superior merit, Bhāsa's *Vision of Vāsavadattā*, and Kālidāsa's *Mālavikāgnimitra*, have collected astonishingly little dust through the centuries. The former contains much the same element of political intrigue as found in *The Minister's Vows*, but is far more inspired in its passages of romantic sentiment depicting a kingly lover and two rival queens. In its theme Bhāsa's play is remarkably modern, for it deals in Proustian fashion with the rival claims of imminence and memory, and in virtually an Expressionist fashion with the similar demands of reality and illusion, actuality and dream. Not a word is wasted in a succinct and almost perfect work of art. In its fantasy it resembles *Twelfth Night*, yet is in some ways more poetic, for it dispenses with the hard, Plautan* core of Shakespeare's play, which, all its Elizabethan fecundity notwithstanding, rests on a Latin foundation. There is great emotional warmth in Bhāsa's romance, resembling in this respect the finest scenes in Beaumont and Fletcher's tragicomedies.

Mālavikāgnimitra has suffered unjustly from some blunt comparisons with Kālidāsa's two other plays, which obviously stand on a higher plain of poetic achievement, not to mention enthusiasm. The lesser play looks like deft craftsmanship in work done on commission, the two others appear as spontaneous art. Yet as contribution to a Spring Festival this light and graceful comedy proves highly gratifying. Though not as rich a drama as *A Mid-summer-Night's Dream*, it occupies a place in Kālidāsa's trilogy of plays comparable, perhaps, to Shakespeare's "Dream" among his more than thirty works. One is reminded, too, of the light comedies by John Lyly with mythological themes presented at Queen Elizabeth's court, as *Endimion*, and *The Woman in the Moon*. Apart from the extraordinary delicacy and sophistication of the Sanskrit play on intrigues within a Hindu harem there is little to perplex a modern audience. The mythology itself is inescapably charming and acted before us, not left in the obscurity of allusion to a faded Pantheon. For example, that so young and sprightly a heroine as we have here will cause a spring-time tree to blossom at the touch of her foot may offend science but seems crystal clear to poetry. Unquestionably the play was often given in India out-of-doors. A more attractive comedy for an out-of-door summer theatre today would be hard to discover. It is light but by no means slight, for such precision of footing is rare.

Unlike *Mālavikāgnimitra*, the majority of Sanskrit plays surviving as potential theatre do more than introduce myth incidentally; they rely upon it as the major element in their story. And this firm basis in myth goes a considerable distance to accounting for their survival, or, in other words, for their nearly timeless, or universal, appeal. The plots are based largely, though not exclusively, on the two great classical epics of India, the *Māhabhārata*, and the *Rāmāyana*. For many centuries these massive poems stood behind a large part of Indian presentational art, their fertility in inspiring at least the folk-arts extending even to the present. Their force was most powerful in the earlier periods of the literary drama. The majority of Bhāsa's plays, the earliest important body of drama known to us, treat these epic themes, as a rule to much advantage. There are, to be sure, relatively poor plays based on the epics. Thus Bhāsa's *The Coronation* reads more like a hastily composed, rapid-fire scenario than a dramatic poem. His *Statue Play*, on the contrary, is a highly sensitive and well composed poetic drama on a major episode in the *Rāmāyana*. Especially after its opening scene, action progresses with the utmost clarity, Rama's story told almost as directly as Shakespeare tells Othello's. The many verbal indirections and understatements are as a rule thoroughly perspicuous to a reasonably appreciative audience familiar with the best idiom of dramatic poetry. Bhāsa's *Karna's Task*, deserving unqualified praise, is one of the most moving of all one-act plays, in some ways not unlike the late, verse dramas by William Butler Yeats. Played with the high seriousness which it demands, it should deeply impress any spectator favoured with a moderate degree of spiritual insight. In substance it dramatizes the *Bhagvad-Gītā*, the most spiritually elevated section of the *Māhabhārata*. Doubtless the original audience experienced the force of this profound drama more deeply than could be expected of a modern audience ; yet even without a philosophical understanding of the *Bhagvad-Gītā*, and even in translation, this succinct little tragedy becomes almost unspeakably moving. Bhāsa's play will always be a reflective and spiritual drama of the highest magnitude, all the better artistically because the predominantly didactic poem that stands behind it is so thoroughly translated into the action of an enthralling drama.

Many pages of the Indian epics are, indeed, far removed from meditations such as the *Bhagvad-Gītā*. Some will seem to modern readers more like the saga mythology of Scandinavia or to resemble the early and relatively savage mythology of pre-Homeric Greece. This violent, primitive, and brutal action at times transfers itself into impressive drama. *Venisamhāra*, by Bhatta Nārāyana, possesses these qualities. To be successfully produced it must, accordingly, be played in a very different manner from any style required by other plays mentioned in this discussion. But it is a moving story, firmly of a piece, full of pain, trouble, tragedy, and despair. Though possessing little of the grace or luminosity found in the works of the more famous Sanskrit dramatists, it comes close to expression which the violent West has long known and knows only too well today. It may remind us of *The Song of Roland*, or even of stark dramas based on heroic incidents of the latest war. Potentially, at least, the play has by no means passed out of the repertory of world drama.

Kālidāsa is exceptional, for he possesses a suavity and dignity, a poetic richness and containment, matched seldom and possibly most closely by Sophocles. Both his two masterpieces are myths for the stage and must be so understood and presented if they are to yield their true meaning. The heroine, Shakuntalā, in other words, must not be made to resemble Goethe's Dorothea, no matter how well the producer recalls Goethe's praise of Kālidāsa's work. Her play is not a romantic drama but a sacred drama. The same holds even more clearly for *Vikramorvaci*, a less elaborated work, though a little more difficult for modern actors to present, especially because of the climax of its poetry, the long soliloquy comprising the greater part of Act Four. The hero, to be sure, vehemently addresses many living forms of nature. But for most of the scene no response follows, unless a barren echo be held an exception. Yet without question, save for minor reservations, *Vikramorvaci* clearly comes within the potential of outstanding dramatic performance today, though still one of the most intensely Indian of all plays.

Although popular India has devotedly cherished the Shakuntalā legend, Indian scholars have expressed scarcely less esteem for Bhavabhūti's masterpiece based on epic sources, *Rāma's Later History*, than for Kālidāsa's *Shakuntalā*. Bhavabhūti's work is a treasure for the theatrically elite, one of the most intense and stirring of all Sanskrit plays and marking in many ways the high-point of the great mountain range of serious dramas on Hindu epic themes. Action is at a minimum. There is virtually no plot, no intrigue, no antagonist, no comic relief. Yet as lyric drama profoundly adapted to stage performance this work has few rivals. Its theatrical qualities, no less than its psychological, moral, and philosophical properties, make it typical of the Indian theatre at its best. A major dramatic poem, indeed almost a miracle of virtuosity, it offers a supreme opportunity for the producer. Little in the play clouds it from modern eyes if only it be performed with a fair degree of imagination and skill. The theme is at heart simply the disintegration and reintegration of family life, revealed in a myth on nature's fertility, the loves of earth and sun. Whereas *The Little Clay Cart* is the most practicable of Sanskrit plays throughout the world, *Rāma's Later History* is the most challenging.

27

A final instance of myth in a play that strikes one first of all as secular and mythological rather than as religious is Bhāsa's *The Adventures of the Boy Krishna*. This apparently was originally performed, as it must be performed today, with a spirit of naiveté, conscious and sophisticated, perhaps, but none the less frankly naive, as though directed, Blake-like, to the child-mind. It is Krishna at play. It relates the miraculous adventures of its hero as a child, one of the symbolic themes most deeply beloved in Hindu art. Much singing and dancing is called for. The conception is that of a pastoral but of a pastoral, like *A Midsummer-Night's Dream*, whose plot is propelled by Puck, vastly enlivened and invigorated by folkore, a play not so close to the decadent, Hellenistic, purely literary pastoral of ancient Sicily as to the folk-dramas of medieval, rural England. The Indian fantasy retains complete freshness and captivating charm. It can best be given today in the Western World before an audience in which there are many children, probably as a production primarily for children, possibly even by children. This is the type of play which everywhere successful directors of theatres for the young, as the inspired and cosmopolitan-minded leader of the famous theatre for children in Antwerp, Cory Lievens, have consistently found popular. Exotic as the play's imagery or fable is to the world at large, its heart is native everywhere and always. For successful performance it calls, of course, for good dancing, good music, and bright spectacle.

Though all the plays dealing with myth partake generously of religious feeling, those just considered do so with some degree of indirection and we naturally think of them first of all as poetic mythology, not religious propaganda. But there are several deeply religious plays explicitly pious and even more fit, it would seem, for the temple than for the court and proclaiming the ascetic virtues of sacrifice, rectitude, non-resistance and contemplation. Their austerities may not be generally put into practice but even today are still powerful and in some respects more compelling to man's conscience than ever. Conspicuous among works that contain such idealism and retain high theatrical potency are Harsa's *Nāgānanda*, and two lyrical dramas a little outside the pale of Sanskrit literature but clearly a part of the great Indian dramatic tradition, the celebrated Tamil play, *Arichandra*, ascribed to Renga Pillai, and the Tibetan buddhistic drama, *Tchrimekundan*, ascribed to the Talelama, Tsongs-Dbyangsrgyamthso. These are very eloquent works, quite capable of presentation today on a poetic stage. The story of the Tamil masterpiece is basically that of *The Book of Job*, with the considerable differences occasioned respectively by their Hindu and Semitic origins. *Arichandra* gives relatively much more attention to the wife and offspring, revealing the central place of family life in Indian thought. The Tibetan drama further presents a contrast between power and mercy.

Nāgānanda requires little or no cutting or arrangement. The two other works, long and episodic, resemble novels in dramatic form. Nevertheless, where both content and theatrical inspiration are initially so strong, adaptation even to the modern stage is by no means difficult or embarrassing. In fact, there is no really authoritative text for either of these dramas, which, like the Western *Everyman*, have persisted from century to century with extensive accretions, deletions, and adulterations. Their initial impulse is powerful and unmistakable, their poetic and theatrical energy no less vigorous. Here are two rich mines, one in the loftiest Himalayas, the other in the tropical lowlands of Southern India, from which theatrical gold may still be extracted. Such plays may be successfully produced in an essentially secular theatre but are possibly best suited for production by actors under sponsorship of a religious institution, for they reach the very core of religious consciousness itself, where all distinctions between sects and creeds vanish before the disclosure of the religious heart of universal man.

All fifteen dramas described in this chapter are of value in challenging the skill and inventiveness of the performers. Hardly any artifice or convention known anywhere to the world's stage is missing in this most synthetic dramatic literature. Soliloquies, asides, the pantomimic creation of scene and stage properties, imaginative choreography, musical embellishment, simultaneous speaking, simultaneous action of two or more scenes, elaborate montage, stylized acting, naturalistic acting, poetical expression, realistic and colloquial expression, impressionism, expressionism, the physical and the metaphysical, the secular and the divine, ritual, humor, emotional intensity, farce, parody, and fantasy— all are carried to advanced stages of development. True, the Hindu drama lacks much that exists in the Western drama, just as it achieves much that the Western drama does not achieve. Character delineation, an expression of uncompromising will power, tragic purgation, satirical sharpness, logical or dialectical thinking, are

29

not carried into their more advanced phases. The emotions implied are much more violent than in most European drama but in sympathetic production are intimated rather than naturalistically expressed, the aesthetic demand for form and control surpassing the indulgence given to direct projection of feeling. The basic theme of all Indian drama is spiritual equilibrium, poise between opposites, rest and fulfillment at the center of violent motion. Sanskrit drama is from the Western point of view that ultimate paradox, a successful contemplative drama. In the acute theoretical criticism of their dramatic art Indian actors are enjoined to stand above the emotions expressed, no matter how violent; both they and the audience are charged to maintain with a severe and spiritual discipline the contemplative view of life. This is a highly convincing aesthetic and the modern world has similarly discovered it to signify an ingratiating outlook in philosophy and religion. Sanskrit plays commence and conclude with prayers to the god of dancing and art, Siva, destroyer and creator. Surely, much is to be gained, whether in the theatre or in life itself, by propitiation of such a profoundly meditated divinity.

their value indiscriminately in relation to time. But they have, of course, a particular relevance for our own time and, as it seems, a relevance of more than usual potency. Not only are they in a broad sense of the word timeless; they are especially timely in terms of recent trends of thought and taste. In grasping for a metaphor, one thinks of the view of Mount Fugi from various areas of Japan. The mountain is always there, at many times veiled or actually hidden, at certain hours with exceptional clearness in the atmosphere becoming preternaturally vivid, approaching the spectator as though it has been violently dislodged. Our own times constitute one of the moments in cultural history when the Sanskrit drama looms in vivid proximity.

For a score of centuries, drama in the Western world has, even in advance of other art forms, favored an objective view of experience. It has in general depicted life in social terms and at times analyzed it in intellectual terms. Its address has been to the social consciousness or to the mind of the audience. It has not, except in certain cases of the religious drama, addressed itself directly to the soul of the individual spectator. Its form has been narratory; it has favored direct projection of action and has emphasized the difference between persons, the contentions arising from these differences being found the very essence of drama itself. Western drama, in short, has depicted the clash of personalities, stressing the view that different men wear different masks. Its conception has been antithetical, for example, to the lyric of self-expression. Criticism has contended that each major playwright, to be sure, stamps his works with the mark of his own personality but maintained that their basic meaning is objective rather than autobiographical.

While the Western drama delights in surprises and looks outward, Sanskrit drama takes the opposite course. In content it is psychological and spiritual rather than social, ethical, or intellectual; it aims to establish the felicity of equilibrium in the soul of each spectator. It stresses the likenesses, not the dissimilarities, of men, depicting them as different only insofar as the exigencies of its myths demand. Its final goal is to proclaim the unity within the universe itself and thus to refute what might be called the multiverse assumed in the secular drama of the West. It depicts the soul in repose, not in action; its image is the seated Buddha, not the javelin-throwing Zeus, or at least the god Siva dancing within the circle of his own sovereignty, not the charioteer urging his horses through tempestu-

ous waves. Its ideal form is neither narratory, dynamic, nor centri-
fugal but, metaphorically speaking, musical, plateresque, and
magnetic. In its structure all lines lead inward as if to the center
of a circle, to the navel of the body or the chalice of the flower.
This form may at first seem to defy the very principles of drama
themselves and indeed if drama be as Aristotle declared it, the most
celebrated of Sanskrit playwrights are among the least of dramatic
poets. But the modern mind is strongly tempted to pass beyond
the Greeks. Clearly, within our own century much of the most
admired dramatic poetry has moved with an ever increasing volume
in the direction of the Sanskrit.

To begin with a view of British and American drama one may consider Dylan Thomas's remarkable poetic play, *Under Milk Wood*,
conceived, to be sure, as a poem for radio recitation but more than
once seen in versions more or less overtly theatrical. The work
complies with almost all the characteristics outlined in preceding
descriptions of Sanskrit drama except, possibly, in its extreme use
of local color, which may well lead the spectator to feel, here lies a
Welsh village, not the City of Man's Soul. The satirist intrudes
upon the role of the idealist or dreamer. Much the same holds true
for the plays of Samuel Beckett. Here the pessimism, to be sure,
is extreme; but pessimism is by no means absent from oriental
religious thought, though Sanskrit drama on the whole outwardly
stresses a more cheerful view of existence. *Waiting for Godot* is
not a play about an action. It is precisely a play about no action,
as its title suggests. It ends as it begins. Its remarkably theatrical
qualities lie in the style, not in the action; or, to express the thought
differently, in the pantomime or "business," not in a story which
simply does not exist.

Chiefly through music-drama and the irresistible tendency of
man to unite music and the theatre a half-oriental form makes
itself felt and all imperatives of the Aristotelian form are dismissed.
The Gertrude Stein-Virgil Thompson, *Four Saints in Three Acts*
illustrates this. It is more a pageant than a play and more a shifting
of tableaux than a pageant. Above all it is a symphony made visible
or a dance with elaborate music and spectacle. Each act has its
own mood (the Sanskrit "rasa", the European "movement").
In its inspired initial production this was widely recognized as
providing a thoroughly gratifying theatrical experience. The new
school of metaphysical poets has clearly contributed the most to

33

this departure from orthodox Western drama. In this category few writers are more typical than Conrad Aiken. His notable play, *Dr. Arcularis*, is, to be sure, in one of its phases merely a detective story, a type of art essentially melodramatic and overwhelmingly Western. Sherlock Holmes was no Bodhisattva. But insofar as the entire play is conceived as a dream or vision at the point of death as experienced by a fairly representative man and as symbolical meditation upon the cardinal conditions of human life, it resembles the meditative theatre of India. The heart of Aiken's play is spiritual and non-objective.

Aiken, to be sure, shows a penchant for autobiography and autobiography is a type of expression distinctly foreign to the impersonal impulses of the Sanskrit stage. The personal confession of both Catholic and Protestant, the one leading to verbal confession to a priest, the other, to written confession to edify a reading public, alike belong to a civilization built upon self-consciousness, antithetical to the mystical cultures of the East aspiring to super-consciousness. Hence the leading dramatists of relatively modern times using the stage for autobiography at once approach and diverge from the oriental stage. Insofar as they become to a large degree non-objective, they approach the Oriental; insofar as they tend to magnify rather than to nullify individuality, they prove violently occidental. Strindberg is here the supreme case in point; his expressionist plays violently wrench Western drama from its traditional position. But one is never quite sure how far *To Damascus* and *The Dream Play* are intended as autobiography of a distressed Christian or as outlines of universal man. These elusive plays might be collected under the ambiguous title, "Strindberg or Everyman". Both of Strindberg's two revolutionary tendencies in the theatre, one toward self-expression in the theatre and the other toward symbolism, announced a revolution. The first merely divorced his plays from the outlook of the Renaissance. The second pointed clearly in the direction of the East. His essentially poetic vision weaned him from the naturalistic theatre and cast his thoughts toward music. Avowedly he conceived many of his mature plays in relation to musical sentiment and form. *Easter* is a progression of scenes based upon the marvellous passion music of Haydn, *The Ghost Sonata*, a similar work indebted to Beethoven. In both cases inspiration moves also toward the Orient.

Another great European playwright moved, as he became increasingly the poet of the theatre, in a similar direction. Pirandello was passionately devoted to music and for a considerable period in his life attempted to work out a film projection of the Beethoven symphonies. That this project in course of time passed largely into the unscrupulous hands of Hollywood, with Walt Disney and Stokowski as its servants, in no way diminishes its aesthetic importance. Pirandello's own last work, his incomplete *Mountain Giants*, is his own unfinished symphony. It calls for considerable musical accompaniment and betrays much of the oriental concern for "rasa". The acts are movements, each with its own emotional tone. This is not "straight" Western theatre. It is a theatre increasingly bent in an Easterly direction.

The preoccupation with a form capable of being abstracted and stated in more or less musical terms, as variations upon certain themes, is conspicuous in Eugene O'Neill's most revolutionary play, *The Iceman Cometh*. There is a sense in which here little or nothing happens. Or, to put it differently, the most dramatic changes lie in the lighting, not in the action. At the end all but two of the chief characters are seated on the stage just as at the beginning, though the illumination is dimmer than ever. The characters sit exactly as musicians in a chamber orchestra. One man, weaker, or possibly stronger than the rest, has committed suicide. Another has come and gone, distinguished from the rest chiefly by his superior power to personify their common predicament. He is the *deus ex machina* of a machine that from the humanitarian point of view conspicuously fails to work. The movements (one cannot properly speak of the "action") are cyclical. There is no "intrigue" or "plot". Only O'Neill's violent pessimism, relieved, to be sure, by some finely humorous, cynical irony, conceals from even the most superficial glance the playwright's marked approximation to the form and spirit of the Sanskrit stage.

Before entering upon the later and more definitive parts of this exposition, it will be well to remark that in the present chapter observations on the Sanskrit theatre itself made in earlier sections of this book, especially as to its thematic structure, will be assumed and attention turned chiefly toward revealing analogies in the theatre of the West. Yet it may be wise to re-examine at least briefly certain formal devices in construction of the typical act of the Sanskrit play which distinguish it from act-construction in Western drama. In a word, the act division has considerably

35

more significance in the East than in the West. That each act has its prevailing *rasa*, or mood, that it requires the use of special formulas for its introduction and only to a less degree for its conclusion, are conspicuous features. Each act is required to develop certain themes belonging to the play as a whole, to recapitulate in its beginning what has already occurred on the stage, or, more often, what has occurred in an intermediate time off the stage. No Sanskrit play is merely a sequence of one-act plays, although several of Bhāsa's short works were quite possibly given as parts of a longer entertainment. But despite this articulation, the act in the typical play has all the completeness of an ideal movement in a musical composition. It may well be that Western music in the last three hundred years has achieved a sophistication in form comparable to that of the Sanskrit stage and that the Indian theatre itself in this regard actually forged ahead of Indian music. In any event, the Westerner seeking an intimacy with the Sanskrit theatre discovers that Western drama provides him with less fundamental aid than Western music. To look to *Shakuntalā* for what the West regards as basically musical qualities rather than essentially dramatic qualities is no poor strategy nor in the end a derogatory comment on Kālidāsa as a playwright.

The Western dramatist and poet closest to the spirit of the Eastern art is, presumably, Federico Garcia-Lorca, especially if attention is focused on his longest play, *If Five Years Pass*. The emotional violence of his three tragedies on Andelusian women is indeed far from Eastern practice and more nearly approaches that most typical of Western dramatic forms, melodrama. An underlying primitivism in Spanish thought, whose most conspicuous outcropping in recent years is in the art of Picasso, seems indeed far from the gentle sophistication of the Sanskrit *nātaka*, although farce is much the same the world over, whether in Lorca's puppet-plays or in the bawdy trifles delighting popular audiences in ancient India. As the most highly conventionalized and impersonal type of theatre, the *commedia dell'arte*, which Lorca closely approaches in his light and witty entertainments, *The Shoemaker's Prodigious Wife*, and *The Love of Don Perlimplin and Belisa in the Garden*, the most nearly approximates the abstraction of the Indian stage. But it is not in this respect that the most revealing analogies are to be found. The plateresque quality of his form and its musical structure and spirit are the qualities chiefly apparent in *If Five*

Years Pass and are so firmly based on his thought and work as a whole that a few comments on his life and non-dramatic poems are useful as introduction to the analysis of his powerful "surrealist" play.

Lorca knew how to write plays of the most varied sorts and how to follow patterns developed on various stages of the Western drama. The narrative elements conspicuous in the "Andelusian" tragedies rest on the firmest basis of Western tradition. Influence of the golden age of Spanish drama, with Lope de Vega and Calderón at its head, appear in the relatively tame, early and derivative piece, *Mariana Pineda.* He was skilled in almost pure *commedia dell'arte.* Never, of course, does he stray into the fertile field of the comedy of manners nor into the stony area of the problem play in the accepted sense of those words. Nor does he write strictly neo-classical drama, though the choral elements in two of the Andelu-sian plays and the two levels of style reflected by the alternation of verse and prose suggest in turn the Greek and the Elizabethan manner. No matter how he writes, however, he is even within each individual work highly versatile and always the poet; thus in two very general respects comparable to the Sanskrit dramatists. His radical experiment with form in *If Five Years Pass,* where he boldly deserts orthodox European practice and turns toward the East, is most strongly revelatory of a mind steeped in the very essence of music.

Lorca was a gifted pianist, an amateur composer, a favorite pupil of Da Falla, a sponsor of musical performances and research, and equally devoted to popular and sacred music, to the music of the flamenco dance and of the Catholic mass. Whatever he wrote, showed the impact of music upon him, whether the essay, the short poem, the longer poem, or the play. He delighted in musical accompaniment for the reading of poetry, sharing with his country-men as a whole a fondness for that best of accompanying instru-ments, the guitar. Though poetry, drama, and play-directing were his professions, he was in a sense a professional in nothing and an amateur in everything, during his brief life reaching considerable dexterity and skill in all the arts, including painting. Better than any other figure of his times he exemplifies the tendency of the age to a synthesis of the arts. He wrote in color and painted in caricature. His colors sing; he can write a narrative ballad inspired by the color green. White and black are passions to him. Whereas Michelangelo

37

declared that a single majesty inspires all the arts, Lorca takes a less platonic and a more pragmatic position. He finds practical relations between the arts and thus achieves the total theatre of movement, speech, color, form, dance, and music, both vocal and instrumental. No art as he employs it is ever out of sight of its sister arts. His conception of the theatre in these respects, he seems never to have formulated for print but its significance in terms of inter-continental culture remains clear. The Granada of his birth is historically the link between the European peninsula that is Spain and the African-Asian world symbolized by the Alhambra. Lorca idolized the Islamic tradition. In so doing he presumably never realized that he was also in his own terms effecting a passage to ancient India, where the synthesis of the arts, both in theory and in practice, was achieved more firmly than at any time in the West.

Music, then, was merely one, though presumably the chief, of the arts whose influence swayed the course of his writing and at least in his own eyes operated greatly to its advantage. He was wholly accustomed to think of such relationships and even to act upon them quite unconsciously, as part of his birthright. A large proportion of his minor poems have received musical settings; all his more popular plays have received operatic settings, a few of them several times over; successful dances have been composed on the inspiration of both his poems and plays. The latter have been the special delight of stagedesigners and producers. Like Kālidāsa, Lorca thought in the most comprehensive of aesthetic terms. He thought also in terms of relatively intense and short-winded literary and dramatic units, in this regard again suggesting the influence of musical compositions. It is almost as though his strong lyrical sense tempted him to accept Poe's celebrated dictum on the impossibility of the long poem. Most of his poems are brief. His plays are also brief and sharply divided into acts. The chief of his non-dramatic poems, his *Lament for Ignacio Sanchez Mejias*, is in strict sonata form, the first movement dominated by the harsh theme, "at five in the afternoon," the second, by the bitter theme, "I will not see it," the third, by the heavy oppression of allusions to stone, the last, by exhilarating themes of revival, announcing that the stone has been rolled away from the door of the sepulchre. That this is one of the most profoundly musical of modern poems is obvious to any sympathetic reader but the condition is still further manifest when, as on certain phonographic recordings, it is chanted by a fine Spanish voice and with the accompaniment of an elegiac guitar.

If In Five Years proceeds from the same hand and mind that fashioned the great chant for the dead bullfighter, though the play is, of course, less essentially tragic and more bitterly ironic, never passing in its mood beyond the astringency of the poem's second movement. There is really no narrative. In the first of its three acts A loves B, while B is cold; in the third and last act B loves A, while A is cold. These are the two major figures. Both are sensitive beings caught in the trap of time. In Act Two a pair of vulgar and insensitive beings wear themselves out in their own animalistic passion, the girl meanwhile deserting A, hitherto her unrewarding lover. Every figure represents a new inflection of the unifying idea, the invidiousness of time, not so much because all things are time's victims through death—though this thought supplies a minor level for the action and a symbolical character or two—as because time decrees that there is no stability for either the human heart or mind. One character lives on memory, another on anticipation; another, a vulgar sensualist, on attempts to snatch the passing moment. Still another, the "Old Man," a slightly more sympathetic character than the rest, is unconvincingly resigned to the luxuries of retrospection and the unrealized surprises of a future as yet unthinkable. The symbolic figures associated with death express time's ultimate irony. These are, in Act One, a dead cat and a dead child, in Act Three, a clown wearing a death's-head and a harlequin, who plays a "violin" with two strings while chanting repeatedly certain theme lines in verse. An imposing but brittle department-store mannikin that can neither live nor properly die supplies the secondary theme of supernaturalism in Act Two. The play is all a very conscious artifact yet by no means dry or concocted. Emotions are strong and tender. No character bears a personal name. All are treated as musical motifs. And all breathe the impassioned life of music itself. The form is scarcely known to Western literature outside the twentieth century. It approximates the most nearly to Western music and to the Sanskrit stage.

As already indicated, the treatment of the individual acts strongly supports the analogy to music, just as the treatment of the four parts in the great *Lament*. Act One is pensive and melancholy; Act Two, bitter and satirical; Act Three, supernatural and tragic. Gestures are repeated, always with a difference. Words and phrases are echoed; at times the words are inverted, exchanged between different characters, or subtly turned around upon themselves. The first few lines of the play are a quiet crescendo, or montage, the last few lines, in a corresponding but inverse form, a quiet diminuendo. Every page and line of the dialogue is alive with musical sentiment, as all actions and gestures proceed with rigid but not too rigid musical precision to the swift conclusion.

This play, written largely, it appears, in 1929, seems in some ways to have been fifty years ahead of its times. Lorca himself withdrew it from rehearsal not on the ground that it required rewriting but that with the actors, facilities and means at his disposal it could not be produced to his liking at the time. He also gravely doubted that it would be popularly applauded in aesthetically conservative Madrid. Moreover, he well knew that plays on Andelusian themes, with their strong coloration in terms of local folkways, would be warmly received. Subsequently he wrote three powerful plays less conspicuously inspired by music and less strongly symbolic, *Blood Wedding*, *Yerma*, and *The House of Bernarda Alba*, together with the patently musically inspired but far less elaborate *Dona Rosita, the Spinster*, or *The Language of Flowers*. Abruptly his life came to a violent end. The surrealist play was only posthumously published and has never received a truly analytical appreciation from its critics nor an adequate representation on the stage. Nevertheless it is perhaps the best of all fantastic dramas of our century, at least the equal in moving force and artistic excellence of any expressionist play from the North of Europe or any surrealist play from the South. The most musically profound of all Lorca's plays, it is almost alone among them in not having received some successful transposition into a musical or choreographic form. But such is the history of Federico Garcia-Lorca's works and no comment on comparative literature, aesthetics, or dramatic art. In its disillusioned tone the play differs greatly from Sanskrit drama and approaches O'Neill or the early T. S. Eliot. It is also clearly a tour de force, a prodigious effort of a somewhat isolated genius in Madrid working against the main current still flowing through his time and place of living. Yet it is conspicuously modern in the sense that European abstract art is modern, that expressionism, impressionism, subjectivism, surrealism, and neo-metaphysical poetry, and the music of Stravinsky are modern. It seems still prophetic of things to come. It is also reactionary in that it harmonizes with the fundamental qualities of Sanskrit drama as these were unfolded over a thousand years before and many thousand miles from Lorca's homeland. The play, like the character of its "Old Man," looks both forward and backward in time. It is both rear guard and *avant-garde.* Although the significance of this particular work has, owing to the fantastic inadequacy of criticism, never been widely recognized, it epitomizes I believe, better than any other both those tendencies in our artistic life rightly declared "modern" and those which look backward to a possibly still richer flowering in the gardens of the Sanskrit stage. It would be too tame a description to call it a passage to India. For the careful reader it affords a firm bridge.

5 | *Sanskrit Drama and Indian Thought*

THE POETIC drama of India during the period defined in the West by the first Christian millennium would be better understood if one of its major qualities had not been habitually overlooked in Western criticism and in the East presumably at first taken for granted and later allowed to rest largely unnoted. This is best described as "equilibrium," a balance achieved by opposing forces found to the aesthetic imagination to be in harmony and not in collision. This signifies in the general scheme of the play that the action is neither progression nor montage nor marked by either the rise or fall of excitement but by a paradoxical poise that customarily takes the form of circular motion ending close to the point of its beginning. It appears further through elaboration of detail in a symmetry achieved with sharp juxtapositions. However bold the contrasts or conflicts, they are never restless; they operate on a radically different dynamics from those in Western drama. Indian drama suggests the smooth revolution of wheels, Western drama, a mounting progress of the dramatic vehicle to a destination greatly unlike its beginning. Movement and contrast, the essence of dramatic form, are, indeed, conspicuous in the great drama of all peoples, for drama is essentially action and contention. But the treatment of these basic qualities differs vastly according to the philosophy and temperament of different civilizations. The Indian stage is so deeply committed to the profound cultivation of its own form, which in turn reflects a formula for life itself, that it dispenses with many attributes held at various times essential to the serious drama of the West, as characterization, naturalism, heroic accomplishments by exertion of the will, and sharp effects of climax and surprise. Time is conceived in Western drama as a forward-moving vista, as if viewed from a moving plane, whereas in the Eastern drama it resembles a dome continuously visible though pre-eminently expansive.

The simplest and by no means least revealing mode of expressing the contrast is to note that the Western stage in its traditional comedy and tragedy deals typically in narratives that terminate in marriage or in death, recording either a wooing or a plot ending in mortality, while the Eastern stage deals in narratives that hinge on separation and reunion. Its typical focus is not upon wooing but upon the family. It celebrates not courtship but social stability. The lost are found, the generations bound together; the stories echo the seasonal and cyclical myths. The contrasts resemble those in the procession of the year, a circular dance of months and days. The play is not a river ending in the sea, either in mystical union with God nor in fulfillment of human ambition. Rather, it is a celebration of cosmic poise, a highly formal and unmistakably aesthetic projection of life idealistically conceived. Western drama when most eminently serious is heroic, a celebration of action strongly propelled by volition; Eastern drama when equally serious is idealistic as a meditation resolved in peace, possibly presenting a mirror of great calamity and suffering but of disasters overcome by the restoration of normal and harmonious relations, a sentiment of repose overpowering the storm. Thus Indian drama is never tragic in the Western sense of the word nor is it in its lighter modes hilariously comic or Aristophanic. Much as it dwells upon the emotions and shuns violent dialectics or dialectics in any form, it avoids the exuberance typical of Western theatres. It has neither the dialectical exuberance of Bernard Shaw nor the emotional indulgence of Federico Garcia-Lorca.

Equilibrium is an aesthetic or possibly a spiritual ideal, not a logical nor an ethical conception. There can be no problem plays in the Indian theatre, for there is basically only one problem, the celebration of poise. Great scope remains for the playwright's ingenuity and intelligence in achieving the balance of elements and parts but little or no room for moral strife. Forces morally opposed face each other as in a tournament or game. Possibly contrary to a superficial, *a priori* view, no Aristotelian ethical doctrine to the effect that extremes are bad and the mean is good is stated or implied. Instead, the hero may go to the utmost limits of ecstacy or grief and such are assumed entirely normal, as in

William Blake's celebrated apology for emotional unrestraint. But these extremes must somehow balance each other with a balance paradoxically but pragmatically resulting through aesthetic terms in a cancellation of violence itself.

Partly as corollary to this balance is the unmistakably aesthetic conception that emotions are not romantically or sentimentally expressed and that neither actor nor audience experiences the emotions of the play to be those of real life. Indian criticism is explicit on this point and the virtuosity of the equilibrium, which in Indian eyes constitutes dramatic beauty and the very core of drama itself, precludes the familiar Western outlook. Even performances of Indian plays themselves in the West have frequently shown obliviousness to this outstanding aspect of the sophisticated Indian theatre. The plays are dedicated, as the introductory and concluding prayers show, to Siva, patron of music, art, and dance, who in the well-known image balances himself upon one foot while dancing in a ring formed by a fiery serpent, whose head consumes its tail. One ear-ring is masculine, the other, feminine. He is god of destruction and rebirth, of continual, unfailing movement within the magic circle of immovability, the very deity of spiritual equilibrium.

Some further difficulties in interpretation arise from a deceptive predisposition to suppose Sanskrit drama in some way broadly representative or typical of Hindu culture. Although as we shall presently see, unmistakably the offspring of this culture, it is no more typical of it than Elizabethan drama is typical of Elizabethan thought. In this connection it is helpful to recall that, from causes neither altogether clear nor dark, the world of Elizabethan drama is very unlike the general world-outlook represented by Elizabethan literature as a whole or even by the Elizabethan dramatists themselves when writing for other media than the stage. Thus while Shakespeare's sonnets at times echo his plays verbally, they are really very unlike them, even in point of language, and his two longish narrative poems come by no means close to his great plays, though one of them may be read as a preliminary exercise for the rhetoric of his earliest dramas. Broadly examined, Indian literature and culture likewise present enormous diversities and the most glaring contradictions. There are many religions and schools of philosophy, many levels of culture, much primitivism, much urbanity, much worldliness, much other-worldliness, four castes and many centuries to be considered. Some Indian traditions have obviously persisted longer than others. The tradition in drama described in these pages is really nameless; it is only roughly associated with the Sanskrit tongue, for much that is fundamental in it holds true also for plays extending geographically from the languages of Tibet to the Tamil of Southern India. Yet a main stem persisted, by the most conservative estimate from about 200 to 900 A.D.—we cannot be sure of the dates, especially where origins are concerned. The great drama seems always to have owed much of its genius to court cultures. With an enormous indebtedness to music and dancing, out of which it may well have grown, it reached an outlook more purely aesthetic than that of virtually any other branch of Hindu expression, in this respect also comparable to the Elizabethan theatre in the total picture of Elizabethan cultural life. It clearly reflects both the typical folklore and philosophy, the manners and religions, of its native land. But it had its own unique accomplishment as well as its own peculiar apologists, as in several important treatises on the theory and practice of the stage.

The accomplishment is so unlike any to be found in the West, that at least perceptible aid is supplied for Western readers when passages in some degree related to the philosophy of the Hindu theatre are recalled from important religious, philosophical, and speculative writings. From their native culture the dramatists naturally picked up valuable threads that must profitably be associated with them. The myths, largely derived from the *Mahā-bhārata* and the *Rāmāyana*, are reworked until they assume quite new aspects, much as Shakespeare reworked his sources in Plutarch and Holinshed. The religious and philosophical statements are more explicit in their bearing on the theory of equilibrium than are the stories ; a few of the former suggesting this theory may be recalled.

The conception is approached in the *Isā Upanishad :*

Unmoving, the One is swifter than the mind,
The sense-powers reaching not It, speeding on before.
Past others running, This goes standing.
In it Matarisvan places action.

It moves. It moves not.
It is far, and It is near.

It is within all this,
And It is outside of all this. . . .

Into blind darkness enter they
That worship ignorance ;
Into darkness greater than that, as it were, they
That delight in knowledge.

Knowledge and non-knowledge—
He who this pair conjointly knows,
With non-knowledge passing over death,
With knowledge wins the immortal.

Into blind darkness enter they
Who worship non-becoming.
Into darkness greater than that, as it were, they
Who delight in becoming. . . .

Becoming and destruction—
He who this pair conjointly knows,
With destruction passing over death,
With becoming wins the immortal.

That most seminal work, the *Bhagvad Gītā*, contains these statements :

He whom the world fears, who fears not the world, free from exaltation, anguish, fear, disquiet, such a one is beloved of Me.
Who exults not nor hates, nor grieves nor longs, renouncing fortune and misfortune, who is thus full of love is beloved of Me.
Equal to foe and friend, equal in honor and dishonor, equal in cold and heat, weal and woe, from attachment altogether free.
Balanced in blame and praise, full of silence, content with whatever may befall, seeking no home here, steadfast-minded, full of love, this man is beloved of Me.

The *Majjhima-Nikāya* (*Sutta* 63) contains this suggestive passage :

I have not elucidated, Mālunkyāputta, that the world is eternal; I have not elucidated that the world is not eternal ; I have not elucidated that the world is finite ; I have not elucidated that the world is infinite; I have not elucidated that the soul and body are identical ; I have not elucidated that the soul is one thing and the body another ; I have not elucidated that the saint exists after death ; I have not elucidated that the saint does not exist after death ; I have not elucidated that the saint neither exists nor does not exist after death.

In a famous passage of the *Samyutta-Nikāya* concerning "the Middle Doctrine" we read:

That things have being, O Kāccāna, constitutes one extreme of doctrine ; that things have no being is the other extreme. These extremes, O Kāccāna, have been avoided by the Tathāgata, and it is a middle doctrine he teaches :

On ignorance depends *karma ;*
On *Karma* depends consciousness ;
On consciousness depend name and form ;
On name and form depend the six organs of sense ;
On the six organs of sense depends contact ;
On contact depends attachment ;
On attachment depends existence ;
On existence depends birth ;
On birth depend old age and death, sorrow, lamentation, misery, grief, and despair. Thus does this entire aggregation of misery arise.

But on the complete fading out of cessation of ignorance ceases *karma* :

On the cessation of *karma* ceases consciousness ;
On the cessation of consciousness cease name and form ;
On the cessation of name and form cease the six organs of sense ;
On the cessation of the six organs of sense ceases contact ;
On the cessation of contact ceases sensation ;
On the cessation of sensation ceases attachment ;
On the cessation of attachment ceases existence ;
On the cessation of existence ceases birth ;
On the cessation of birth cease old age and death, lamentation, misery, grief, and despair. Thus does this entire aggregation of misery cease.

47

Such passages as these, and there are many, indicate both the spirit and essential form and rhetoric of the Sanskrit theatre.

The surprise which may at first be felt on realizing how much in Sanskrit drama is elucidated by the theory of equilibrium and yet how little it is discussed in the extensive and highly sophisticated critical works produced in India itself should not embarrass the validity of the view. Two civilizations differ in ways that neither realizes fully until they have existed for a considerable time side by side. Moreover, in any culture there is always much that is so completely native as to be taken almost entirely for granted. The Greeks scarcely realized the uniqueness of their emphasis upon logical thinking nor the Greek dramatists their further emphasis upon emotional tension strung lengthwise on the coordinate of time. The Sanskrit dramatists, it seems, hardly realized to what a pronounced degree they relied upon precisely the opposite outlooks, discovering spiritual integration between apparent and logical antinomies, and finding peace that flows from contemplation to be the unifying element even in their narrative and dramatic art. The dynamics of the Western stage draw the breath in, creating the tension of flexed muscles ; the dynamics of the Indian stage let the breath out, creating relaxation and repose. The idealism of the one is heroic, that of the other, contemplative. In each case the work of art is organic, developed from a single seed ; in each case we are confronted with the spectacle of opposing forces. The organisms themselves, however, differ as widely as day from night. Each presumes its own way of thinking and feeling. In each culture the critics justify the outlook known to them and define that technique as the best which most fully realizes the native ideals. But it is the technique that is clearly stated rather than the outlook, as the aesthetics of Aristotle or Cicero, of Bharata or Sāgaranandin, clearly show. It is only when one system is confronted with the other that certain of the most deeply ingrained properties of each become clearly apparent.

Although the purpose of this brief chapter is to state the principle of equilibrium, not to trace its application at large or to describe the multiplicity of its manifestations, a few examples showing its application will naturally be demanded. The circular motion of separation and return must, however, be conspicuous on even a rapid inspection of the most celebrated Sanskrit plays. To begin with the earliest playwright to whom any considerable number of works has been ascribed, Bhāsa's masterpiece, *The Vision of Vāsavadattā*, describes the supposed death of a beloved queen and her final recovery of the husband convinced that he has lost her. *The Minister's Vows*, another of Bhāsa's notable plays, repeats much the same theme. The "happy ending" of almost all Sanskrit plays operates in this behalf, for where a story falls within the mould of tragicomedy, the action will naturally pass from felicity to misfortune and back to felicity again. Sanskrit criticism itself states that the end of the play should in some way recapitulate its beginning. Bhāsa treats the epics that have the same patterns, as the *Rāmāyana* so conspicuously shows. Rāma loses Sītā twice, first when she is abducted by Rāvanā and second when she is exiled by Rāma himself at the malicious instigation of "the populace". On each occasion she is, of course, recovered. These are themes in four outstanding plays, two by Bhāsa, two, considerably more powerful, by Bhavabhūti.

Shakuntalā and her lover are first happy and devoted to each other, then the dark eclipse of forgetfulness sets in, and at last their reunion is achieved. Purūravas loses Urvacī, only to find her once more. In Harsa's *Nāgānanda* the lovers are separated by a gulf deep as death itself, only to be united, proving, to cite an aphorism in another play, *Rāma's Later History*, that misery and joy are encompassed within the same dominion. What is most remarkable, even in a political play, as *Mudrārāksasa*, where the estrangement is not between two lovers but between two ministers of state, the end of the play depicts their reconciliation, peace being restored by public unity.

The larger part of the significance of the theory of equilibrium cannot, however, be realized until the detailed working out of a single play is examined. This is most clearly seen in the most gigantic of Sanskrit dramas, *The Little Clay Cart*, a work of transcendent virtuosity and choreography. Here every item has its counterpart, though the themes are themselves frequently so complex and subtly interwoven as to escape instantaneous recognition. We presumably experience the integrity of the form before realizing its causes and in fact the symmetry will exhaust the most intense scrutiny. Scene balances scene, as the two perigrinations of Vasantasēnā through the streets, once when pursued by the villain, once when a thunderstorm pursues her as she is in quest of her lover, on each occasion being accompanied by a *vita*. On each occasion, too, there is a trio of voices speaking with dialectical peculiarities. The balance of flesh and spirit is evoked in the single role of the gambler turned ascetic. The theme of the unlucky but faithful servant, itself a foil to the ultimately lucky Chārudatta, is developed in the story of an impotent but valiant servant who is twice beaten because of loyalty, first to the heroine, second to the hero ; on each occasion he declares that he has done all he possibly can. In the important character of Sarvilaka, thievery and idealism are contrasted with exquisite humor. Chārudatta's poverty is contrasted with Vasantasēnā's opulence, his dilapidated house with her thriving palace. One *gharri* is set off against another, a clay cart is the foil to a golden cart, every incident and almost every speech is a foil to another. The repetition of stanzas under the varying circumstances, the balance of design, for example, in the processional scenes at the four gates of the city, the near-deaths of hero and heroine, each invoking the name of the other, all, even in point of the most minute verbal parallels, support the underlying theory of equipoise. Chārudatta was once rich ; he falls into poverty ; he recovers his riches with interest. In the language of William Blake, who alone among English poets reiterates all the essentials in the cyclic pattern of Hindu thought, even Vasantasēnā was doubtless both virginal and sexually honest once and is in the end elevated to what is deemed the highest moral honour of woman, matrimony. In short, *The Little Clay Cart* preserves the cyclic theme common to almost all serious Sanskrit drama but does so less spectacularly than in the unsurpassed subtlety and consistency with which it develops the factor of equilibrium within the multiple threads weaving its garment as a whole.

The Tamil drama, *Arichandra*, the Tibetan drama, *Tchrimekundan*, are both, like *The Book of Job*, stories of tribulation surrounded by happiness. The hero in each case falls from his splendor only to be restored to it. With much less subtlety than the Sanskrit plays themselves and more indebtedness to the bare increment of folklore, these justly illustrious works follow the same basic pattern as the main stem of the serious Indian theatre.

Equilibrium, as the Indian drama reveals it, is exemplified, then, both in the conception of the plots and, what is considerably more important, in the execution of detail. It is followed, in other words, in the dramatic narratives and in the details of style and execution. Sāgaranandin declares the highest type of play to be that employing the maximum number of dialects and styles practically available, that is, the play containing the largest number of conflicting elements to be reconciled, for Sāgaranandin himself uses the image of the whole work as developed from a single seed. The conflicts, as analysis reveals, are harmonized by playing opposites off against each other, as summer-winter, light-dark, right-left, war-peace, or whatever the most available contrasts may be. The essence of aesthetic success is conceived as the poise between opposites, somewhat, it may be observed, as in the paradoxes of Kierkigaard. This is at once the form of art and the formula of life, according with the choreography of man's world and that of the stars. For this reason, too, the plays are so vital. Their form and meaning, body and soul, are one. Art has seldom served an ideal purpose more fully. Yet the morality is fundamentally aesthetic. Morality may well be in the subject-matter of the plays but their delightfulness springs directly from their form as art.

6 / *Achievement in Equilibrium*

INVESTIGATION OF the main features of Sanskrit drama may follow one of two major paths : we may consider how closely the plays themselves realize the somewhat confusing but abundant and often searching theoretical and philosophical writings on the drama by Sanskrit thinkers themselves, or, however highly their critical writings are appraised, we may prefer to proceed from fresh premises. It is true that the ancients must in many respects always be regarded as their own best critics and interpreters. As A. B. Keith has observed, their literature in general is highly self-conscious. Indian dramatists were certainly well aware not only of countless specific precepts and admonishments by the theorists but of many profound generalizations regarding art and life which they were pleased to exhibit, wherever practicable, in their plays. Many of the theoretical comments are of high importance not only historically but even for the present time. Nevertheless critical thought on so stimulating a subject does not end with the Sanskrit thinkers themselves any more than such thought in the field of Greek drama terminates with Aristotle. This chapter, though frequently indebted to the Indian thinkers, proposes an investigation from at least a number of new angles. Starting with several observations from the ancients, it aims to press forward with new generalizations. Indeed, were this not the case, such a study could hardly be justified, or at least be justified only in sorting out and interpreting certain remarks of the ancients acknowledged to be less than fully clear. Our comments are, then, at least grounded on some of the most familiar and impressive views of the ancients themselves and from those proceed further.

Any general review of the old Indian drama recognizes that its aims are primarily neither intellectual, moral, tragic, satirical, nor naturalistic. On the contrary, purely aesthetic principles are highly potent while the goal is a pleasure that is also held spiritually purifying. Attendance at the theatre is designed as an act of enjoyable edification or edifying joy ; the fruition of the play is both aesthetic and religious ; hence its achievement cannot be summed up in terms exclusively aesthetic or theological ; it is neither art for art's sake nor simply wisdom and indoctrination. The delight or joy to which the playwright aspires is equally of the aesthetic sensibilities and of the soul. Furthermore, the Indian playwright desires neither the more harrowing depths of tragedy nor the irresponsible hilarity of pure comedy. His ideal implies a phase of the serenity to which the deeper spirit of Asia has from its most venerable traditions been dedicated. There is in this drama, that is neither essentially tragic nor comic, a potent but elusive poise with which the drama of the West is unfamiliar. In some of the lesser plays there certainly occur strong elements of day-dreaming or trance, an island of illusion such as alcohol or drugs may induce. But these descriptions clearly fail to do justice to the major works of the Sanskrit stage.

No one following the theoretical comments scattered through the Sanskrit writers themselves can escape being impressed by the analogies, both explicit and implied, between music and the stage. Even if it be erroneous to hold that drama develops from the dance, it is clear that it develops in close association with it, and much as music is in many respects wedded to the dance, so it appears the mistress and inspiration of much of the Indian feeling for the stage, with its strong inclinations to stylization and abstract form. The theatre is conceived as functioning much as music, at once artful and therapeutic, and, indeed, much more than merely therapeutic, for it is not only a means of relieving or obliterating pain but of confirming well-being and happiness proceeding from an image of spiritual health and strength. The play is to induce us to feel through the harmony of its art the harmony presumed to reside equally in man's soul and in the religiously conceived universe. The end of its art, to repeat, is neither mimetic nor rationalistic, neither strictly moral nor intellectual, but a pervasive awareness of an inner harmony, with the refreshment from an experience in which the spirit is at the same time active and serene, an experience valid far beyond the games and toys of childhood and yet as gratifying and smooth in its operations as a game played with complete mastery of the conditions encompassing it.

If this is, in substance, the goal of the Indian dramatists and possibly of all the arts as conceived in the climate of Indian philosophy during the first millennium of the Christian calendar, how, it will be asked, do the playwrights proceed to attain their difficult goal or at least to approximate it ? The premise of this study is that a close examination of the goal itself much assists in explaining the more technical strategy of the dramatists. They aim at poise or serenity by the creation of an aesthetic equilibrium throughout both the major and minor features of their work. A principle of balances often seems to underlie the mythology and theology of the East. To a still greater degree this principle becomes the strategy of artists who make of these formulations in life the form and structure, even the very life, of their art. The tensions in their drama produce the symmetries of its composition. In each play there is observable not only a pervasive sentiment, or *rasa*, concerning which the critics have much to say, but a persistent and readily observable equilibrium between opposites, a condition with which the same critics seem to have been much less consciously concerned. In other words, the dramatists, being true artists, were wiser than either they or the contemporary critics were aware. Surely the playwrights were wiser than we ourselves are aware, for it is always timely to recall that the best key to art is that it has no key. But such ultimate caution by no means debars partial explanation. Let us see how far and how safely the simple formula of equilibrium as achieved by balance in likeness or antithesis carries us in unravelling the basic problems of the plays. The proposition, then, is that each play is based with exceptional rigidity upon a leading dichotomy, maintained in equilibrium, and on a large number of related and secondary patterns. Some such formula may, of course, serve for the elucidation of a large part of all drama and is by no means unrelated to the description of drama itself as conflict. But this interpretation fits the Indian stage more fully and reveals it more amply and suggestively than any other body of playwriting to which it may be applied. It is noteworthy that every one of the major Sanskrit plays presently to be analyzed is based on the formula, so familiar in myth, of separation and reunion. This applies not only to those plays most clearly utilizing popular myths themselves, as *Rāma's Later History*, *Shakuntalā*,

Vikramorvaci, and *Nāgānanda*, but even the political drama, *Mudrārāksasa*.

The argument can scarcely be conducted with an economy that remotely promises success unless the field of reference is quite sharply delimited. This is primarily because of the exceptionally glaring inequalities of merit within the Sanskrit drama which, after all, is the harvest of nearly ten centuries and of writing over a large part of a vast sub-continent. The conditions are anything but those of the trim little garden of the Greek theatre, with its four playwrights, all from a single city, from barely three generations, and each author represented by plays all clearly of a high level of merit, plays themselves, it seems, winnowed by time operating in one of his most rational and least capricious moods. Many of the Sanskrit plays mentioned, for example, by A. B. Keith are negligible as works of art or of philosophical insight and no one in his right mind could seriously apply to them the observations already made in these pages. But if the total body of drama is, to use a phrase from the English "Metaphysicals," a "dreadful miscellany," modern criticism and, one judges, the ancient critics as well, arrive at widely accepted views as to who are the chief dramatists and what works are their masterpieces. In most cases the larger part of the problem is prearranged, for with a single dubious exception no major playwright has left more than three plays and several are known only by one. A useful statement can certainly be made without placing a large number of plays under consideration. A bare half-dozen dramatists represented by seven plays provide an exceptionally substantial body of work. Such are Bhāsa represented by his masterpiece, *The Vision of Vāsavadattā*, Kālidāsa by his *Shakuntalā* and *Vikramorvaci*, Sūdraka by *The Little Clay Cart*, Harsa by *Nāgānanda*, Bhavabhūti by *Rāma's Later History*, and Visākhadatta by *Mudrārāksasa*. These are acknowledged as major plays ; several are long works ; all are impressive ; and few scholars will question that they provide abundant material for the proposed investigation. Each will be briefly considered, in what may possibly be the order of their composition, and the longest and most richly compounded of them thereafter examined in comparative detail, not only in respect of its major balancing of opposites but as regards the principle of equilibrium manifested in several aspects of its thought, narrative, architectural structure, and choreographic, theatrical and poetic style. The method itself can scarcely be regarded as unorthodox but the result of its application to this group of plays will, it is held, justify the view that they possess highly unusual and attractive qualities both as drama and as poetry.

I

The vision which Udayana enjoyed of his queen, Vāsavadattā, gives the title to Bhāsa's most celebrated play but the presence of her name and absence of his happily signifies the direction in which our attention should chiefly be drawn. The king himself does not appear in the first three acts, or, to put it differently, fails to appear until the play has run nearly half its course. Looking within his mind, we see, not him, but the images of his two queens. This is a work with an exterior and an interior, possibly of equal value. From the external view it represents the relations of two queens, one, Vāsavadattā, the earlier, seen in disguise as ward to the second, the princess Padmāvati, in the play's course becoming a queen. In the usual course of human relations Vāsavadattā would be jealous of Padmāvati, and Padmāvati, on realizing her husband's unalterable devotion to Vāsavadattā, would entertain nothing but hostile thoughts of her. Yet both queens are morally speaking heroines, having more than sisterly devotion for each other. Such competition in generosity on the part of these exemplary women is by no means uncommon in Indian drama, being witnessed, for example, on a less notable scale, in *The Little Clay Cart* in the relations between Vasantasēnā, Chārudatta's mistress, and his devoted wife. The second aspect of the ideal of poise in Bhāsa's play is indicated by the word "Vision" in its title. The play comes to its inner focus when its action is viewed in what we have designated as its interior, Udayana's mind. Throughout, the tension is between present and past, actuality and memory, outer and inner sight, the eye of the flesh and that of the mind. Such tension is, of course, metaphysical; the poet's conclusion is that reality, so far as humanity can experience it, is composite of the two elements in equilibrium. The play's structure, extended to the most minute features of its execution, depends upon this balance. Its harmony, both aesthetic and spiritual, hangs upon the validity of this concept. We witness far more than a personal relation between two women or a divided loyalty and devotion within a single mind. The poise presented is at once emotionally moving and essentially abstract. In a word, its closest analogy is music. Here not rival queens but rival themes are associated in such a manner as to produce the balanced composure of parts commonly called beauty. The student of dramatic literature would be hard put to it to discover outside the Sanskrit drama itself a play so consistently composed on the poising of two equally compelling forces, each with its set of facets matching that of the other.

However uncertain the date and authorship may be of *The Little Clay Cart*, ascribed to "King Sūdraka", this great play must often be associated with Bhāsa, since its earlier acts closely parallel Bhāsa's drama, *Chārudatta in Poverty*. Once again a title offers a clue of major significance. To any reader it must immediately be clear that many as are the characters in this exceptionally long and elaborate work, the focus lies to an exceptional degree on hero and heroine, Chārudatta and Vasantasēnā. And here the relationships are almost throughout those of strong contrast or comparison. He lives in poverty, in a broken-down house, she in opulence and in a palace ; he is an aristocrat who until the play's last moments is sinking lower and lower into misfortune ; she is a woman of the utmost success in the material world, who falls upon temporary disaster but also until the play's last moment is deprived of the state which Hindu morality regards as woman's supreme blessing, matrimony. These two, in the most diverse ways wrenched aside from the felicity which life should afford, are at length elevated to their proper station. He is hitherto seen in the winter of discontent, she for the most part in the full springtide and flowering of material prosperity. Each when alone is insufficient ; together they constitute a perfection, a complete rondure, and are, in fact, a symbol for the rotation of the seasons of the year, upon which all life, from the perspective of Hindu thought, depends. She, deprived of his presence, is virtually slain by Samsthānaka. He, deprived of her presence and even accused of murder, is all but slain by the executioner's sword. Although virtually the entire play, as will presently be shown, is woven of dualities, the dualities associated with its two chief characters stand in by far the most significant place. The title of Bhāsa's work indicates the most striking aspect of their contrast, whether the play is viewed chiefly on lines of natural, social, moral, or metaphysical thought ; he is poverty, she, opulence. And much as art itself demands both economy and abundance, the clay cart and the gold cart are two chariots, or *gharries*, that carry mankind through the rough road of experience. The drama's theme is developed as a profound study in equilibrium. To what a large extent its execution embellishes its central theme will be further considered in the second part of this chapter.

Kālidāsa is the Sophocles of Sanskrit dramatists, the most elegant, consistently poised and serene of them all. His dramatic master-piece, *Shakuntalā*, poses the problem of the equally compelling force of passion and obligation, the erotic and the moral values, both phases of experience viewed as in essence good but even in the best of men not at all times felicitously balanced. This is a drama of education by way of hard experience. Hero and heroine err, grieve, and ultimately redeem themselves. Overmuch moved by her erotic experiences, Shakuntalā neglects her social duties as mistress of a hermitage and hostess to its visitors. Dushyanta errs in quite contrary manner. At first he remembers that he is a king but forgets that he has become not only a lover but a husband. This forgetful-ness leads to a still graver fault. He fails to learn or to acknowledge that he is a father. In his case, to be sure, appears what may be regarded as a certain duplicity or sophistry on the part of the play-wright himself. So confirmed was the dramatic theory of his age in its idealization of the hero and the sacredness of royalty that no fault could be laid over-bluntly on the shoulders of a kingly hero. Dushyanta is nowhere depicted as making a false choice. Because of a curse inforced by powerful magic he forgets his obligation. This invention glosses the play's story with a somewhat super-ficial garment of serenity. The problem is, in fact, resolved on a far different and far deeper level than that of mere theatrical and courtly decorum or convention. Shakuntalā spends a long period in penance and in sorrow ; the king spends a period almost as protract-ed in quite as grievous and repentant a state. The reader must look behind the scenes to discover the king's guilt, though in the end neither person is found so grievously guilty as to require any mental act approaching the Christian requirement of forgiveness. Three of the most impassioned speeches in the play, occurring during the scene of its chief emotional crisis, voice Shakuntalā's accusation of her husband, one speech by herself, the two others by her faithful attendants. The audience no less than the king feels the full force of these accusations. Whatever apology is offered in compliance with dramatic theory, to the ancient Hindu reader no less than to the modern reader, Dushyanta as well as Shakuntalā has erred, passing through penance and suffering to contrition and absolution. The two are educated by an experience that is virtually a ritual into the mature and happy life where neither of its two major elements, passion and moral obligation, is actually sacrificed at the other's expense. This ideal condition cannot be better described than by designating it a state of equilibrium. The play walks a tight-rope between the pitfalls of too much and too little. The lovers reach not only the fruition of their love but the all-important establishment of their family through their passionate devotion. Shakuntalā learns that passion must not become selfish indulgence. It is well to observe that Dushyanta in the erotic melancholy of his repentance is almost as neglectful of his duties to his kingdom as Shakuntalā had previously been of the obligations imposed on her as mistress of her hermitage. The kingdom depends upon an heir and also upon its monarch's normal exercise of his official duties. Both Shakuntalā and Dushyanta are rendered morally ineffectual by separation from each other. It is on his absence that she errs and on her absence that the king succumbs to his melancholy and near-madness, from which only a celestial messenger recalls him. The ideal of the play, expressed with such subtle and even consummate art, is itself best described as a condition of harmony through equilibrium.

That *Vikramorvacī* reiterates much of the thought and basic symbolism of *Shakuntalā* is, or at least should be, a commonplace of criticism. In each case we have a seasonal myth, a story of separation in which the first fault, itself still presented as venial, is ascribed to the woman ; in each also a reunion occurs with the intercession of the two enveloping generations, the ancestors and the offspring. It is possibly to the disadvantage of the less popular but scarcely inferior work that the king, Purūravas, grieves but apparently does not repent nor engage in self-accusations. Nor is the moral delinquency of Urvacī examined as closely as that of Shakuntalā. *Vikramorvacī* is less a play on education for maturity and more a play symbolizing nature and its seasonal changes, together with the confirmed belief throughout the Orient that in some way the king's position resembles the sun's, the lord of the world and all living things, passing through the seasonal orbit. *Shakuntalā* is clearly more a drama of the earth and man, *Vikramorvacī*, of the heavens and the gods. Shakuntalā herself is at best only a minor deity, sprung from a nymph and a man. She is all-too-human and too girlish. And Dushyanta is pure king. Purūravas, on the contrary, passes, it seems, a large part of his life in the various halls of heaven and Urvacī is by birth a pure *Apsara*, sprung from Narayana's thigh. Only their son seems the earthly monarch and a creature with the fully recognized limitations of humanity. Nevertheless the play throughout moves artfully between planes of heaven and earth. Though Purūravas is virtually a demi-god, he must die ; though Urvacī is truly a nymph, she wins her wish to live on earth as long as Purūravas lives and to bear him a mortal son. The tensions of her life spring from an inner duality in her nature ; at heart she is half-divine and half-human. The glory as well as the ordeal of his life derives from his two-fold experience of being at once a king on earth and a soldier and courtier in heaven. When she is fully her celestial self, she performs plays in heaven dealing with the gods ; when she yields to her penchant for mortality, she substitutes, as heavenly actress, the name of her earthly lover for that of the god. Purūravas also discovers his chief problem to be that of giving to the gods what belongs to the gods and to mortality what belongs to his kingship. Here is not merely the subject matter of the play but its essence. It might almost have born the title which Lord Byron gave his "Mystery" dealing with the loves of men and angels, "Heaven and Earth." Such is the chief and most distinguishing dichotomy in Kālidāsa's most lyrical, graceful, and eminently poetic play, a work that especially in its last choral scenes seems almost to dissolve into music. Of all possible generalizations regarding it, this statement of its equilibrium defines it best.

Harsa's *Nāgānanda* appears at first glance two plays instead of one ; the first section, Acts One to Three, less serious than most of the chief Sanskrit plays, the second section, of equal length, Acts Four and Five, apparently more serious from a religious or philosophical point of view than the other works in question. The first part deals with an amorous courtship ending in marriage, with the revels of a wedding ceremony, where the attendants no less than the families of the bride and bridegroom are regaled. The touch is light, the mood epicurean. But the red robe of marriage abruptly becomes the red robe of sacrifice (quite as the red robe worn by Chārudatta is described as equally the garment of death and matrimony). Love as amorous play yields to love as mortal sacrifice. Jīmūtavāhana dies substituting himself for the young *naga* sacrificed to the voracity of *Garuda*, the bird of death. Beyond question there is a sex symbol here. The death of the old enters with the conception of the new ; the wheel of existence completes another rotation. Equally true is it that the playwright contemplates two aspects of love, the private, which is erotic, and the cosmic, which signifies the effacement of personal identity in identification with all life, to quote Bhavabhūti, "all moving and immovable things," by which are signified the animal and vegetative kingdoms. Chiefly through a number of unobtrusive devices Harsa artfully and successfully links the two sections of his play. Thus on her first appearance the heroine prays to Gaurī, the mother deity, in whose sacred grove the action occurs. The story comes to its conclusion as Gaurī, at the petition of a repentant *Garuda*, suddenly enters—the heroine at this moment recalling her former prayer—and as *dea ex machina* restores to life both Jīmūtavāhana and all the slain *nagas*. The first part of the play without the second would be too slight, the second without the first too terrible. Together they express a theory and a conviction of the harmony of physical and universal love, of pleasure and sacrifice, which to the logical, pragmatic Western mind presents an antithesis but to Eastern meditation presents the condition of complete equipoise.

Perhaps more than any other play Bhavabhūti's *Rāma's Later History*, also a diptych, is the fruition of certain major tendencies in Sanskrit drama. Especially in contrast with the emphasis on intellect and volition in Western drama or the merciless repression of emotional statement in the frozen melodramas of the Kabuki and the Noh, Sanskrit drama appears an apotheosis of emotional unrestraint. Literally viewed, it is indeed emotion unlimited. More seriously examined, however, the chief Sanskrit plays, as those considered in this chapter, are neither unrestrained nor excessively romantic because of their extreme artificiality and the apparently intuitive gift of the dramatists to realize in spiritual equilibrium the demands of aesthetic "distance" and "abstraction." *Rāma's Later History* shows this most forcefully. Based on an action that to a Westerner strongly invites moral and intellectual scrutiny, it shuns such scrutiny and proceeds to an intensive development on the emotional plane. No play is more tender-hearted. Aeschylus would have abhored it. The first half is engulfed in gloom ; the second half proceeds from joyous energy to the gates of ecstacy.

In their earlier appearances Rāma and Sītā are bewildered by their grief ; in their final appearance they are, of course, no less over-whelmed, but in waves of joy. From a literal-minded inspection there seem no limits to either their sorrow or their ecstacy. Yet the two moods make one play that transcends its moods with a wisdom expressed aphoristically in the first act ; Rāma observes : "Happy is the lucky man who somehow seeks and finds that unique thing, perfect identity of happiness and misery, favorable to all conditions, where the heart finds its solace, the flavor of which cannot be taken away by old age, which ripens into firm attachment after time has removed the veil of reserve." This passage not only describes the relations of man and wife but the basic sentiment within the play itself. In short, life matures in consonance with art's maturity, the clue to each being the attainment of equilibrium. The great scene between Rāma and Sītā in Act Three marks the quintessence of dejection ; the scenes shortly following, introducing Lava and the other youths and occupying so much of the rest of the play, are the elixir of exhilaration. Remarkably, the two moods do not clash aesthetically. On the contrary, they accord, as do the movements in Beethoven's most advanced compositions, with the most startling contrasts in their emotional content. That Bhavabhūti, possibly the most deliberate and even self-conscious of the Sanskrit playwrights, grasped the musical analogy in its full force may be inferred from lines spoken, or chanted, in unison by the confidantes of Rāma and Sītā in Act Three. "Oh wonderful is the arrangements of incidents ! The pathetic sentiment, though one in itself, being modified by various occasions, seems to assume different forms, as water assumes the various modifications of eddies, bubbles, and waves and it is all, nevertheless, but only water." Equilibrium is achieved by variations on a theme, display-ing a balance between two component parts, as life itself, for example, may be construed as a pattern of masculine and feminine elements. In a supreme sense the dramatist of the heart, Bhava-bhūti exhibits Blake's lyrical proposition that "life is made of joy and woe." But the Sanskrit poet is not content to rest with the romantic schism. The two parts of his masterpiece instead of defin-ing a fissure define a unity ; obviously they are two, profoundly they are one. This is equilibrium, at once the art and philosophy of a deeply meditative poet.

Although that excellent and eminently political drama, Visākhadatta's *Mudrārāksasa*, obviously differs widely from any of the preceding works in regards subject matter and temper, it proves helpful in demonstrating in fresh terms the fondness of all the chief Sanskrit dramatists for suspending the mind between rival claims in disparate areas of experience. The play is seasoned with bitter wit and never softened with cloying eroticism. Here the contention is resolved in terms that quite surprisingly introduce at least a touch of tragic sensibility. Rāksasa has sworn an oath to avenge the death of the monarch whom he has served as minister of state. His commitment during the action of the play seems more in terms of the honor of his oath than in terms of political or personal values. The king is dead. Whether Rāksasa could ever have regarded him as a friend as well as a monarch does not appear. But the oath has enormous binding powers. This obligation comes into conflict with the claims of friendship. This theme is announced in the first act and resolved only in the last. One of Rāksasa's aids, to whom he is deeply devoted as a personal friend, falls under the power of the minister who has succeeded Rāksasa and who in substance rules the kingdom. Rāksasa must choose between his honor that binds him to his oath and his affection that binds him to his friend, between an impersonal and a personal obligation. The second tie appears to him—and apparently to the dramatist—as the more binding. One good is sacrificed to another and to the extent that there is a substantial sacrifice there is at least an impingement on tragedy, comparatively rare in Sanskrit drama. This is the closest of all Indian plays to being a "problem play." But there is no debate ; the correct choice is obvious. From the present point of view, however, the main consideration is that with a persistence rarely found in any dramatist, Visākhadatta brings his play to its focus in reference to a duality. Unquestionably he admires both Rāksasa's loyalty to his vow and to his friend. The warm and emotional Indian mind in the end prefers the friendship to the public vow. The play by no means resembles a typical baroque drama contrasting the themes of love and honor, as a rule with decisive preference for one above the other. In the Sanskrit play, the emphasis is not on the superior desirability of one claim over the other but on the irony that two claims of such nearly equal force are made upon a divided and tormented soul. The conclusion is not that Rāksasa betrays the more grim honor but that to pursue this honor further would be in excess. He has done enough—all that his high intelligence and devotion can do. The play ends at the point where it no longer becomes possible for the hero to view such rival claims as existing in equilibrium side by side. Here is a dry test in experiments in living more optimistically presented in the possibly finer and more poetic plays of an earlier date. This is the last great Sanskrit drama. With it the tradition had run its course. In no other Sanskrit play does it appear that the pleasures of equilibrium have been purchased at the somewhat bitter cost of tragic irony.

II

The value of equilibrium in creating the mood of happiness or well-being which is the distinctly spiritual goal of Sanskrit drama has been analyzed with reference to the balance of a sense for memory and imminence in *The Vision of Vāsavadattā*, of passion and obligation in *Shakuntalā*, of heaven and earth in *Vikramorvaci*, of grief and ecstacy in *Rāma's Later History*, of pleasure and sacrifice in *Nāgānanda*, of honour and friendship in *Mudrārāksasa*, and of poverty and opulence in *The Little Clay Cart*. These seem the chief or at least most distinguishing features in the thought-content of the seven plays. In each the achievement of equilibrium colors the major element in composition. But the divisive conception of the problem play, or play based on one theme only, stands on the whole far apart from Indian practice and theory. A deeply poetic drama, as are all the chief Sanskrit plays, declines to be so narrowly confined. The main issue must be luminous and in no respect confining. Equilibrium itself as a condition or quality is present not only in the treatment of the major theme of each play but in its multitudinous aspects. Its dominance appears not merely in the development of the play's chief theme but in the development of scores of lesser themes as well. It becomes conspicuous in almost all phases, as in the play's structure and ideas, its language, action, and choreography.

The general structure of Sūdraka's work is remarkably harmonious though un-European. At the end the plot is not unravelled; instead, the knot is tied. At the beginning no clear problem has been proposed for solution. There is originally no knot to untie. Instead there are what appear to be loose threads which bit by bit, and to the delight of the audience, are drawn firmly together, but never completely tied until the last moments of the action. The

Western stage in its typical form begins with a statement of a problem which is at long last to be solved. The Indian stage begins with what appears to be a miscellany of natural experience, so that only at the last are we convinced that we have at all times been led by a poet's guiding hand. One method starts from the stem and proceeds to the branches ; the other, with at least as firm a sense of form, control, and even finality, commences at the tips of the branches and only at the last unveils the secret of the germinal force. *The Little Clay Cart* has by some Western critics been found wanting in certain elements of form. But is it not possible that a rigidly achieved form complies with the genetics of a principle of art different from our own ?

To summarize all the multiple features of the complex plot would require an expense of words denied this study. Suffice it to say that the duality of the design, placing Chārudatta on one side of the canvas and Vasantasēnā on the other, is strictly observed. The two meet only in the scenes of cardinal importance to the action, namely, in Acts One, Five, and Ten, that is, at the beginning, middle and end. Both come within an inch of death and both are revived. They are alike in showing toward all worthy persons with whom they come into contact a warm generosity and toward their intimates a still warmer friendship. Both are extravagant in this generosity but in the end reap the most unexpected fruits from it. The threads of their kindness reach out in multiple directions which at first seem the merest irrelevances though as time advances interlace to weave a firm fabric. The play is a remarkable construction whose basis is equilibrium. The many balls, some dark and tragic in tone, others gay and smiling, are held poised in space, like planets about a single sun. Whatever may be said on the particular manifestations of form illuminates the achievement of form as a whole and the germ of this form itself as poise. The wheel runs smoothly.

All episodes are held in balance. Two pairs may, to begin with, demonstrate this. Vasantasēnā, journeying, in Act One, through the streets at night, pursued by Samsthānaka, with his parasite and his slave, foreshadows her journey in Act Five through the street at night, accompanied by her parasite and slave. The theme is inverted. One is a pursuit, namely, of her shy lover; the other is an escape, namely, from her would-be ravisher. These situations further define an important balance or juxtaposition, actually vital to the

65

play, the contrast between the civil, refined, intellectual, warm hearted Chārudatta and the rude, coarse, foolish, and brutal Samsthānaka, the hero and the villain of the piece, antithetical to each other in so many studiously considered respects. In the first act the prince challenges the hero ; in the last he drives him to torture and all but brings him to his death. Chārudatta's leniency to the wretch whom he finally thwarts constitutes his final act of generosity.

The second instance of balance selected here is not, like the first, perspicuous, but woven with much subtlety into the fabric as a whole. Sthāvaraka, the servant, is a minor character who, none the less, speaks two of the play's most moving and poignant lines under circumstances meticulously paralleled. In the first instance in a generous attempt to save the heroine he submits himself to a thrashing ; in the second in a generous attempt to save the hero he exposes himself to the same brutal treatment. Each attempt is futile, the effort of a man destined to be generous but powerless, the antitype of Chārudatta, fated to be generous and in the end successful. In each instance the unhappy slave goes off the scene making virtually the same simple remark, that he has done all he can and yet accomplished nothing. He is that contradiction in terms, a humble martyr. A servant in a play has seldom been given so touching a role. For a likeness one should go, perhaps, to *The Cherry Orchard*. But the distinction is that Sūdraka, by balance and repetition, moulds his matter into the Hindu form, based on a comprehensive conception of equilibrium, whereas the Russian dramatist relies on the equally typical Western device of emphasis and climax.

The conception in the Sanskrit, as already urged, is essentially musical. It is to be noted that Chārudatta is at once a connoisseur of music and a performer. The four-times repeated proclamation in the last act is preceded on each occasion with a role of drums and certainly with other turns of musical embellishment and accompaniment. The style of composition renders the characters analogous to instruments in an ensemble.

In most Sanskrit plays, as here, there is a studied juxtaposition of the generations or the ages of men. In the last acts of *Shakuntalā*, *Vikramorvacī*, and *Rāma's Later History*, for example, the hero is flanked on one side by his young son, on the other, by elders of the last living generation. Here Chārudatta finds on one hand his son, who is still, we are several times reminded, in the stage of finding toys his chief delight, and on the other by the bald and elderly brahmana, Maitreya.

The style is based on meticulously studied and elaborate balances. First of all is the opposition, or rather, harmony, between Sanskrit and Prakrits ; then, the similar opposition between the sententious and the colloquial ; and the still more conspicuous alternation of verse and prose. Greek drama distinguishes passages of dialogue from choral passages, the former combining action and poetry, the latter combining music, dance and a totally different species of poetry. The Sanskrit theatre wears a cloth with more threads to the square inch. Its greatest passages are those combining in equal measure its finest theatrical achievements in dance, ritual, action, poetry, musical embellishments, and, almost without question, some species of recitative in strong contrast with the lighter dialogue in prose. Thus the dance-like movements, with artfully fumbling pantomime, in Vasantasēnā's street journey in Act One, the similar affects in her scene in Act Five, and Chārudatta's long procession past the chief stations in the city, bearing the stake for his impalement on his back, to his calvary in "the Southern Cemetery," combine the most inspired choreography, lyric poetry, and dramatic action in the play. In each case, especially in the much extended final death march, are numerous refrains, repetitions, strophes and anti-strophes. If a character is mentioned, he is likely to appear instantly, to the beauty of the form and the distress of the literal-minded. That this form is basically musical is further suggested by certain speeches declaimed in common by two characters, in short, dramatic duets. Thus, the Scribe and Provost in the ninth act are apparently two persons, though almost invariably speaking as one. (Similarly, "two friends" address Shakuntalā in Kālidāsa's masterpiece ; and *Rāma's Later History* contains many long and impressive passages of simultaneous speaking, whereby agreement between the speakers is powerfully underscored). These are among the "operatic" features of the Sanskrit stage. The oft-repeated stanza in which Chārudatta invokes vindication by Vasantasēnā, in this life or in another, a prayer whose potency miraculously leads to her material-ization and thus brings the play to its happy conclusion, is a fine instance of a phenomenally balanced structure within the Sanskrit drama. The repetition not only of stanzas and other speeches but of phrases, so much a part of the tragico-burlesque role of Sam-

sthānaka, points in the same direction, as do the much repeated
and stylized gestures which the action unmistakably calls for.
An instance of the latter is Maitreya's peregrination through the
eight courts of Vasantasēnā's fabulous palace, where each peregrination of the stage denotes a new courtyard, each repeated
gesture between the eight episodes, the crossing of a new threshold.
On each advance both he and his guide repeat a verbal formula.

The organization of the more lyrical passages into strict and
balanced forms appears strikingly in the first scene of importance,
the pursuit of Vasantasēnā. Speeches are in general arranged in
ABC order, Samsthānaka, the Vita, and the Slave each speaking
a distinct dialect. Thus the inevitable analogy is found in ensemble
music, each speaker being a distinct instrument in a calculated and
inclusive pattern. Sanskrit drama is a high-water-mark of stylization, which in turn almost inevitably means a balance of forms.
This stylization does not, however, as that of the Japanese stage,
result in stiffness and repression of a warm humanity. The style
lives. It is a blessed style.

The play yields its scholars such ample rewards that prudence
and economy, not dearth of materials, must put an end to the enter-
prise. It would be almost impossible to list the passages of dialogue
having a lyrical or balanced movement. Of considerable importance,
of course, is the juxtaposition of speeches by Chārudatta's virtuous
mistress and his almost incredibly patient and generous wife.
Maitreya's exchange of terse comments with Samsthānaka in Act
One does much to set the play's action in motion but still more to
indicate its style. The exchange of remarks in the witty talk
between Kumbhīlaka, Maitreya, and Chārudatta in Act Five,
so like wit-combats in Shakespeare between servants and their
masters, or, what no doubt is historically more pertinent, those
between corresponding figures in Greek and Latin comedy, helps
to sustain on a relatively low level the rigidly controlled form
set by the more emotional scenes. The smaller the fragment examined, the clearer the play's general nature becomes. Consider the
last words spoken by Vasantasēnā before an unreal death shadows
her and the final words spoken by Chārudatta on the corresponding
occasion in his own experience. Each is being attacked ultimately
because each loves the other. Each is Samsthānaka's victim. And
each calls upon the other for aid. At the theatre or in an early
reading of the play these parallels may be overlooked. But of

such symmetry, usually bilateral in design, the play is largely compounded. *Gharri* matches *gharri*; toy cart matches toy cart ; man matches man; and woman matches woman.

As motive force in the plot Sarvilaka occupies the central position. His importance is stressed by his use of a style which has been designated as a particularly elegant Sanskrit. He is housebreaker and a thief but also a noble regicide, a liberator of the oppressed, a redeemer of the slave, a pious brahmana and a true hero. (He is housebreaker in the manner of Ulysses.) The keystone of the structure so far as action is concerned, he honors Chārudatta and ingratiates himself with Vasantasēnā, whose favorite slave he frees and marries. His thoughts and actions help to keep Chārudatta and Vasantasēnā associated in the mind of the audience during several scenes in which they remain physically separate. Sarvilaka prefers the claims of friendship to those of his wife, Āryaka to Madanika, as later Chārudatta prefers those of Āryaka to his mistress, Vasantasēnā. Regarding the play, as one undoubtedly should, as a story of hero and heroine, seen in numberless positions of essential likeness and accidental dissimilarity, it is Sarvilaka, more than any other figure subsidiary to the two leading characters, who helps to define the balance between their roles. Samsthānaka is merely the foil, or villain, the antithesis of Chārudatta, and actually holds a less important position in the play as a story, a poem, and a meditation than the energetic housebreaker, whose actions unintentionally set in motion the extraordinarily ironical adventures of Vasantasēnā's jewels and of the chief characters themselves.

Lesser characters are also in balance. Two opposed types highly prominent in Sanskrit thought, literature and drama are the gambler, to whom all the world seems governed by chance, or fatality unexplained, and the devotee or mystic, who believes in and contemplates the inexplicable. The gambler embraces chance as his mistress ; the man of religion embraces a mystic vision that regards chance as an illusion no less than reason as an illusion. One stands within the heart of chaos, the other, at, or approaching, the essence of truth. Although no major Sanskrit play is a strictly doctrinal or theological work, all such plays pay respect to religious doctrine and to the philosophical beliefs that accord with it. *The Little Clay Cart* is on its surface about this world ; it is a clay cart. But it implies a gold cart, the chariot of divine wisdom. So one of its characters in himself defines both of these contradictory coordinates. When first seen, he is a gambler. On meeting the heroine, he changes his way of life as completely as possible and becomes a wandering religious mendicant, an ascetic. His career defines the extremes of worldliness and other-worldliness, sensuality and spirituality, between which the main current of the play flows. This character defines its boundaries. He is the former servant of Chārudatta, the faithful protegee of his patroness, Vasantasēnā. Thus equilibrium, both philosophical and theatrical, is found even in one of the admittedly lesser figures of this calculated play, calculated indeed, but perhaps no more so than the half-dozen other mas terpieces of Sanskrit drama in turn more briefly examined in the first section of this chapter.

A construction in equilibrium out of contrasted or conflicting elements : such to these playwrights is the secret of art and the essence of wisdom. But above all they are artists and their artifacts are highly abstract, even when the imagery, as in Sūdraka's play, is at times naturalistic. To them equilibrium is a poise that is not a pose, for it is far more intuitively than logically discovered. To them also it resembles the harmony of music, the ordering of heaven or the stars. The successful embodiment of this equilibrium gives the plays their unique flavor and lasting charm.

7 / Sacred Drama

APPRAISAL OF the classical Indian drama demands more than passing recognition of the attraction of a type of playwriting fully answering the description of sacred drama. True, so pervasive is the religious consciousness in all ancient Indian thought that no play of consequence lies wholly outside the pale of religious influence. Virtually all areas of experience stand within this circumference, including the political, social, economic and emotional life. Conversely, the most conspicuously religious plays reveal much of the political and social order and are far more than explicitly theological or devotional. The serious Indian drama falls in these respects into two classes : plays depicting a court culture more clearly than the religious culture and those revealing religious thought more conspicuously than the morals and manners of a court. Scarcely a single drama is without Brahmins or ascetics of some description among its important characters and all are dedicated to and overshadowed by a mythology still forceful in the lives of their audience. The more national or widely popular the play, the closer it cleaves to a folklore essentially religious and reveals a culture profoundly influenced if not even dominated by a priesthood. Certain plays, in short, are conspicuous for their distillation of the religious life of the community. Emanating from a monastic or at the least an ascetic philosophy, they successfully project its emotions and ideas in dramatic form. For their sources they rely relatively less than other works upon the epic material, more upon avowedly religious texts.

That the social genesis of the chief division of Sanskrit drama, whatever may be its content, is secular rather than religious appears from a survey of plays generally acknowledged as masterpieces, notably those by Bhāsa, Kālidāsa, Sūdraka and Bhavabhūti. With the fairly conspicuous exception of the two concluding acts of Harsa's *Nāgānanda*, such is also the quality of that important author's works, who, it will be recalled, was himself a king. On turning to the most specifically religious plays which are also of literary distinction, one is drawn to two pieces well outside the area of typical Sanskrit drama, to the chief play in the Tamil language, flourishing in Southern India, *Arichandra*, and the chief work in the Tibetan offshoot of Sanskrit, *Tchrimekundan*, the former a product of tropical India, the latter of the bleak mountains across her northern border.

These works have considerable dramatic power. They are, accordingly, distinguishable from a number of plays written in the late, declining period of Sanskrit drama, which tend to be dry, allegorical, intellectual, non-theatrical, and, at least in our own eyes, indisputably pedantic. The two masterpieces in question resemble, roughly speaking, the great and stirring religious Mystery Plays in thirteenth-century Europe, with their subjects taken from biblical narrative ; the decadent Sanskrit plays, which may be neglected with such slight loss, resemble the pedantic allegories, commonly though not very felicitously termed "Morality Plays," produced in such mechanical profusion throughout the waning years of the Middle Ages.

These two Asian dramas share so much in common that there is obvious economy in viewing them under the same head. Each could better be described as a national drama or possibly even as a folk drama than as a product of sophisticated literature. That each is ascribed to a known author, the Tibetan work to the sixth Talelama, Tsongs-Dbyangsrgyamthso, a poet and general dilettante flourishing in the seventeenth century, and the Tamil play to a scholar, Renga Pillay, has actually small significance. Each play is certainly far older than either of these writers. The Tibetan ascription is presumably honorific ; that to Renga Pillay alludes merely to a rewriting in a metre different from that of earlier versions. Each is a profoundly traditional drama strongly reflecting the established religions and the religious institutions of its own country, each an apology for an outlook partly Brahmanic which, as far as the popular drama allows us to judge, proves remarkably alike in each land. Each tells the story of a prince who is, in our own eyes, more a religious than a secular leader, whose conduct is

more befitting a saint than a king. On his faithful obedience to
religious precepts depends both the physical and spiritual welfare
of his kingdom. His piety is of primary concern in the seasonableness
of the rains and fruitfulness of the crops, in the moral and religious
discipline of the folk.

The stories are remarkably alike. A prince at the beginning and
end of the play possesses seemingly infinite power and riches,
although during the greater part of the action he withstands in the
name of religious piety the most extreme trials and tribulations.
Especially the Tamil play resembles the story of Job. Both monarchs
carry with them into their misery their devoted queens and their
offspring. Here it proves of no great consequence that one king
has only a single child, his son, the other, three children, two sons
and a daughter. In each case pious devotion compels him to accord
to any petition from Brahmins or sacred men, even though their
petitions are from the rational point of view excessively cruel and
immoral. Each sacrifices his material prosperity to what he deems
his sacred duty and his sense of an ideal of righteousness. Each is
recklessly extravagant in his charity, giving away his boundless
wealth. In each case the wife is renounced and the offspring placed
in virtual slavery. The prince himself suffers the utmost physical
hardship and indignity, wholly contrary to the decorum in the
courtly dramas based on the *Rāmāyana*, the *Mahābhārata*, and
developed from the main stem of Sanskrit theatrical tradition, with
its solicitude for a serene, courtly and aristocratic type of idealization. The distinction between the two types is almost as great as
that between *Le Morte d'Arthur* and *The Little Flowers of Saint
Francis*. A cynical or even a Marxist interpretation of the Tamil and
Tibetan dramas would readily pronounce them an apology for the
superiority of the priestly over the princely caste. Such a view
would in all probability, however, be at best partial. The plays are,
or at least in their origins were, obviously sincere in religious and
metaphysical inspiration.

Clearly, each grew ; it was not made in the sense in which a
sophisticated literary work is made by a single author. Each was
performed year after year, even century after century, in towns
great and small throughout a wide geographical area. Only in
relatively recent years was the Tibetan drama confined to an
annual ceremonial production in the capital, Lhasa. The Tamil
play, it must be confessed, is a trifle less a folk play and more a

73

literary drama ; it seems to have lost its wide theatrical currency well before our own century. *Tchrimekundan* survives in several manuscripts, though it has seldom been printed and at that only in comparatively recent times. The versions differ widely. None, so far as is known, is a conventional dramatic text ; all read somewhat as a narrative, with "he said," and "she said," introducing speeches and with an appreciative amount of pure description. Yet about ninety per cent of the work is in dialogue and no doubt whatsoever exists that the reader holds a play in his hands. What he holds, to be more specific, is the groundwork for a theatrical performance, never reduced to a standard version of any sort, either in written or spoken form ; the actors are invited with much license to enlarge and improve on the basis of a firm core of traditional material.

Interestingly enough, this by no means signifies an impromptu acting and improvisation. The performers were often monks and presumably literate. Each could enlarge or subtract as he saw fit. In recent productions it is said that Tibetan actors held long manuscript-scrolls in their hands from which they read their parts. There seem to be no reliable reports on how much or little the version discovered in Outer Mongolia by Jacques Bacot in 1912 has been heard by Europeans or even used in modern times. To all appearances, the Tibetan drama enjoyed a literary renaissance some six hundred years ago and from this era the greater number of the transcriptions at least descend. There is every likelihood that popular, choreographic and spectacular features have in modern times materially reduced the poetic texture of the performances. Theatrical conditions probably changed less radically in Tibet, however, than in India, the dramatic legends of Tibet undergoing less of a deterioration in popular presentation than in the lands to the south. But it is also highly probable that the strictly literary quality of the Tibetan stage at no time approached the ripeness of plays by Kālidāsa, Sūdraka, or Bhavabhūti—or, for that matter, of *Arichandra*.

The Tamil masterpiece is known to fewer scholars than the great Sanskrit plays and to English readers only through the translation made nearly a century ago (1863) by Mutu Coomara Swamy. This translation is of good literary quality, though somewhat freer than the version of *Tchrimekundan*. The translator of *Arichandra* acknowledges and even specifies a few inconsiderable omissions and even admits some slight interpolating phrases of his own to smooth the play's course for his reader. Nevertheless his scholarship, both as a translator and as an annotator, seems creditable even by the stricter twentieth-century standards. His version is eclectic. According to his own account, he used several manuscripts in addition to printed texts. These circumstances might be thought almost tangential to the present inquiry, which is aesthetic and philosophical rather than scholarly or linguistic, were it not that they so clearly indicate the kind of work with which one deals. It is virtually a sacred gospel over which no Jerome exercised a critical censorship.

In the intensive but loosely organized religious life of India the producer no more demanded a standard text for such a work than the singers of British or American ballads demanded a text for their favorite pieces. Certainly the plays existed in scores of widely different forms. The vitality lies in the focus upon a potent myth and on an accumulation of poetic eloquence to which several centuries and innumerable hands have contributed. To use European analogies, both Indian plays stand midway between the Passion Play and *Everyman*. This further describes both their peculiarly compelling force and their relatively naive quality. Although they may be read today with much pleasure and edification, or even enjoyed upon a hypothetical stage, they were written with authority not on paper but in the hearts of two great and religiously inspired peoples. They stand midway between the extravagantly sophisticated art-works constituting the classical Sanskrit stage and the mountains and forests that formed the cradles from which they rose. They are part of a social landscape ; one may compare them in turn to a monastic town crowning a mountain in Tibet and to a richly carved temple itself almost a part of the jungle of tropical India. In short, they are an art that merges into the history of a people. This further accounts for much of their dignity.

It is possibly no more than an accident that even in the styles of the two works there lies a contrast in terms of their native landscapes. In the versions most available to us, the Tibetan play has a northern austerity. It is relatively brief ; episodes are short ; action is brisk ; the poetry has few ornaments ; there is a stark simplicity and relentless focus on the central theme. Persons preferring a forthright statement may take peculiar satisfaction in it. One is reminded of the straightforward brevities of the

75

Gospel according to Saint Mark. The Tamil drama, on the contrary, is much longer and far more elaborated. To be sure, in production the Tibetan work, aided by pageantry and dance, quite possibly consumed a longer time than the Indian. It is said to have been regularly extended to a festival production for three days. But nothing in the text which we possess indicates the extensive elaboration of episodes or proliferation of fancy found in *Arichandra*. Of primary importance, however, is not the distinction in verbal style but the strong unity of purpose inspiring each work throughout. Their emotional effectiveness is said to have been extraordinary. Stoical Tibetan mountaineers are reported to have wept bitterly at the pathos of their beloved national drama and the same was unquestionably the case with the more volatile audiences witnessing the Tamil play.

The contrast between the austerity of the style and the pathos of effect in the Tibetan drama proves especially remarkable. This work is severe not only in style. It is also abstract to a far more pronounced degree than *Arichandra*. A plausible explanation for this is that the form in which we possess the Tibetan play descends only from the later years of the Sanskrit drama, when allegory of a scholastic or even pedantic manner was much in fashion. The profound emotional and religious conviction of Tibetans presumably helped to save their national drama from dryness, yet allegorical to a strong degree it certainly is. The names of both people and places are fashioned on the basis of abstract nouns. Naturalistic touches such as abound in the warmer drama from the south are strikingly absent. No one seeing or hearing *Tchrimekundan* could infer anything whatsoever of the manners or customs of the country from which it derives. The poet's stern devotion to his subject dissuades him from any humorous or tangential embellishment. He launches directly upon his theme and concludes his work (at least in the version referred to above) with a summary invocation.

As in a seasonal myth, the hero is exiled, here for twelve years (the time, incidentally, marked by the separation between Rāma and Sītā or, to put the case differently, the time required for their offspring to reach puberty. The twelve revolutions of the moon should also be noted here). To relate the story—one can hardly say, plot—only illustrates the succinctness of the whole. A son and prince of altogether legendary generosity gives away a vast portion of his estate. Moreover, he gives a prince known to be an enemy of his own country a magic jewel which grants its owner the fulfillment of all his wishes. It is thus the insignia of infinite power. Tchrimekundan, the Son and redeemer, is exiled by his father (God, the Father) at the instigation of an evil counsellor (Satan), though a kindly counsellor, a conciliatory spirit, grieves at this harshness. The hero's saintly charity is subjected to a series of tests. In turn he gives away all remaining possessions, together with his children and his wife, though the last is promptly returned. Those petitioning him are for the most part Brahmins, or at least so appear to him, for several are later discovered to have been gods in disguise.

To a blind Brahmin the princely saint gives away his own eyes, hoping thereby to gain the third eye of religious vision. There are vivid and essentially symbolical pictures of the severities of the desert and mountain landscapes through which he journeys to the city of his ultimate penance. After faithfully sustaining his ordeal, the term of his exile being ended, he returns to his native kingdom. Overcome by the spectacle of his generosity, the enemy prince returns the jewel that grants all desires. The meaning here is that Tchrimekundan's own desires are at last chastened into pure spirituality, the desire of the ego totally effaced, together with all cupidity for material things. His treasures, his eyes, his children, and his wife are all restored, augmented with a new blessedness. Father and mother receive their son, who is crowned king.

The play is a pageant of holiness, an imitation of a mental action, not of an historical or a social action. If any naturalism whatever can be detected, it is in the descriptions of the wasteland scenery, the incomparably rugged panorama of the Himalayas. Such scenery supplies the ideal backdrop for the austere philosophy. No one need accept the doctrine to realize the human validity of the thought, which proves as real and emotionally convincing as sublime passages in the three proverbially associated German composers, Bach, Beethoven, and Brahms, or, if one prefers to turn elsewhere, in the most moving scores of Monteverdi, Handel, or Gluck. Of Mozartian grace, elegance or sophistication there is little or nothing. But of spiritual nobility there is much ; such drama measures the grandeur of the human soul against the sublimity of Everest. The play is a parable of non-resistance, pacifism, resignation, peace.

In certain of its facets it looks not toward the past but toward the future. Should the world of the atomic age learn the lesson of peace, it may well be remembered that this was written in the gospel-drama of the Lhamas, wherein man is enjoined to live with his fellowmen harmoniously under the constant threat of an inimical nature. Should the world of the atomic age, on the contrary, turn with altogether unprecedented violence to the betrayal of humanity in atomic war, then the more than stoical resignation of *Tchrimekundan* would more than ever come into request. It is hard to deny the nobility of the conception. But the reader may well wish to supplement its bleak abstractions with a warmer and more pliant humanity. Even its pathos remains inflexible. The tears freeze on the cheek.

Arichandra preaches the same doctrine in a far different spirit, but, all its elaborations to the contrary, with equal point and force. The version presented by Coomara Swamy is doubtless representative and certainly generous in scope. As in the Tibetan play, action progresses steadily without aid from such conventions of the Sanskrit theatre as act divisions. With much astuteness the playwright provides a long preliminary action depicting the hero's opulence, his marriage to an ideal and even seductive princess, and his wise and prosperous reign. This with calculated contrast sets off the distressing episodes to follow. The scene shifts abruptly to heaven, where, as usual in Hindu mythology, the saints mingle with the gods. The singularly austere saint, Wis Wamitra (known elsewhere as Shakuntalā's father) is jealous of one of his fellow sages and generally skeptical of human integrity. Wis Wamitra holds that there is no honest man on earth, no, not one. Vasitta, his rival, maintains that King Arichandra is incorruptible. The god Indra pronounces that Wis Wamitra is licensed to tempt Arichandra in order to determine whether this saintly monarch will at any time fall into sin. The play's action is suspended on the wager between the two sages, overseen by the celestial umpire, Indra.

Arichandra, most resolute of mortals, is tormented like Job and tempted like Saint Antony. The main question is simply, will he yield to cupidity, sensuality, or any falsehood whatsoever in order to extricate himself from his distress ? Will he deny any request, no matter how unjust, made by a Brahmin ? Will he succumb to any alluring temptation ? Will he yield to any torture, physical or mental, so that he departs from "truth." Incidentally, the word "truth" or its antithesis, "lie," may not ideally convey the poet's meaning but possibly no better words in English can be found.

The unfortunate king is forced in turn to give away his riches and his kingdom, to go into exile, to sink into poverty. The gradations of his torment are studied with extraordinary skill, each episode adding a greater grief. He is tormented first by his painful journey. Actual physical torture is represented but this only half-way through the story and far subtler cruelties are progressively applied. By degrees he is reduced to the very lowest order in the caste-ruled society, becoming the burner of corpses and for his food given only the rice stuffed in the mouths of the dead. He loses his prime-minister, who has been his most faithful follower and friend. In turn he sells himself, his only son, and his beloved wife into bondage, each to a loathsome member of the lowest rank. There is remarkable pathos in the scenes of parting.

The action is admirably scaled and timed according to a principle of playwriting widely practised in many languages. At first leisurely and descriptive, the style grows constantly more brisk and accelerated. The scenes, too, become less conventional and more naturalistic, less artificial and more poignant. Arichandra's small son is forced to go into the dangerous woods to gather grass for sacrifices. Bitten by a snake, he dies. The mother discovers his body. She requests the keeper of the cemetery that the body of the boy should be burnt. Only after an interval in this gruesome conversation do the woman and the guardian of the graveyard discover to each other that they are man and wife, the one-time king, Arichandra, and his one-time queen, Sandramati. Arichandra refuses to burn the corpse because the mother can offer no fee such as the law requires. On her way through the woods she discovers the body of the son of the ruler of the city in which she and her husband are exiled. She is promptly apprehended and accused of murder. Thereupon she is brought back to Arichandra, this time for decapitation. But as, once more in pious obedience to the law, he raises his sword to kill his own wife, the sword itself is suddenly transformed into a string of superb pearls. "The Gods of Heaven, all Sages, and all Kings, appear suddenly to the view of Arichandra." Siva himself now declares that Wis Wamitra has lost his wager, for Arichandra has proved incorruptible. The god restores the dead son to life and the king and queen to their original thrones, with augmented wealth and blessings.

Although the play is without the sophisticated or self-conscious art of the great Sanskrit masterpieces, it is none the less an impressive work. Its many episodes all serve one end by means of one of the most colossal montages in dramatic literature. A play which begins as a courtly romance marches with relentless pace into the area of deeply human and profoundly religious drama. Pathos is much more natural and less austere than in the sister drama from the mountains of Greater India. The grotesque delineation of the brahmin tempters is unique and theatrically admirable. The chief among them are gods in disguise.

The dual personalities of these important figures exemplify a condition of much importance for the Sanskrit theatre. In the more secular plays, as the politically orientated *Mudrārākṣasa*, disguise similar to that commonly found on the Elizabethan stage is used. But quite another device at once subtler and more fundamental in its imaginative force is employed where deities are concerned. According to firmly established Indian theology, a god may manifest himself as any creature at any time and place. Especially in such religious plays as *Tchrimekundan* and *Arichandra*, this divine power became a notable feature of the presentation. The dual personality was quite probably on certain occasions realized through the use of masks. Masks seem not to have been commonly used in the courtly Sanskrit plays but were extensively employed in the more popular, explicitly communal dramas of Tibet and of southern India and Ceylon. Vestiges of the practice survive even to the present day, where primitive looking masks constitute an important feature of the performances. Theatrically brilliant revelations occur in the last scene of *Arichandra*, as naturalism is transformed into philosophy and supernaturalism. The hateful pariah, Veravakoo, turns out to be in truth Yama, God of Death, the odious, low-minded brahmin, Kalakanda, to be Agni, God of Fire. These transformations, it will be recalled, have strict parallels in *Tchrimekundan*. In the Tamil play even the tormenter, Nekshetra, disciple of Wis Wamitra, is condoned on the ground that he is only "the tool of another." Fate has controlled all, operating to the ultimate good of all. In the end this play becomes an extraordinary conjunction and synthesis of the natural and the abstract, entertainment and edification, the secular and the divine. It is beyond doubt a major work of art.

8 / *Deficiencies*

IN INTERPRETING or appraising a dramatic literature as unusual as the Sanskrit even its merits are seen the more clearly when those qualities appearing to our eyes as defects are taken into account. It is not only that a judicious judgment is sought. The highlights are defined by the shadows, the strength itself in often obscure ways is associated with the weakness. Much the same forces that on the one hand led to the greatness of Sanskrit drama led on the other to its defects. Its merits epitomize what India has chiefly to give in terms of the spirit to the world, its blemishes as seen from a cosmopolitan point of view spring largely from the characteristics limiting a considerable part of it not only to the peculiar taste of India itself but to India of the Middle Ages. The attraction of this drama derives in large measure from its religious idealism ; much of its unattractiveness proceeds from an evasiveness in morality attributable with almost equal plausibility to either an optimism or a pessimism that is an offshoot of a religious view of life. In the course of these studies passing references have been made to certain aspects of the Sanskrit stage lowering it in the estimation of the modern mind. The subject should be sufficiently rewarding to justify a brief, independent investigation.

A few relevant considerations, even though fairly obvious, require preliminary statement. The grammar of Sanskrit and the extraordinary dialectical peculiarities of the plays make translations even at their best unsatisfactory. Although the difficulties are less than those presented by Chinese or Japanese drama, they remain considerable. Yet a few quite successful versions, as Revilo Pendleton Oliver's translation of *The Little Clay Cart*, and Sri Aurobindo's translation of *Vikramorvaci*, attest that solutions may be found. In quite different terms, Indian criticism itself, as already observed, makes the sharpest distinctions between the major and minor plays. Roughly speaking, four or five hundred plays survive, about half of which have been printed and less than a quarter translated into English. Of these, again, the works of undisputed excellence number hardly twenty or thirty. The gap between the strongest and weakest Sanskrit plays known to us is almost unthinkably wide. The best rise to the heights of the world's finest theatre, the poorest with almost equal abruptness plunge into puerility. If the problem of evaluation were throughout as simple as the foregoing statement, however, small incentive would exist for the remarks to follow. But the case is much less drastic and more complex than at first appears. The masterpieces themselves reach their eminence without gratifying us in many of the ways in which we are accustomed to be inspired by the most rewarding theatre. Provocative distinctions lie between the Indian plays which seem most valuable to the West and those held in highest estimation by the Indians themselves. The latter must have merits which, whether undervalued by the West or overvalued by the Indians, must at least repay not only historical but critical examination. There are several plays well worth consideration which producers may not as a rule care to stage nor critics to praise. Though they cannot be expected to yield the keenest delight, they may quite possibly evoke fruitful ideas.

Before viewing these pieces of merely average stature in any detail it is wise to define the general issues at stake or, in other words, the outstanding qualities of the Hindu theatre that fail to satisfy the West or which even arouse its distaste. Probably the two foremost qualities of this description are the fatalism that dampens the will and its corollary, a deficiency in strong ethical conviction. Characters are insufficiently free to make dramatic choices and insufficiently convinced of the ethical importance of their choices when made. Evil is limited, as, in consequence, is the moral imperative. Not only is the drama as a whole unintellectual, it is without a sense of animated debate. In these respects it stands at the antithesis not only from Ibsen and Shaw but from Euripides and Racine. Whereas Western drama appears to be in our own eyes all the more dramatic in being an arena wherein ideas are debated and issues fought out, Indian drama is a stage whose main issues have been fully solved long before the play begins and where equilibrium and stability are the qualities to which the theatre itself is primarily dedicated. In the contemplative Indian drama action seems incidental or at best a means to an end, whereas in the strenuous theatre of the West action constitutes less a means than an end. With the conception of action itself Aristotle begins his definition of serious drama. The Western mind is loath to accept the premises of the Sanskrit stage, which is probably the most contemplative of all the great dramatic literatures. Even the Chinese and Japanese theatres give an impression of a more advanced objectivity.

The Sanskrit play must, according to imperative tradition, have a hero but in Western eyes this hero looks a trifle pallid. The most obvious explanation is that the protagonist lacks a really sinister antagonist. Indian drama affords no real equivalent for the Western villain. It is notable that in by far the greatest of the Rāma plays, Bhavabhūti's masterpiece, Rāvana does not appear. In the works where he does appear he more nearly resembles a hostile force in nature than a hostile force in society or an enemy of the people. Significantly, during the long centuries of decline in the Hindu stage Rāvana became in popular presentations a god to be placated or even a half-humorous figure. Like the serpent, he becomes symbol of healing rather than of death. Though the acute George Meredith observed that a tragic tale needs no villain, there obstinately remains in Western criticism the idea of the tragic fault in the protagonist. But the hero of the Sanskrit stage is required to be almost, if not completely, blameless. (Homer in the first book of *The Iliad* mentions "the blameless Ethiopians" but leaves them strictly to their own devices, preferring to follow the fortunes of those eminently fallible heroes, Achilles and Ulysses.) The Indian view is likely to appear in Western eyes not only intellectually and morally weak but positively undramatic and even to smack of insipidity. The Hindu drama seems slippery and soft; our tradition instructs us to look for a sterner and more angular statement of life.

If these observations apply to the heroes, still more strongly do they to the heroines. Most Sanskrit dramas possess a heroine; in her the passivity, at no time completely absent in the hero, is magnified ten fold. As he is obedient to fate, she is obedient also to him. This is not so much her choice as her destiny as woman. Conflict between the sexes, a major theme in both the comedy and tragedy of the West, does not exist on the Sanskrit stage. It is scarcely a misrepresentation to state that most of the heroines are little more than privileged members of a harem. Their privileges are few, their freedom of action and choice is severely limited. Devotion to husband and child as a rule circumscribes the boundaries of their emotional life. From this condition the dramatists develop the most masterful and moving scenes of pathos and reach lyrical heights of the purest joy. But Shakuntalā is no Juliet. And of course a Lady Macbeth, a Cleopatra, a Medea, or a Clytemnestra becomes unthinkable for the Indian playwrights. Although many of the most celebrated and moving episodes in Sanskrit drama are focused on women, here in particular the light that strikes them is only too likely to seem comparatively pale. Pathos is gained at the expense of force.

Which philosophy of life is to be preferred, that of the contemplative East or of the active West, is not the subject of this essay. Neither is any ultimate evaluation of the two dramatic literatures intended. Perhaps the best available conclusion is merely the provisional one that the West must in some degree shift its philosophical outlook if it is to derive from even the best of the Sanskrit theatre as keen an aesthetic pleasure as it does from its own. Yet in many and grave terms of appraisal the Sanskrit stage appears equal or even superior to that of the West. This is a theme for later chapters.

Especially outside the confines of India itself a further reservation respecting Sanskrit drama springs from the rigidity of its conventions, determined both by critical precept and long-established practice. Seldom, if ever, is a dramatic tradition so firmly grounded as that extending through centuries from Bhāsa's *Vision of Vāsavadattā* to Bhavabhūti's *Rāma's Later History*. Not only are situations, theatrical devices, and even phrases repeated in play after play; the initiative of the creative artist himself seems to be discouraged by the rigid formulas of his art. Characters are repeated in a long, descending procession, as the hedonistic king, the jealous queen, the obedient mistress, the scheming and devoted prime minister, or the clownish *vidūsaka*. Even their very names are reiterated, as names in the *commedia dell'arte*. The playwright recreates as much as he creates; he imitates as often as he invents. Even the most commanding figure, as Kālidāsa, cleaves strictly to familiar usages, while his own most successful passages, as Purūravas's soliloquy inquiring of beast, bird and tree for a report of his lost love and Dushyanta's aerial journey, are duplicated endlessly by even the most imaginative playwrights succeeding him. Kālidāsa seems more representative than original. Moreover, even where we may suspect a device to be used for the first time, it does not follow that it is therefore better or worse than in its subsequent appearances. The formulas are, to be sure, as a rule highly effective. The over-all impression remains something that of an exquisitely conceived traditional dance. But the signature of the individual workman, so important in the eyes of connoisseurs in other quarters of the civilized world, remains comparatively faint. The result, however, is not a flat terrain of vast extent. Relatively few plays of the highest categories, as the *nāṭaka* and the *prakaraṇa*, survive and among these still fewer rise to classical stature. Even India in time appears to have wearied of its magnificent achievement, whose freshness it was unable to maintain. The loss of a play by Shakespeare constitutes an irreperable calamity in the history of the theatre. The loss of a hardly less effective play by Bhāsa or Kālidāsa signifies much less of a calamity, for others take its place. Whoever has studied carefully a judicious selection of some thirty Sanskrit plays may rest assured that he has achieved a substantial knowledge of what this dramatic literature has to give. The remainder echoes the masterpieces with diminishing force. Especially after Bhavabhūti the drama presents only a sad attenuation.

The inequalities within the Sanskrit theatre become particularly conspicuous as one turns to the work generally ascribed to Bhāsa himself, earliest of the important playwrights. Indeed, so glaring are the discrepancies here that most thoughtful critics will probably hold serious reservations regarding the single authorship of the Trivandrum Plays. Something has been said in earlier pages in commendation of *The Minister's Vows* and *The Statue Play*, and praise can scarcely be too high for *The Vision of Vāsavadattā* and *Karna's Task*. With the exception of the first-mentioned, primarily a light-hearted entertainment, these are serious works based on mythological themes. Intrinsically, the finest is also the most religious, the extremely brief *Karna's Task*. These considerations faithfully indicate the most fruitful source for the greatness of Sanskrit drama as a whole. A courtly and sophisticated lightness of touch notwithstanding, power lies chiefly in the undercurrent of religious and meditative inspiration. When epic subjects are treated as mere narratives, as in Bhāsa's obviously superficial,

85

The Coronation, inspiration lags. Western readers have from time
to time professed to find in the Sanskrit epics themselves passages
rivalling the dignity and force of the epics of Greece and Scandinavia, but all have, I think, acknowledged that these qualities are
by no means sustained. The epics, of course, long preceded the
plays. And where the latter based on the epics reflect the religious
and metaphysical thought which the epics themselves occasionally
express, they frequently ascend to great heights. Where, on the
contrary, they reflect only the narrative elements, they are likely
to lose interest for any person outside the Indian tradition itself
or at least for any reader lacking the most intimate acquaintance
with the original literature. The Western epic, like so much of the
Western drama derived from it, as Greek tragic poetry leaning the
most heavily on epic sources, is an expression of violently asserted
will, of extreme exertion and energy, producing the quality by which
classical criticism most successfully defined the impact of tragedy,
namely, the sublime. Achilles' wrath provided such a triumph.
From causes now sufficiently clear, this quality is absent from even
the most moving of Sanskrit plays. The want is most sharply felt
when no factor of comparable force or dignity takes its place and
where the very epic subject-matter of the piece places the deficiency
most strongly before the Western mind. Moreover, there is a less
penetrating consideration that may pragmatically be almost as
significant where Bhāsa is concerned. Several of his short plays seem
merely fragments chipped off the monumental epic stone. For
full comprehension they require a wider acquaintance with other
material than is consonant with the aesthetic doctrine requiring
an art work to be self-contained. Such plays seem footnotes on a
parent work, mere decoration for the architectural ensemble that
is the epic poem itself.

Some fine Sanskrit dramas are emotionally slight or, in rather
loose terminology, not tragicomedies but comic romances. Of these
works Kālidāsa's *Mālavikāgnimitra* offers the most flattering example, though Harsa's *Priyadarsikā* and *Ratnāvalī* and possibly the
three early acts of his *Nāgānanda* effectively exploit this tradition.
The Hindu stage delighted in such delicately carved trifles, resembling works in ivory, and excelled in them. But the tradition of
lightness in time weighed heavily. In general perspective it is
almost as though, to turn to Shakespeare for a figure of speech,
half their plays were Midsummer Night Dreams. Bhāsa also relied

heavily upon his lightness of touch. Although his *Avimāraka* has a plot quite similar to that of *Romeo and Juliet*, it never remotely approaches the grandeur of Shakespeare's work. The mood is hedonistic or pathetic rather than tragic or sublime, nearer to *The Arabian Nights* than to *Hippolytus*. Similarly, that charming play, *The Adventures of the Boy Krishna*, though dignified by its incursion into the venerable field of folklore and unquestionably possessing much vitality, shows a theatrical sensationalism and studied naiveté belonging to a domain which the West, at least, commonly regards as the low countries of the imagination. The Trivandrum Plays are, clearly, not all wrought in pure gold. Their inequalities probably seem even more apparent to Western than to Eastern eyes.

Even the masterpieces of Kālidāsa fail entirely to escape the reservations already made concerning Sanskrit drama in general. Their amorality extends to an extreme, marked by a haze, now bright, now dark, as optimism or pessimism prevails, but always remaining within a relatively neutral zone wherein no moral imperative is heavily enforced. Serious Western criticism, to be sure, is on the whole harsh toward any confusion between art and morality. The complete antithesis of the Sanskrit play is the melodrama, that mischievous step-child of the Western theatre on which serious criticism looks solemnly askance. The approval of the West falls, it seems, the most warmly on works that are neither amoral nor sensationally moral but possess a mean in which social and personal values are present by implication and all the more powerful for a freedom from melodramatic overemphasis. Speaking in terms of morality, to modern taste the moral metabolism of Kālidāsa's plays is too low, that of the typical melodrama, too high.

Bhavabhūti's masterpiece, *Rāma's Later History*, is within its own highly specialized terms so powerful that small discussion of it is invited here, where the subject is the inherent weakness of the Sanskrit stage. An Indian drama of the highest order, ranking with *The Little Clay Cart*, it craves an affirmative appreciation and in this spirit will be examined in a succeeding chapter. His earliest play, *Rāma's History*, its many beauties notwithstanding, illustrates how clearly Sanskrit drama depreciates in value as it leans heavily on action and drifts away from the main preoccupation of Indian thought, religious or metaphysical experience. Much more instructive from the present point of view is his popular, moving and elo-

quent *Mālatī and Mādhava,* which has the sensational qualities
of a baroque opera or gothic romance rather than the moral obses-
sions of melodramatic sensationalism. For several centuries which
followed its composition, presumably in the eighth century, it was
possibly unsurpassed in popularity by any Indian drama whatsoever. Bhavabhūti was evidently a man of unusual originality as well
as of strong imagination, a man of intense emotions and considerable
seriousness, though certainly not of the "high seriousness" recommended by the most insistent moralist among distinguished
British poets, Matthew Arnold. One infers that he took himself
seriously and possessed not only less lightness of touch than his
predecessors but considerably less of a sense of humor. Contrary
to general Indian practice, his plays which have come down to us
have no *vidūsaka,* or clown. His epic themes and penchant for
seriousness keep his imflammable fancy within bounds in his two
plays based upon the *Rāmāyana.* But in writing his *Mālatī and
Mādhava* fancy broke loose. Here we enter a world that Orlando
might have inhabited when he was also Orlando Furioso. The
scenes are heightened with terrors—highly artificial—such as a
patient and sagacious reader encounters through the delectable
experience of reading through all six books of *The Fairie Queene.*
A tiger chases a lady. One character readily impersonates another;
indeed, a man, as in Ben Jonson's *The Silent Woman,* is disguised
as a woman and married to another man. Two magicians, one evil,
the other good, vie with each other in miracles. The love of man and
woman is great but (*vide* Beaumont and Fletcher) that of man and
man seems even greater. The heroine is captured by a lascivious.
monster and spirited away to almost inaccessible mountains.
Thither comes the hero in hot pursuit. Hero and heroine in turn
despair, trembling on the verge of suicide. Black magic torments
them until white magic saves them. The poetry has a perfervid
eloquence; its style is prodigiously rhetorical. Music joins forces
with horror to swell the emotional appeal. There is a highly operatic
witchscene that stands midway between a Walpurgisnacht and the
cavern-scene in *Macbeth.* Several passages occur to which Dryden
might be imagined to have contributed a poetic effect or two and
Purcell a musical accompaniment. The lovers are young and short
of princely rank. The heroine is urged to violate convention and
assert her own will. One previsions the violence of *Die Räuber.*
This is and is not typical of the Sanskrit theatre. It is certainly not

typical of the most serious and distinguished Sanskrit drama.

Notably, the earliest of extant Sanskrit plays, such as *The Vision of Vāsavadattā*, stand among the most delicate and sophisticated. From the sixth century onwards the theatre declined as it moved in three directions : toward pedantic allegories, as *Prabodhacandrodaya*, by Krishnamisra Yati; toward lascivious trifles, as *Karpūramanjarī*, by Rājasekhara; and toward unabashed, sensational, extravagant melodramas, as *Mālatī and Mādhava*. Of these three relatively inferior types of plays the third is undoubtedly the most rewarding and Bhavabhūti's drama ranks among the notable works in Sanskrit and almost certainly stands in the forefront of its kind. It is palpably a production of genius. But in *Mālatī and Mādhava* the emotional intensity, as found in his own *Rāma's Later History* concentrated and heightened by control of the most austere art, is released and virtually exploded. The fires that should warm us are no longer present. The fireworks are brilliant but cold. Art there is in abundance but it is an art in decline. Even the maddest of Western melodramas scarcely flys to the excess of this extraordinary piece. Once more one observes that a seed planted in tropical soil develops with a unique luxuriance. Of two further conclusions we rest assured : the Western scholar readily recognizes the play for what it is and, though it will be supposed that he will appreciate its brilliance, he will know it to be a masterwork only of a lower order of merit. Of baroque drama and of romantic melodrama the West has accumulated enough and to spare. Although our economy in dramatic art will be vastly enriched through importations of the undoubted masterpieces by Bhāsa, Kālidāsa, Sūdraka, and Bhavabhūti himself, it already groans with prodigies in the general manner of *Mālatī* and *Mādhava*. Hindu emotionalism here breaks through the frame of the finer Indian art-consciousness. Indeed, after this explosion Sanskrit drama, once so great, virtually ceased to be of cosmopolitan significance.

9 / *The Art of Swooning*

THE PATTERN of a major work of art is often so complex that a comprehensive analysis of the whole proves overambitious and less fruitful than a view focused upon a part. Certainly the style of a painter, for example, is enjoyed best by experiencing his whole canvas. It is, however, frequently best understood intellectually by examination of a small section. This general conclusion applies nowhere more strongly than in the instance of such intricate and sophisticated works as the masterpieces of the Sanskrit stage. Comprehensive analysis of an entire play may easily be protracted to several times the play's own length and the trees be lost in the wood. Even a conspicuously minor theme may give better results.

When these circumstances are recalled, the relish of expectation may greet a glance at one of the less conspicuous though possibly not the less revelatory features of the Indian drama. A brief scrutiny of this may even disclose important features of other schools of the theatre as well. Detail further dilates in importance until it yields a commentary on the choreographic character of the Indian drama, its invitation to inspired acting, its emotional power, poetic imagination, and exceptionally synthetic genius. Much as a spoonful of water gives a faithful sampling of a well, the part abstracted from the whole proves more intelligible though certainly not more enjoyable than the whole itself deprived of such anatomizing.

That Sanskrit drama is a notable meeting-place of the firmest artistic control and the greatest emotional abandon is clearly indicated by the frequent appearances of swooning, appearances so numerous and formally designed as to constitute a theatrical convention. Characters and scenes of the utmost emotional mobility are held tightly in the playwright's hands. His play achieves the spectacular aspect of a dance, its gesture and pantomime almost as exquisite or powerful as its poetry. With so many other technical refinements of the drama, this convention grew in currency through the years, ultimately exhausted, at least in part, by its own excess. The critic is attracted first to the historical and philosophical background of such episodes and thereafter to their refinement and use.

Swooning would seem considerably more frequent in the theatrical arts than in real life and one of life's more extravagant gestures attracting the playwrights. Yet conclusions are difficult, since there is little documentation of the matter today and almost nothing from times past. It is here far easier to ask questions than to answer them. Are women, for example, more given to swooning than men? What actually constitutes a swoon and what varied phenomena are popularly included under the term? If history, as usual, is inconclusive, it is also by no means silent. Decorated green bottles of smelling-salts were seldom out of reach of Victorian ladies and fiction leads us to assume that those formidable and wily creatures when under emotional strain not only often lost consciousness but quite as often pretended to do so. The smelling-salts were indubitably real; how faithful are the interpretations would be hard to say. Frequently, high-strung children also fall over the edge of excitement into swooning. At times it becomes difficult to distinguish swoon from trance, to know when the patient is totally unconscious and when possessed with illusions while in completely negative relation to the outside world. Western audiences have witnessed swooning along the wide gamut from Shakespeare's *Othello* to Charlie Chaplin's farces. Certainly some older literatures are surprisingly rich in scenes of fainting. Heroes and heroines of medieval romance and balladry and of still more venerable epic poetry habitually plunge from excitement into swoon. The sturdy champions in *The Song of Roland* time and time again faint from excess of joy or pain. Such scenes are extremely common also in the literatures of the Near East, where various types of trance are distinguished. Thus we are carried across a long bridge, heavy with many travellers and a weight of years, to the theatre of ancient India.

As will presently be shown, the Sanskrit playwrights have an unsurpassed liking for the swoon. This will immediately be recognized as related to their mental occupation with the soul and its adventures, for the soul is in a sense the major subject of all their plays.

The soul may, by religious discipline, become the oversoul or achieve with the mystic effacement of consciousness complete *Nirvana*, which, with some license, may be designated a religious swoon. A surprising part of their thought is metaphysical. Repeatedly characters are presented as confusing reality and illusion. Dreams are of much importance. Time is relative. Life is much more mobile than the Western Man has conceived it to be. The typical swoon is a pause in excitement, when the spirit rests, recuperating exhausted powers. The Hindu climate proved ideal for subtlizing on the subject.

To appraise the matter properly some half-a-dozen plays must be cited. Swooning appears in the earliest dramas, as those ascribed to Bhāsa, but as common practice magnified it into a convention, it became increasingly employed. It is already conspicuous in Sūdraka and even in those acts of his brilliant comedy, *The Little Clry Cart*, which belonged originally to Bhāsa's *Chārudatta in Poverty*. The hero, Chārudatta, for example, somewhat extravagantly swoons when reminded that the stolen jewels, central to the plot, were left to him in trust. The heroine, Vasantasēnā, and her maid, Madanikā, similarly faint when the report of the robbery in Chārudatta's house leads them to fear for his life. (It is a delicate point that at this critical moment these admirable women give no more thought for the jewels themselves than did Chārudatta.) The *masseur* is knocked unconscious, producing, roughly speaking, a species of swoon. In the later part of the play swooning is several times introduced, as when the villain, Samsthānaka, grasped in the neck by the not-too-formidable Vita, loses consciousness out of sheer terror. The Vita himself faints on hearing Samsthānaka's boast that he has murdered Vasantasēnā. The hetaera, supposed dead, is in fact unconscious while buried under a heap of leaves. In the final scene Chārudatta precipitately falls to the ground, momentarily unconscious, when he fears not death but disgrace for himself and his family.

Kālidāsa, the arch-poet among the dramatists, makes shrewd use of swooning as a theatrical device. In *Shakuntalā* the king Dushyanta when at the lowest point of his despair falls into a swoon, overcome by his anguish. Only the intervention of a supernatural messenger restores his mental activity. The episode is the hinge or turning point on which the entire action is suspended. The heroine in his *Vikramorvacī* first enters while still in an unconscious or at most semi-conscious state, overpowered by the shock of her violation. Her noble and kingly lover, Purūravas, swoons when perceiving that he has mistaken news of her spoken by a mountain echo which has been merely the echo of his own voice and faints again in abject despair immediately before the happy ending of his long, unhappy quest. Only Urvacī's voice restores him to consciousness. This is likewise the turning point in the play's action. For the last time he faints when threatened in the final scene with Urvacī's departure after the recovery of their son. These are the most crucial moments of tension in the play.

Harsa, one of Kālidāsa's most eminent successors, uses the device profusely in his most original play, *Nāgānanda*. During its early scenes the heroine faints when her love for the hero suddenly appears hopeless. The mother of the doomed naga, Sankhachuda, swoons twice from the force of her grief. When the hero himself appears irrevocably doomed, we twice read of his family, "they all faint." For good measure, Sankhachuda swoons along with the rest. In the play's final act the hero is gradually dying of wounds inflicted by the direful bird-god, Garuda. Exhausted by his efforts to realize his goal of complete unselfishness and shortly before he expires he passes into a temporary swoon. It should be recalled that death itself may to Indian thinking resemble a swoon. In Harsa's play the female protective deity, Gaurī, as *dea ex machina*, brings the hero to life much as a man might be recovered from a fainting fit. On being sprinkled with holy water, he returns to life with augmented strength.

The last of the great Sanskrit playwrights, Bhavabhūti, in his masterpiece, *Rāma's Later History*, makes by far the most impressive use of a formula that by the time of his writing had become one of the most firmly established theatrical conventions. Repeatedly a climax in the action is marked by a swooning. There are sixteen such episodes. Sītā, the heroine, faints seven times, Rāma, the hero, four times, his attendant, Vāsantī, twice, his mother Kausalya, once, Sītā's mother, Prithivī, the Earth Goddess, once, and on one spectacular occasion an entire army is completely stunned by "the weapons of stupefaction." The conspicuous place of these incidents proves how important the convention had become.

Sītā faints from fear as she dreads the result of a combat in which her favorite elephant is engaged. Forgetting that she has for twelve years been separated from her husband, she calls him to the aid of her former pet immediately before losing consciousness. A few moments later she swoons from joy on hearing Rāma's voice. In the scene's calculated reversals, she swoons with grief immediately after her husband faints. Once more she swoons when Rāma expresses his wish to depart. Again she faints when she herself is urged to leave. In the play-within-a-play in the last act, she faints shortly after child-birth and again for the last time in the arms of the Goddess Earth in pity for her own plight.

While in the forest of Panchavatī, Rāma swoons twice, overcome by the bitter thought of the happy life that has passed and his present bereavement. With his infallible gift for varying his themes, Bhavabhūti places the first of these swoons off-stage, the second on-stage. Although each time Rāma recovers at the touch of Sītā's hand, there is no repetition here either, since on the second occasion occurs the weird episode of the clasping of hands. By magic, Sītā is invisible yet is both heard and to this extent even felt. Twice also he swoons in the final act, first, at sight of Sītā's pitiful condition in child-birth in the play-within-the-play and, second, when in the same action he witnesses her descent to the world of the shades beneath the earth. From the second of these swoons he is for the last time rescued by Sītā's touch.

The incidents with the lesser characters are hardly less striking. The attendant minor deity, Vāsantī, faints on hearing in whispers, unheard by the audience, the news of Sītā's exile and again when in the scene in the forest she recalls this cruelty. Kausalya, Rama's mother, faints on recalling the ills that have beset her son and her family. Virtually at the play's climax, Prithivī, the Earth Goddess, faints through intensity of sympathy for her daughter, Sītā. The episode of the "weapons of stupefaction" has, naturally, a quite different character. Precisely what constituted the stage picture here cannot be ascertained but in all probability an elaborate pantomime represented the weapons as missiles thrown by one group of dancers and the army as another group of dancers prostrated, or rather frozen, by their magic force. Later in the same scene, at Rāma's request and his son's command, the army is restored from its swoon to normal vitality.

The prosaic enumeration of these episodes by no means indicates the full force which the idea of stupefaction holds for the play. Swooning becomes a topic for discussion and imaginative thought. The major episode of the mural paintings in Act One is prophetic with its references to swooning. Two scenes in which Rāma fainted with grief at Sītā's abduction are shown in the pictures and discussed by their viewers. Rāma himself describes an experience derived from Sita's touch which virtually constitutes a swoon following on ecstasy, prophetically using much the same words which he employs later during the supernatural incidents in Act Three. His elaborate apostrophe to Sītā asleep shares in this train of thought. In the commencement of the remarkable Third Act, the river goddess, Murala, sets its key : "in every fit of distraction that comes upon good Rāma, refresh his life with breezes from thy waves." To this the second river goddess, Tamasā, adds : "a radical means of reviving good Rāma is at hand today." Her reference is to Sītā's visit to the same locality.

Swooning, then, is not only visible to the eye of the audience; the poet analyzes the peculiar conditions of mind that accompany it. His poetry subtlizes on various types of stupor that do or do not embrace consciousness. Sītā observes : "my heart as it were forgetting its own sorrows is indescribably bewildered." Rāma paints a mental state which "spreads over me forcibly some indescribable distractions of heart. . . the frame of my body is falling asunder; I think the world to be a void; my helpless soul sinks and is, as it were, engulfed in pitchy darkeness, and the distraction paralyses me from all sides." Later the poetry describes the sensation of "numbness," which clearly applies both to the hands of the lovers and to their minds and spirits. The Sanskrit poets are in truth discriminating psychologists. Their characters, who are keenly introspective, not only experience various states of mind pertaining to the swoon but observe them objectively and make discerning comments upon them.

Of the purely theatrical aspects of this convention the playwrights themselves are highly self-conscious and refine their procedure with a technically adroit method. On the one hand, it is possible that they had only small actual experience with fainting, though this is mere conjecture. On the other hand, they had certainly made deep studies in the theatrical effectiveness of their practice and its utility as a language of emotional expression in complete harmony with dramatic poetry. The word never obstructs the action nor does the action intrude upon the word. Similarly, Bhavabhūti twice, in crucial moments of his great play, reduces communication between his characters to whispers inaudible to the audience.

Although the audience hears nothing, the silences are in the context more impressive than words just as the unseen is often more harrowing than the seen, the unheard more eloquent than the heard. The audience knows precisely what is whispered. In fact, to make the whispers audible would subject the audience to artless repetitions. Bhavabhūti is by no means alone in employing this device.

The swoon itself is clearly a moving appeal to the eye. It takes command of the stage where action passes smoothly beyond words, where emotion actually reaches its climax and where pantomime and choreography take over the stage. The faint is treated in an extremely formalized fashion, resembling less an action in real life than a series of descending tones in music. It is no vulgar representation of one of the most awkward and unpleasant incidents in human experience; instead, it becomes a triumph in choreography or stylized action, what is merely beastial in reality becoming the perfection of art. The astute dramatists who made designs of the blunderings of the *Vidūsakas* and of fools such as Samsthānaka knew best how to treat such dramatic material artfully, making of life's blemishes the beauties of art.

There is an interesting possibility that their convention of the swoon derived in part from the traditional origins of Indian drama itself in the puppet play. No doubt at all times Indian puppetry has exercised a perceptible influence on practices of the live stage. It is well-known that puppets with great expressiveness pass from the most animated action to complete passivity. A doll may swoon or die with an emphasis scarcely attainable on the stage of live actors. As the master of the strings (the Sanskrit word for play-producer) leaves the strings hanging loose, his figure may well be said to swoon. This is the closest analogue to the actual effect of theatrical fainting on the human stage and may well be one of the chief sources of its remarkably refined use.

There is only the merest handful of cases in which an actor is required to fall to the ground in anything approaching the violent thumping with which Elizabethan stage convention required melancholy characters like Hamlet to grovel on the ground. Rāma is once "discovered" prone on the earth. The audience is not permitted to witness the indignity of the king's fall. As a rule the victim of the swoon is beside a friend into whose embrace he falls, precisely as a ballet dancer into the arms of her porteur. Also, he is not allowed to remain long in this negative state; such words as "take comfort, my friend, take comfort," invariably cause his prompt and full recuperation. Both dialogue and stage direction show the precise moment in which the character faints and when he regains control. There is a formula for both the swoon and the recovery.

Since the playwrights are keenly aware of the high theatrical value of contrast, a hero is often instantly aroused from the most complete swoon or trance to the most vigorous or violent action. This is the case, as previously mentioned, with Dushyanta in Act Six of *Shakuntalā*, and with Purūravas in Act Four of *Vikramorvaci*. That contrast is of the very heart and essence of drama is fully realized. The swoon is a color to be contrasted with its antithetical color. Design is skilful in the extreme.

There is every indication that these scenes of extravagant and abandoned passion were themselves executed with a perfection of grace : "for in the very torrent, tempest, and, as I may say, whirl-wind of your passion, you must acquire and beget a temperance that may give it smoothness." Shakespeare certainly apprehended this theory but there is every indication that Elizabethan acting, great and artful as it doubtless was, was more violent and naturalis-tic than that of the Sanskrit stage. Indian aesthetics is most ex-plicit in insisting that whereas the subject matter of art is impas-sioned its proper manner is temperate, conscious, and controlled, and that neither actor. nor audience is to feel the emotions clearly indicated though never prosaically duplicated on the stage. A study of the swoon demonstrates, as any other detailed study in the field must, that Sanskrit drama is not a mere imitation of nature but a meditation upon it, not a duplication and proliferation of our ills but a device by which these very ills may be transcended and by the ritual of the theatre cast aside. Such drama is never a romantic escape from reality but is a passage through it, elevating the audience, both aesthetically and religiously inspired, upon an altitude above life's storms. Its aim is through disciplined restatement of passion to create spiritual serenity, through images of tempest-tossed souls to establish an equilibrium not merely personal, as the equilibrium attempted by the modern psychologist, who views life as a romantic individualist, but an equilibrium of the religious sage who seeks harmony with the universe. To the man of the world life not infrequently seems a shambles, to the inspired Sanskrit playwright it becomes a dance. This familiar truth we learn again from the art of swooning as achieved by Sūdraka,

Kālidāsa, Harsa, and most admirably of all, by the last master of the Sanskrit stage, Bhavabhūti. Tragedy, insisted W. B. Yeats, himself acquainted with much Indian thought, is gay. The deftness of this dance of swooning as achieved on the Sanskrit stage must itself have instilled aesthetic gaiety, intrigued the sense of comedy, and lightened the burdens of lugubrious existence. It signified a new flowering in magic, the withered blossoms returning refreshed to their stems. What a delight it is to contemplate these achievements of the masters!

IO / Theatrical Technique on the Sanskrit Stage

FEW PLAYWRIGHTS approach the Sanskrit in the amount of conscious thought given to theatrical technique. Their plays are well grounded in their philosophy of life, still more clearly elaborated in their literary style, but presumably most sophisticated of all in formal and artificial adaptation to the theatre. The stage conventions are many and strictly binding. Although innumerable variations are played upon these formulations, lending the plays the impression of spontaneity and creative energy, they cleave to patterns long tried in the pragmatic laboratory of the stage. These pages examine a few characteristic features important from the strictly theatrical point of view.

"Give me my robe. Put on my crown. I have Immortal longings in me." These will at once be recalled as the opening words of Cleopatra's death-scene in Shakespeare's tragedy. They contain in substance a stage direction. The words offer direct commentary on the actions, the actions on the words. It is well known that this manner of dramatic composition has proved itself highly fruitful and has been more or less freely employed by a large number of successful playwrights. That few European dramatists exhibit it more conspicuously than Shakespeare should lend it our favorable consideration. At times words literally describe simultaneous action or gesture, at other times merely suggest them. There are clearly degrees and degrees in this practice. But one conclusion may be asserted with full conviction : Sanskrit dramatists carried the usage to its farthest extremes. Long passages in their plays are self-descriptions. The action of whole scenes is virtually defined by the dialogue. This becomes a conspicuous manner or even mannerism. How artful it is and how truly synthetic in the organism of the drama will appear from inspection of a few examples in major works.

In this regard *Shakuntalā* is typical throughout. The technique is employed so gracefully, naturally and easily that few persons will be aware how continuously it is employed. Whatever elements of naturalism there may be suffer little or nothing from this turn in the dialogue. It is an art that at least from the casual eye conceals itself. On retrospect the reader discovers to his surprise that he may almost as truly be said to have seen the play as to have read it. He has perforce learned how the characters are costumed, and what is their appearance, complexion, facial expression, together with their movements, gestures, acts. He knows not only in what physical context the persons are found but the detailed appearances of the scenes, as the woodlands for hunting, the penance groves for devotion, the cool banks of streams, their vegetation, and the atmosphere and light at the various hours of the day. The smoothness with which these conventions are used shows highest skill in polished workmanship.

Scene one of *Shakuntalā* is both an action and a description. One may think of its dialogue almost equally as real talk or as stage direction, as documentary evidence from the play or as an account for the performance of a dance. Dushyanta and his charioteer are in pursuit of a deer. The wind stiffens their horses' plumes as they fly. Dust cannot impair their speed. The deer itself is clearly in sight, though in performance presumably in the mind's eye only. His posture in running is vividly described. The chariot jolts and labors over uneven ground so that the deer gains in the race; but as the hunters near the hermitage the ground becomes level, they gain speed, and bring the deer into bowshot. The little episode reaches its dramatic climax when, as the hero is about to shoot his arrow, a hermit loudly beseeches him to let the deer go, as they are on sacred ground where all animals enjoy safety. Word and movement throughout are synchronized and timed with the utmost felicity. The scene is a miracle of studied artifice.

This is a famous passage, launching the play in the most graceful manner possible. Almost as widely admired is the complementary scene opening the last act, which meticulously balances the first. Here is not a pursuit but a return. Although the hero has had experiences checkered with joy and grief, he has throughout the play grown in dignity. Here he rides not over the earth but through the air. He is returning to his kingdom as victor in celestial warfare to which he has been summoned by the foremost of the gods, Indra. His charioteer is no longer a mortal but a demi-god, Matali, roughly an equivalent of the Greek Hermes. Passages of almost pure description occur, as the remarkable lines depicting terrestrial objects enlarging themselves as the flyers approach the earth and appearing to rush towards the chariot, denying the truth that the chariot is rushing towards them. The lines resemble those depicting horizontal movement in Act One. No action on the stage can explicate these lines of verse. But much of the dialogue, as in the hunting scene, describes the actors' pantomime as they appear to plunge through the air. The words are deliberately fitted to the deeds.

Throughout the entire first act, the speeches provide an elaborate, moving painting of the action, with both the stage scenery and the characters prominent. The reader not only hears the characters speak; he discovers almost as well how they appear, their facial expressions, gestures and actions. So in the beginning the hero divests himself of his ornaments on entering the precincts of the hermitage. The labor of watering her favorite plants fatigues the heroine. Entirely typical is the momentous little incident at the act's close, where the heroine pretends to have snagged her dress on a thorn, her true motive being to delay her enforced departure from her lover and, like the deer chased by the hunters, to glance backward at the eager Dushyanta. In such cases—and they are innumerable—the words seem accompaniment to the action. In fact, the more closely in performance they are fused, the better. Their conjunction becomes a basic principle of the style. The same principle holds true, of course, throughout acts two and three, which bring the wooing in the hermitage to its happy conclusion. The Commander, for example, gives a vivid description of the king: a hero in the finest of health and clad in the becoming costume of a hunter. Dushyanta in turn describes Shakuntala. We see her friends fanning her and later witness her action in writing her lover a letter on a lotus leaf.

Act Four marks in these terms even an advance over the preceding. For here is very literally a ceremony, the rite celebrating the departure of the bride from her paternal home and the beginning of her journey to her new home, where she is to assume the functions of wife. The occasion is doubly ritualistic, for she is not only assuming her wifely duties but concluding her religious duties as priestess in a religious society. She bids ceremonious farewell to the creatures sacred according to the law of a singularly naturalistic and animistic religion. Her last respects must be paid to beast, bird, flower and tree and above all to her devoted fawn. We see her clothed item by item in her ceremonial costume and witness the various parts of the ritual demanded by these events. The entire text is a reflection of itself, like an image mirrored in still water. Even more than in the earlier passages, it proves hard to distinguish between the mere description of the imagined stage scene, or naturalistic background, with its unmoving or inanimate parts, and the words actually describing the movements of the actors. All is fused in an extended passage equally literary and choreographic.

The action reaches a climax in Act Five, which presents Shakuntalā's repudiation by her forgetful husband, the king. Although the episode lacks the obviously picturesque quality of the scenes in the forest hermitage and has more the appearance of "straight" drama as commonly conceived by the Western World, a somewhat closer inspection shows almost as strict a harmony between text and action. The king, weary of conscientious performance of his royal functions, rouses himself to a pious reception of the mission from the hermitage. His gestures are singularly easy to imagine. But Shakuntalā is herself the focus of the sharpest attention. She enters reluctantly ; shows hesitation and fear in every word ; is first unveiled ; next makes the futile gesture to present the fateful ring ; breaks at length into tears, and finally rouses herself to righteous anger. Her tragic exit, befriended by none, concludes a role whose every feature has been strictly previsioned and provided for by the playwright.

Dexterous interweaving of stage-business and dialogue appears on examination of the long and subtle Act Six. This progressively depicts Dushyanta's remorse deepening to despair after the recovery of the ring brings the realization that he has betrayed Shakuntalā. Despite the act's eminently psychological character, many incidents built into the dialogue attract the eye. The whole is prefaced by a scene of flower-gathering in the palace garden, full of stage conventions. The long episode of the king's half-finished painting of Shakuntalā and her friends, with its interval of the deluded bees, persistently combines language with deed. The act concludes with the surprising scene of Matali's attack on the unfortunate Vidūsaka, during which Matali is disguised as a demon. Matali, to be sure, is not seen in his demon form, in which capacity moreover he acts only off-stage, but the king's abrupt recuperation and arming to protect his friend provide a lively action about which the words cluster, to use a favorite Sanskrit metaphor, as the vine around its tree.

The spectacular nature of the last act insures the liveliest interplay of word and physical movement or sensational effect. Following the king's aerial journey is the scene in the earthly paradise where dwell the divine ancestors of gods and men, Kashyapa and Aditi. The description of the ascetic Kashyapa is noteworthy. All that concerns Dushyanta's meeting with his young son is made especially vivid by both language and action. The boy enters playing intrepidly with a lion cub. Further stage-business is associated with the youth. We see his beloved toy, the china peacock, whose name suggests his mother, Shakuntalā, and witness the incident of the magic amulet fallen from his wrist in his sport. The King innocently picks this up, with no ill effect. He is told that the absence of miracle is here a miracle, since none but the boy's father can pick up the jewel and remain unharmed. In the case of all others it turns at once into a venomous serpent. Still Dushyanta is loath to believe that he has actually recovered his son. Particularly moving is the appearance of Shakuntalā herself in mourning dress and braided hair owing to her long absence from her lord. The play's last moments, as fitting, possess greater splendor but less poignancy than the first reunion of the lovers. There is a general congregation of rejoicing mortals and immortals. Yet everywhere is the striking union of the action and the poem.

Kālidāsa's other dramas illustrate the same usage though in slightly different ways. In no plays does the background of nature receive more brilliant word-painting than in his *Vikramorvacī*, though obviously space denies a prolonged demonstration here. As initial statement it may be remarked that Act One is laid in the air, on the clouds, and on the mountain-tops ; Act Three is drenched in moonlight ; Act Four offers a magnificent painting of the forest in the rainy season, the woods crowded with bird, beast, and flowering vine ; while in Act Five, the last, occurs a brilliant word picture of a marauding bird imagined as seen by the persons of the play.

Throughout the work the characters also are brought vividly to view by the language. Particularly effective is the picture of the heroine at her first entrance, when she appears riding in the hero's chariot in a swoon, supported on her sister's arm. The praise which the nymphs bestow on Purūravas makes him shine so much the more brightly in our eyes. His chariot-flight is even more exhilarating than Dushyanta's. The poetry dilates the spectacle, a projection of things seen, an invisible glory that is merely an extension of the glory visible. The sensuous character of the nature-description is matched by the sensuous word-portraiture, especially that of the heroine, Urvacī. Similarly, the heavenly charioteer, Chitrarath, enters at the close of Act One :

> My lord, I hear a rumor in the East
> And mighty speed of chariots. Lo, one bright
> With golden armlet, looking down from Heaven
> Like a huge cloud with lightning on its wrist,
> Streams towards us.

When has an actor enjoyed a more glamorous introduction ?

Act Two paints a garden only less colorful than untamed Nature as painted in the celebrated Act Four. The long episode of the leaf, extending through half the act, is a thoroughly conventional stage-business on which, as usual, Kālidāsa lavishes rare poetry. Among the visual elements embellished with poetry in Act Three are Urvacī's entrance, when wearing her trysting dress, and the devotions of the repentent Queen to the moon, denoting her obeisance to her husband's will. The act is as drenched in ceremony as its scene is in moonlight conjured wholly by words. The final act is largely pageantry delineated alike by poetry and stage-spectacle. Or in other words, it unrolls the ceremony in which the jewel Union stolen by the vulture and recovered by the youthful son of the godlike king is the sacramental kernel, worshipped by all. During the central episodes action is brisk and sharply delineated by the speeches. First are the embracings of the child magically recovered by his parents, followed by Urvacī's tears and the king's swoon, as they are abruptly faced with parting. This parting is indefinitely deferred by the triumphant entry of the god Narad, who in addition blesses with his presence the ceremonious investiture of the youth as king. Heaven and earth join in the celebration. The scene is only surpassed in theatrical and poetic opulence by the roughly similar conclusion of Bhavabhūti's *Rāma's Later History.*

That play may without exaggeration be said to be largely descriptive poetry, much of which is intimately wedded to the actor's movements and guise. In this regard it will hardly seem in the least fortuitous that the first act is entitled "The Picture Gallery". Some of the description, to be sure, is not of an action simultaneously seen but of one beheld later than the words here considered. Thus is constituted a species of theatrical syncopation. So the chorus of heavenly spirits in Act Six describes a battle which is more or less symbolized in the stage action immediately following. The description of Prince Chandraketu occurs in Act Five, his first entrance in Act Six. This is the familiar device in Indian drama whereby an imagined action off-stage is described by speakers on-stage. It may or may not be witnessed later by the audience. From first to last in this play the portraits of Rāma and of Sītā are painted and repainted, each describing the other. The forest of Sītā's exile and Rāma's visitation is most elaborately described in Acts Two and Three. Many features of the natural scene, as that of the embattled elephants, enter into the actions of the characters. The swoonings of both Rāma and Sītā and Sītā's recuperative touch, thrice applied, belong in the category of pantomime and are also adorned with poetry. This poetry brings most vividly to eye the chorus of old people, the ancestors, lamenting the tragic history of the *Rāmāyana.* Martial scenes have scarcely in the greatest epics been more forcefully depicted than in the word-painting of the acts devoted to the chivalrous strife between the cousins, Lava and Chandraketu. Among the figures brilliantly described but unseen on the stage is the ceremonial horse, pursued by the young ascetics. The vignette is a masterpiece of naive poetry, employing that adjective with a connotation somewhat different from its use by Schiller. The words depict the impression which a horse is assumed to make upon imaginative children seeing a horse for the first time. In the last act the projection extends to the play-within-the-play. Here the dialogue amply describes the action, though with a phenomenal economy of words. We are told of Sītā's plunge into the waters of the Ganges. Presently we behold her rising supported by her mother, the Goddess Earth, and the deity of the Ganges, the patron of her husband's family, each goddess bearing one

of her newly delivered twins in her arms. Shortly thereafter we
see Sītā on the verge of going into a new exile beneath the earth,
again in the protection of her mother. The inserted play has
been a ceremonial device to reintroduce Rāma to Sītā. The
play-within-the-play is abruptly ended with this happy consummation. The poetry depicts the splendor accompanying the event
as action and word together express the core-meaning of the
myth.

Sūdraka's virtuosity in this technique, as usual in all theatrical
skills of drama, is unsurpassed. What characterizes other Sanskrit
playwrights on important occasions in their work characterizes
him almost habitually. Hence it becomes unnecessary to call
attention to special instances where almost any passage taken at
random tells the same story. The dialogue makes gesture continually
explicit. The technique might be thought a mannerism were it
not so highly successful and so clearly a masterful achievement of
dramatic art. From first to last the figures are continually in motion
and continually talking of their behavior. The spectacle would
presumably be restless were it not so firmly held under control.
Minor actions are typical of the whole. Vasantasēnā inspects the
painting of her lover ; he is first seen sprinkling sacrificial grains.
Much of the action concerns costumes, as Chārudatta's scented
cloak or the red robe of the ascetic. Another angle of approach
suggests the observation that stage properties, great and small,
are continually in use. From one of these the play derives its title.
It will be remembered that the toy cart is last seen loaded with the
very jewels that will later hang about Chārudatta's neck as he is
led to execution. The exchange of the *gharris* and all that concerns
them adds important instances of this technique. Several scenes
are laid at night or in the evening. This is true of Acts One, Three
and Five. During these scenes occurs considerable fumbling in the
dark, always a fruitful subject for pantomime. Samsthānaka's
pursuit of Vasantasēnā, her conflict with the storm, Sarvilaka's artful
house-breaking, the escape of Āryaka, Samsthānaka's grotesque
antics in the park, the trial scene, and Chārudatta's execution are
all vigorous actions where word and deed are knit together with
an almost unparalleled firmness and persistency. Perhaps the most
striking incident of all is the minor episode of the escaped gambler
who pretends to be a statue and who is later caught in "the gambler's
circle." Following this is the blinding of the eyes of the gambling-

master with dust. All point in one direction : the complete fusion of speech and deed.

In this regard the early and the late dramatists differ little from one another, Bhāsa, for example, from Harsa. The chief scene in Bhāsa's masterpiece, *The Vision of Vāsavadattā*, which gives the play its title, illustrates Bhāsa's use of the method. The episode of Udayana's delusion that he is under a delusion and that the real Vāsavadattā is only a dream of her is a prolonged and truly intricate action, centered upon the bed where Padmāvati is presumed to be lying, where Udayana is in fact lying, and which Vāsavadattā visits, mistaking the king for the queen. This is all a fantastic pantomime yet wonderfully effective as psychological drama. The words, to repeat, are little more than eloquent stage-directions which themselves tell the entire story. This is essential theatre, the very core of theatre, realized with profundity and developed with the highest sophistication.

Of Harsa's electic *Nāgānanda* a brief comment must suffice. The early scenes in the sacred grove and garden in general much resemble those of *Shakuntalā*, although some of the stage-business, as the identification of the lover by a picture, more nearly resembles *The Vision of Vāsavadattā*. Several such scenes occur in Sanskrit plays. The fooling with the Vidūsaka provides the usual low comedy, highly visual in its appeal. The supernatural scenes in the play's second half possess the usual ceremonious character, with focus here upon two sacrifices, the hero's sacrifice on the rock of the Nagas as the red-clad victim of Garuda, and the sacrificial immolation of the hero's entire family in the sacred fires. Disaster is transformed to joy on the appearance of the protective deity, Gaurī, entering with a flourish of ritual itself brilliantly described in the text. This conjunction of poetry and pageantry suggests European medieval drama but the conjunction is not aesthetically frigid, as in many of the Christian allegories. The Sanskrit stage successfully combines the charms of the medieval and the Elizabethan, being formal as one and fully alive as the other.

In the theatre, where artifice is of the essence, the passage of time, always vital in any presentational art, is treated with no less sophistication than the conjunction of act and speech. Time in the poetic theatre is clearly not that of real life. Western classical theory, of course, allows only a minor compromise with the most literal views of time and place. The play, presumably consuming two or three hours, is to represent no more than the passage of a single day and moreover each event must follow its neighbor in literal sequence. The hands of the clock cannot be rushed violently forward or ever set back. Imagination is curbed. All must suggest the transit of time flowing forward at virtually its normal pace. Action is essentially historical, not mental. If intervals are needed, these must be achieved through a division of scene from scene. A short vacancy of the stage, the fall of a curtain, the introduction of a chorus, or some other instrumentality clearly divides the action in time. Scene and act divisions, so persistent in Western drama, as a rule denote shifts in time or possibly in place. It has become a marked exception to the rule that the conventional divisions of the action be merely intervals of rest for the audience, the action being resumed precisely when and where last seen. Act division in Sanskrit drama is, on the contrary, merely a shift in subject matter and mood, as the divisions between the movements of a symphony or a dance. Time and place are incidental. Meaning is the essential factor.

Since drama intensifies life, time is seldom prolonged on the stage ; but on the poetic stage it is frequently abridged. This often distresses literal-minded audiences and critics. In Sanskrit drama messengers come and return in the twinkling of an eye. The story suggests this and thus it is. The literal are offended, the imaginative, possibly grateful for this efficient shorthand. Such treatment of time in the trial scene of *The Little Clay Cart* has been subjected to considerable harsh criticism and even ridicule from Western writers. No one in India would think of advancing such an objection. And, given the principle of stylized art, the objection does, on the whole, seem prosaic and weak. The Indians like their dramatic actions to fall out pat. Merely mention a character and he is as likely as not to materialize on the stage at once.

Sanskrit dramatists start with presumptions about time very unlike those of prosaic Westerners, with their own particular species of naturalism. Further evidence of this occurs in what may be termed the chronological parenthesis. Here again the happiest examples appear in *The Little Clay Cart*. In the first act we observe Chārudatta in his house conversing with the Vidūsaka. Abruptly action shifts to the street, where Samsthānaka is pursuing Vasanta-sēnā. This episode constitutes a long parenthesis. At its conclusion action returns without the least interval or break to the Chārudatta-Maitreya episode. The two men resume their talk with the words at which it has been sharply broken off. The device is used repeatedly in the course of the play, notably in the trial scene and the execution scene, comprising Acts Nine and Ten respectively. The multiple stage certainly aided this practice. But the multiple stage may be more concerned with space than with time. Thus in Act Four, where Vasantasēnā, looking from a window, overhears talk between Sarvilaka and Madanikā, time flows naturally and smoothly onward without serious break ; Vasantasēnā merely comments in an aside to the audience on the interview which she sees while remaining herself unseen. The technique as practised in Act One and elsewhere is more drastic and more artificial. It also suggests the repeat or the return in music. The extent of the insertion compels us to readjust our feeling for time in terms of some artificial parenthesis. Two episodes are not simply parallel, occurring during the same time interval. The play's action, it is clear, may at any moment be subjected to inserts. The playwrights discover a special instrument on which to perform a decidedly sophisticated music.

Even though all the details of Indian scenographic art are by no means clear; its general features admit little doubt. As previously noted, there was at least some form of multiple staging. Especially is this true for a dualistic stage. It would be merely burdensome to ennumerate the many instances in which two groups divide the stage between them. As a rule one sees the other, as when, in *Nāgānanda*, the prince and his Vidūsaka observe, unseen, the princess and her confidante. Subtlizing on this theme gives us the entire remarkable third act of *Rāma's Later History*. But such is not necessarily the case, as when Chārudatta is merely told of the summons to his trial. Here one part of the stage represents the vicinity of the hero's house, the other, the courtroom. Similarly, Vasantasēnā learns of her lover's execution in an episode inserted into the execution scene. It is long before her haste brings her within sight of "the Southern Cemetery." Possibly small stools were used to elevate characters at one point of the stage. In Act One of *The Little Clay Cart* Samsthānaka declares that from the terrace of his palace he will overhear Maitreya deliver his ultimatum to Chārudatta. Although no speech or stage-direction indicates that the prince does so overhear the delivery, this is virtually certain, since the provision is explicitly made that he does. Some such treatment must account for the window at which Vasantasēnā stands while overhearing the conversation between Sarvilaka and Madanikā, and again, the very same window imagined in Act One comes into use when Sthavaraka views the procession to the place of execution and jumps boldly to the ground or where, shortly thereafter, his master views a later stage of the same solemn procession. Although "stations" in the manner of classical comedy or medieval mystery play were unknown in India, at least the Sanskrit stage used symbolic divisions in its playing space effecting a divorce from the strict naturalism of either the most conservative classical theatre or the thoroughly literal stages occasionally seen in the nineteenth or twentieth century.

It is of the essence of the imaginative Sanskrit theatre to induce the audience both to hear and see more than is literally said or seen. Although the expansion of things unseen is far more important than that of things unheard, the principle remains identical in both cases and neither type of artifice should be slighted. The plays contain interesting instances of whispers which the audience thoroughly understands but does not hear. This device is not only to hasten the play along where information already known to the audience is imparted to a character on the stage. That such is not the case might even be inferred from the actual repetition of important speeches or stanzas for the sake of emphasis. The words whispered are often terrifying and become all the more so as they are left to the imagination. One receives an impression that the air is too frail a medium to carry such dire news. This is instanced when the messenger in Act One of *Rāma's Later History* tells Rāma what "the citizens and country people" have determined of Sītā's fate. The same harrowing news is whispered in the following act during an interview between two of Sītā's female friends. The convention is employed with varying shades of meaning in other plays, demonstrating anew the force of pantomime in the Sanskrit theatre. This was at once an intensely literary theatre and an intensely choreographic theatre, combining the greatest possible attraction for both ear and eye. One medium is never sacrificed to another. No doctrine of the golden mean is found applicable here. The maximum of weight on both sides is thought by no means too heavy for the play to carry.

The factor of the unseen is far more important than the merely whispered word, for, after all, why whisper if nothing is to be heard ? Pure pantomime, with action alone eloquent, may be supposed to suffice. To state the case bluntly, a considerable amount of activity in the Sanskrit drama is conducted off-stage. Not only is no murder and no scene of advanced physical dalliance permitted. A positive use is made of what lies behind the curtain, with the result that of all theatres this is probably the least compressed within a frame. The mind leaps beyond what is seen to conceive an ample world in unbounded space. Many devices are employed to minimize the tyranny of the dividing line between seen and unseen. A world without limit demands a stage without walls.

To aid this mental outlook quite frequently a character is heard speaking before he enters. In such instances he often repeats on the stage the sentence which he has just spoken behind the curtain. In short, he is first realized as a voice and thereafter as a physical being endowed with speech. His soul precedes his body. Not only death but other awesome events are realized off-stage. So the irritable sage who is cause of all the woe in *Shakuntalā* is heard only as a loud voice ; he is never seen. One of the visible actors walks off to speak with him and later reports her interview.

Many significant variations on this theme occur. Conversations are conducted between speakers on and off-stage. At times the speaker off-stage is heard ; at other times he is unheard but his words are immediately reported by a character on stage, as though the audience was informed of the silent half of a telephone conversation. Frequently a character is seen and described by a person on stage well before his entrance, the entrance being thereby prepared. This poetic device proves especially useful where important figures are concerned, as heroes, villains, or supernatural persons. In *Rāma's Later History* several minutes of poetic description take place before an impatient audience is permitted to see the rival heroes, Lava and Chandrakētu. The same technique introduces the aged members of Rāma's and Sītā's families. This type of poetic description, whetting the audience's anticipation, becomes one of the outstanding features of Bhavabhūti's highly rhetorical style, although found in less sensational form in all Sanskrit dramatists. Here again there is no sacrifice of word to spectacle or spectacle to word. It is found effective at times to perform each separately, as in a fugue one part is heard and then another before the two parts are joined. Expectation is increased. Both the word and the thing seen are accentuated, rendering their final union all the more moving. One is reminded of the Vita's advice to Vasantasēnā, stating that the sexes should lead each other on by alternate advances and retreats. Distinctions are analyzed before being resolved.

An unexpected refinement in the interpretation of imagined sights brings the licentious stage under aesthetic control and realizes anew the intense love of nature in the Indian soul. Many of the acts begin or end with verses of a lyrical sentiment, conjuring images of some phase of the day or night. An act may begin at evening and end with dawn, or, more often, begin with dawn and advance toward the heat of noon. Act Four of *Shakuntalā* commences with an exquisite encomium to the dawn; Act One of *The Vision of Vāsavadattā* concludes with a delightful speech by the religious student, the equivalent of a hymn to evening. This usage is handled at all times with remarkable tact. Again is demonstrated the control by which, all its poetic license notwithstanding, artifice commands the Sanskrit theatre.

There are still further unexpected refinements of the unseen. Speakers may not only talk to characters unseen because they are behind the curtain. They may even address persons assumed to be on the stage who are not actually there, just as their talk imagines physical objects viewed from the stage for which no actual physical symbol or representation exists. This is the manner of pure pantomime extended to the imaginary evocation of people no less than of properties or things. Furthermore, the myth of invisibility, present in all folklore throughout the world and well known to that mightiest of magicians, Shakespeare, proves highly familiar on the Sanskrit stage. Just what garment or symbol connoted invisibility is apparently unknown today but that the usage was common, thoroughly accepted, and well understood remains perfectly clear. Sarvilaka, the all-accomplished thief, conveniently possesses an ointment producing invisibility. Sītā and her confidante are invisible to both Rāma and his friend Vāsantī throughout the longest act in *Rāma's Later History*. Invisibility very naturally presents no difficulty to such an airy goddess as Urvacī. She and her heavenly friend instantaneously transform themselves from invisible to visible in the course of Act Three of *Vikramorvacī*. The noble god and celestial charioteer, Matali, becomes an invisible being in an important off-stage scene towards the close of *Shakuntalā*, Act Six. It is of the nature of the Indian poetic theatre, symbolical, mythological, and irrational, to be the more profound for being also magical. Magic and the theatre, as that excellent thinker and scholar, Brander Matthews, insisted, have much in common, magic being in a sense ideal theatre since it most fully induces an illusion and a conviction of belief.

The deeply metaphysical spirit of Sanskrit theatre further subtlizes by conjugating intricate interrelations between "real" life and theatrical life, the audience and the play. This is the familiar technique known from *The Taming of the Shrew* and Ben Jonson's court masques to Pirandello and Brecht, but developed in India with special nuances. Here a statement of the general point of view will suffice without exploring the many formulae by which Sanskrit playwrights provided that the forescene should dissolve into the play. The Producer at times evolves into a character of the play. His remarks may introduce a sophistical relation in time between the present and the play's imagined past. Still other characters are introduced who straddle the two worlds. Thus Maitreya is an off-stage character who speaks in the forescene of *The Little Clay Cart* and promptly becomes the first character to appear in the play itself. The Producer is often represented as interrupted in his address to the audience by the voice of an unseen person in the play. He usually introduces his wife, who is assigned a role in the drama. In *Shakuntalā* and other works the season of the year is mentioned as a tie between the real and the ideal world. In this instance the season is early summer. The Producer declares a song about the summer appropriate and finds the actual song so ravishing that he loses all sense of present actuality and hence is the better prepared to accept as actual the vision of the play. The abstraction of music induces the magic of the stage. Frequently a metaphor establishes a bridge between prologue and play, as in *Shakuntalā*, where the song is said to draw the Producer's mind as powerfully as the flying deer leads on the eager huntsman-king. The forescenes also have as a rule some reference to the author of the drama, which likewise links the present to the ideal world. All plays begin and end with prayers that unite in religious sentiment the entire assembly, the playwright and his audience, the persons on the stage, and those in the auditorium. Actors, imagined characters, and spectators alike pray for blessings that constitute the prime ends of existence. All is brought into focus by the vision of the religious mind. The purpose of the play is to induce the serenity or equilibrium of the enlightened soul. This is the meaning of the two prayers, that which begins and that which concludes the performance. A clever convention of the theatre denotes also a deep conviction of the soul. With this final thought we may fittingly bring to an end this brief study of technical conventions of the Sanskrit poetic theatre.

II / *Sanskrit Dramatic Style*

PROBABLY NO other dramatic style is so complex as that of the Sanskrit playwrights. Much as their language itself is highly inflected grammatically, so is the language-style of their works considered as art. The over-all form of dramatic composition, including their plot construction, is also elaborate and sophisticated, but of that at the present time nothing will be said. The following pages deal with certain general principles of their literary style, especially the playwright's fascinating manner of incorporating various tonalities or levels of speech into a successfully theatrical context.

Sanskrit dramatic theory makes no idol of simplicity. Although the contemporary criticism emphatically affirmed a need for unity in the play as a whole, in general the best and most skilful play was described as one which synthesized the largest number of distinct elements. The richer the harmony of parts, the better. In accord with this view and as a particularly conspicuous manifestation of it is the variety of dialects used. Broadly speaking, the most exalted characters, as deities, both male and female, and the heroes, speak Sanskrit, this being the standard liturgical and literary language ; the women and lesser characters speak in the more popular Prakrits. A play may employ only one of these lesser dialects, in which case it is that best known in the time and place of its origin. But variety of dialect peculiarities, as will shortly be noted, is sometimes employed to excellent advantage, especially where various servants and persons of the lower classes are speakers. Speech is to this extent determined by rank, not by scenes or even by the specific nature of the particular utterance. Each character is faithful to one dialect assumed to be understood both by everyone on the stage and the entire audience, though in the declining centu-

ries of the great Indian theatre the Sanskrit was understood only
by a minority of the spectators. When the aesthetic problem is
seen from a sociological angle or, so to speak, from the rear, the
use of Sanskrit and Prakrits reflects on the stage the caste system
in society and even italicizes it. The practice endows the plays
with a peculiar elegance though at possible cost of rendering them
at least mildly esoteric.

Readers of modern English poetry may be reminded of Sanskrit
and other tongues occasionally used in the verse of T. S. Eliot and
Ezra Pound, upon whom, one presumes, a veritable gift of tongues
descended. But on the whole a polyglot character in modern verse
is quite likely to appear snobbish or affected, whereas Indian life
and practice made their usage seem at the same time natural
and artful. It is hard to deny that the Indian usage adds in the end
to the stature of the plays as art. The text clearly becomes on this
account more artificial. Unfortunately, many of the features
of this technique of necessity are rudely obliterated from translations. The most familiar device is to use a slightly more elevated
style for the Sanskrit passages. But this is actually more feasible
in distinguishing the verse from the prose, especially if in the
translation prose is used throughout. The relation of verse to
prose has in the plays themselves no direct bearing whatsoever
on the relation of Sanskrit to Prakrits, the two distinctions operating
on completely different levels. In other words, almost all characters,
including those who speak Sanskrit, use both verse and prose.
The distinction by scene so commonly made in Elizabethan drama,
where in general some scenes are in verse and others in prose, does
not properly apply in Indian practice, by which at least the greater
number of scenes employ two dialects as well as the two forms,
verse and prose. Indian drama enjoys here virtually a unique
dimension, though the Noh Plays and other Oriental schools of
playwriting may afford distant analogies. Although the dialect
pattern of Indian dramas is of much importance and bears a vital
relation to other aspects of their art, it will not be examined
further here. The problems raised by the peculiar treatment of
the verse are both more important and much more accessible to
revealing analysis.

Several noteworthy comparisons should be made between the
Indian usages and at least three leading schools of poetic drama in
the Western World, those of Shakespeare, Calderon, and Sophocles.

In their ricn eclectic quality and profound humanity the Indian plays stand closer to the Elizabethan than to the Spanish masterpieces. Yet, the frequently religious spirit of the Sanskrit comes closer to the similar spirit in the Greek or Spanish. And while the Indian use of both prose and verse accords with the British, the distinction between two leading types of versification in the Spanish plays at least vaguely suggests the two dialects in the Indian. The authors of *The Vision of Vāsavadattā*, and *The Ring of Shakuntalā* would surely have recognized, had they been able to make their acquaintance, their affinity with such plays as *Life Is a Dream*, and *The Mighty Magician*, while the heroic melodramas of Bhavabhūti have at least considerable likeness to such Spanish works as *The Devotion of the Cross*, and *Life After Death*. Although Kālidāsa is probably nearer to Shakespeare on a profound level than to Calderón, in certain formal aspects he stands nearer to the illustrious Spaniard.

The verse-prose relation and above all the peculiar usages in verse itself undoubtedly give the Indian plays their chief stylistic distinction and hence these features repay special attention. Also, it is worth considering that these matters have been much less discussed than other features of the Indian drama, far less important, so that here more than elsewhere fresh comments are possible. Even here, however, a few factual statements, somewhat commonplace and essentially descriptive, are of use before interpretative statements can be attempted.

The proportion between verse and prose differs considerably from one play to another. Generally speaking, the more heroic or lyrical is the spirit of a play, the more verse there will be and the less prose. Some of the less pretentious works ascribed to Bhāsa, for example, as the delightful *Vision of Vāsavadattā*, have a large preponderance of prose, while Kālidāsa's idealistic drama, *Vikramorvacī*, abounds in verse. Roughly speaking, the parts are as a rule about equally divided. Relatively more prose appears than in a typical Elizabethan tragedy. Certainly the contrast with Greek tragedy, which is entirely in verse, proves drastic. Indian playwrights themselves, as we have observed, eagerly seek contrast, and hence find the admixture of prose and verse, the more naturalistic and the more stylized dialogue, distinctly attractive.

Here too, the Indian achievements can initially be grasped best by comparison with the work of others. In keeping with the tropical profusion of variety in the Indian plays, the number of meters employed proves considerably greater than in the typical Elizabethan drama. There a ten syllable iambic line predominates, with occasional couplet rhyme and a large predominance of blank verse. The blank verse itself is favored as time advances and grows considerably more licentious, or, in other words, closer to prose. And there is on the whole less prose in Caroline drama of serious complexion, that is, in tragedy and tragi-comedy, than in Elizabethan and Jacobean tragedies. The tendency was to oblite-rate distinctions. Incidental songs of various metrical construc-tion are, of course, introduced into English drama, yet, are com-paratively unimportant and add little to the over-all picture of the serious English stage. Only a few passages in Sanskrit drama appear to have been sung. The music for that drama seems to have been important but was largely instrumental accompani-ment and aid to the stylized acting and dance.

Style in European poetic drama has its taproot in the versified harangue of Greek drama, itself largely inspired by the fondness for grand speeches in Greek epic and narrative poetry. The grand harangue, derived essentially from the ancients, penetrates serious English drama and even extends to those eloquent speeches in plays by Bernard Shaw which Charles Laughton has within vivid memory delivered with such applause from his audiences. This oratorical tradition, primarily public, forensic, and at times even logical and argumentative, has no parallel in India. Even the epics supplying the subject-matter for several of the Sanskrit plays have themselves comparatively little use for the hortatory style. Nor are the dramatists themselves by any means as much indebted to the style of the epics as to their thought, their narra-tives, and their mythology. It is noteworthy that when seen in comparison with European practice speeches are relatively brief. The Sanskrit provides nothing remotely approaching the harangues of the great Spanish stage.

Style in the verse passages of the Indian works may first of all be described as poetically heightened above that in the prose dialogue. The verse is more metaphorical, sententious, emotional, and imaginative, and above all more formal or stylized. As seems most reasonable, the prose style is more colloquial; the verse style, more palpably artful. Although much of the verse is in Prakrits and a moderate amount of prose in Sanskrit, the proportion of verse in respect to prose is considerably greater in Sanskrit than in the popular dialect. Especially is this true in a writer of such exalted and poetic drama as Kālidāsa, most of whose verse passages occur in the role of the hero, who speaks in the learned tongue.

As clue to the chief feature of Indian dramatic verse it should be recognized that the sources for its aesthetic values lie primarily not in epic or romantic poetry but in the lyrical and epigrammatic. Here is its unique and most inspiring feature. Even the most casual glance at the pages of the plays should indicate this basic procedure. The style suggests a sky half clear and half ornamented with fine cumulous clouds ; the open sky is the prose, the clouds, the formations of verse scattered across the smoother but less sensational surface. Here a revealing distinction should be noted between the use of Sanskrit and that of verse. Both heighten the dramatic effect but each in its own way. The speeches may be extremely brief or fairly long. The prevailing tendency or norm of the verse elements is to be of at least a fair length, comparable in Western terms to the stanza or distinctly short lyric poem. Occasionally when stanzaic structure or its equivalent is actually found, several strophes may occur in sequence. In general, however, the unit of verse-speech resembles a lyric or at the very least a verse epigram, not the more elaborate ode. The average length for the unit is more or less that of a sonnet. These elements of verse lie like verdant islands in a bay, profusely scattered over the surface of the whole.

Such a procedure justifies the conclusion that Indian drama is generically one of the most lyrical in the entire history of the stage. By this is not meant, of course, the literal view that its verse was sung, like lyrics in *The Beggar's Opera*, but that such verse consists of various types of the literary or sung lyric accommodated to dramatic usage. A play is thus at once a firmly knit dramatic unity and at least potentially an anthology of short poems. Literally considered, these parts cannot well be extracted from their setting. One would seldom, if ever, think of doing so. Yet an analytical reader will almost certainly be surprised to notice how truly in the spirit of lyric poetry these passages are. Each is likely to express a mood, to employ a heightened rhetoric, to have in itself a roundness of form, a beginning, middle, and end, in short, to be a pearl in the jewelled pattern that is the play itself. The audience steps from one such passage to another with complete ease, nevertheless enjoying at each step a pause and a rhythmical arrest highly gratifying. No two passages are strictly alike, save in the delicacy with which each is designed as a cell, or minor organism, within the greater organism. A single unit may, to be sure, be repeated but this stands in our computation as one. We walk across the surface as over a floor inlaid with painted tiles. Such is the basic pattern of the play's verbal structure or decoration. How this patterning came about poses a question to which literary or theatrical history can hardly be expected to supply a conclusive answer. Quite possibly the choreographic and musical backgrounds of the plays supply at least some clues to their rhythmical development. The passages in question resemble poses or distinct movements in a dance or distinct periods within musical composition.

How much more artistic than its rivals the Indian poetic drama proves, may—with some partiality or unfairness, one must admit—be explicated by reference to that abortive experiment on the early Italian stage, the madrigal opera, a form of theatrical entertainment consisting entirely of short lyrics. Certainly among the closest analogues to the Indian speeches are the extraordinary and aesthetically gratifying Italian madrigals. Like the Indian speeches, the madrigals express in brief compass and perfected form almost every conceivable emotional state. But the very nature of the polyphonic madrigal presented insuperable obstacles to the construction of music drama exclusively out of madrigals. Whereas the Italian venture in this kind proved merely exploratory and academic, the Indian practice, with single parts, or airs, and intervals of prose, fructified completely in terms of drama. Many arrangements contributed to the successful assimilation in the Oriental plays, chief among them being the more pedestrian prose settings in which the verse elements are naturally and firmly embedded, as carefully selected stepping stones lead across a garden path. Italian classical music developed its fullest richness in polyphonic patterns awkward for theatrical assimilation on a large scale. It suggested choral scenes, not dialogue, and fitted the oratorio far better than the stage. It favored the musical as against the verbal element. Indian drama was, however, above all a drama of speech and dedicated to the Lord of Speech. On a few very rare occasions, notably in Bhavabhūti's *Rāma's Later History*, two characters deliver the same verse-speech at the same time. To Western ears this sounds distinctly operatic. It may well remind us at one and the same time how lyrical in inspiration Indian verse dialogue is and yet how far it stands divorced from the choral theatre known to either Aeschylus or Verdi.

Much Sanskrit literature by no means suggests to Western eyes a verbal economy. On the contrary, it tends to the diffuse, the expansive, even the interminable. Drama is a presentational art, tied to the wheel of time. When creating its drama, India perforce learned profound lessons in economy not learned elsewhere. Out of the materials of the interminable epics, the *Mahābhārata* and the *Rāmāyana*, plays of eminently manageable proportions and theatrical style were devised. A partial but presumably important explanation lies in their happy use of inspiration provided by the short poems of their own literature. Sanskrit and the native Indian dialects are peculiarly rich in development of the eminently short poem. Indian song, especially that allied with the lute, is rich in short pieces. It is safe to maintain that no literature is better stocked in witty verse-epigram than the Sanskrit. If not quite as ascetically condensed as the Greek anthology, much of which is in the manner of inscriptions, the short Indian pieces are more varied than the Greek and to this extent more useful as inspiration for a dramatic style. The true enjoyment of Sanskrit plays is greatly increased by attuning the mind to this strong vein of lyrical feeling crossing it from every side. Moreover, it is virtually impossible to doubt that such was the intention of its authors.

A revealing method of examining the lyric style more closely is to view the various inflections which it receives at the hands of a few major dramatists. This raises at once the question of its manifestations among the oldest playwrights and so in view of the accepted conditions of Indian dramatic origins launches such an analysis on a twilight of uncertainty. Drama indubitably flourished in India long before the composition of any surviving plays. The thinker is precipitated into pre-history. From the Trivandrum Plays ascribed to Bhāsa, however, some inferences may be drawn, as well as from analogous evidence elsewhere. The lyric style as used in the main corpus of Sanskrit drama presumably developed through a number of centuries. It represents so difficult and sophisticated an achievement that spontaneous origin becomes almost unthinkable. Moreover, the integrity of dramatic texts as such is generally a late cultural development. Some of Bhāsa's plays themselves read almost like scenarios, outlines to be filled in during actual performance with considerable expansion of both spectacular and verbal elements. In general, the lyric element is much less prominent in these early dramas than in the later masterpieces. Although the lyrical parts are comparatively sparse in the texts, speeches relatively brief, eloquence at a minimum, and dramatic effect commonly achieved by terse and poignant statement, there may conceivably have been some expansion on lines of lyrical expression. Similar conditions are suggested by surviving versions of Tibetan drama, where the text is set down primarily as a romantic narrative and the actors almost certainly are invited to enlarge on the actual script, using either improvisations or traditional expansions of the dialogue. In some cases a text may be little more than a skeleton to which performance adds flesh and blood. It is true that the Tibetan texts themselves are comparatively recent yet some likelihood exists that they parallel early or primitive conditions in theatrical achievement. Yet with all allowances for defective evidence, the strong presumption is that the lyric style in drama went through many stages before reaching its ripest fruition or highest development and indeed considerable differences exist in its treatment by the masters who followed in Bhāsa's footsteps during the succeeding centuries.

Kālidāsa shows the style already in an advanced form and even betrays special evidence of interrelationship between the true song and the merely lyrical element in dramatic dialogue. Unforgettable in its appropriateness to its context is the spring-song incorporated in the forescene of *Shakuntalā*. True songs are heard in the ceremonious fourth act of that play and are conspicuous in both Kālidāsa's *Vikramorvacī* and his *Mālavikāgnimitram*. These sung passages blend smoothly with those recited in verse and the latter were probably rendered in a heightened manner of delivery not quite recitative but at least quite distinct from the dialogue in prose. A closer correlation occurs here between the Sanskrit and the verse elements than in most Sanskrit plays. This is owing in part to Kālidāsa's fondness for the role of the hero, who overshadows the surrounding characters, especially when eloquence is a consideration. Like Sītā, Shakuntalā herself, though the ring given her by the hero gives the play its title, is a character of comparatively few words. The heroine is, in Indian practice in general, a woman of relatively modest speech, a character more to be seen than heard, more spoken about than speaking. The further the play descends to comedy, the more the heroine is likely to speak. Vasantasēnā is far more loquacious than Urvacī. Save in the fourth act of *Shakuntalā*, where the king does not appear and the leading male role is that of the voluble Kanva, by far the greater number of the verse passages are spoken by the king himself. He is supported in verse chiefly by official figures, as his chamberlain, his counsellors, and, in the last scenes, by his celestial charioteer. It is the king who, in Sanskrit, carries the main line of the verse. And the greater number of his speeches, in the elevated and metaphorical language favored for such poetry, have lyrical integrity, or, in other words, may theoretically be detached from their context and enjoyed as lyrical expression. His role is, accordingly, comprised in large part of an anthology of these potential lyrics offering an extended commentary on the phases of love and conjugal emotion. It is somewhat as though Shakespeare had composed a play in which his own sonnets had been incorporated into the dialogue to constitute the highpoints in its emotional progress. Here, as throughout Indian drama, the tendency is for the lighter passages to be in prose and for prose to provide the comic relief, as notably in the role of the *Vidūsaka*, or jester. Verse carries the chief burden of the play's emotion, which signifies that it falls in large part to the role of the hero. It also proves useful in passages of heightened dignity, official or ceremonious expression, and religious sentiment. The divine ancestors prominent in the exalted finale of *Shakuntalā* naturally speak in verse. Verse is always appropriate for the *deus ex machina*, a figure that may be said to belong to Sanskrit drama as well as to the Greek, though to be less prevalent in Sanskrit. Kashyapa in *Shakuntalā*, Narad in *Vikramorvaci*, Bhāgīrathī in *Rāma's Later History*, and Gaurī in *Nāgānanda*, all answer this description and are all unthinkable without the appropriate majesty which verse confers.

Lyric sentiment is strong in Harsa's plays and still stronger in Bhavabhūti's. Both playwrights show lyric feeling in their many passages describing nature, as of penance groves, forests, mountains, atmosphere, storm, birds, and beasts. This accords with the deeply entrenched Sanskrit tradition of a lyrical nature poetry and hymns to the forces of nature. Harsa's method shows here little advance from Kālidāsa's. Bhavabhūti, in this as in other respects a radical, marks a further stage in the enrichment of the lyric style, an evolution best exhibited in his masterpiece, *Rāma's Later History.*

The play contains an unusually large proportion of verse, owing in part to the absence of a Vidūsaka and any explicitly comic passages of emotional relief. Poetic descriptions are peculiarly lush and extensive. The characters invite both Sanskrit and verse, since many are supernatural and many also heroic. Thus Rāma, the hero, by no means monopolizes the verse passages, as Dushyanta is inclined to do in *Shakuntalā.* Kusa and Lava, his sons, speak much of the heroic verse. The supremely lyrical third act presents four characters speaking a large amount of verse, Rāma, Sītā, the goddess Vāsantī, friend of Rāma, and the river goddess Tamasā, confidante of Sītā. At the conclusion of the act the two goddesses utter the same words in unison, though addressed to Rāma and Sītā respectively. Everywhere the speeches tend to fall into strophe and antistrophe and to be themselves in symmetrical proportion, as a rule neither abrupt, as in a colloquial idiom, nor expansive, as in a declamatory manner, but comparatively brief and strongly emotional, warm, imaginative, symbolical. The total effect resembles a cantata composed of lyrical numbers. The poetry has a singing tone. Each verse-speech is an integer in itself although a more closely woven fabric of distinct pieces is hardly imaginable. On the one hand it resembles a textile decorated with medallions ; on the other hand, in its accumulative force, with its remorseless montage, it is a work strung on the coordinates of time, a masterpiece of presentational art, an instance of the triumphant union of lyrical and dramatic style.

Much the same technique, though developed with more simplicity and less virtuosity, dominates later acts, in which the twins, Lava and Kusa, and their cousin, Chandrakētu, play leading parts. The quarrel-scene between Lava and Chandrakētu includes passages of pure duet, where the two rival warriors speak identical words simultaneously. The battle that follows is obviously less a military engagement than a war-dance, where the verse is conceived as lyrical and is fully assimilated into patterns of dance and music. The effect from a literary point of view is that of pure stanzaic verse. In the first act, designated "The Picture Gallery," verse is apportioned with approximate equality between Rāma, Lakshmana, and Sītā. The prologues to the acts, or *viskambhakas*, have also strong lyric feeling. That to Act Six, for example, where celestial spirits flying in the air describe a battle, is especially choral in quality suggesting choral passages in Greek tragedy or the celestial choruses of Rumours and Recording Angels in Thomas Hardy's *The Dynasts*. As will later be considered in some detail, the lyric feeling need not be confined to passages in verse. So pervasive is this sentiment in Bhavabhūti's play that even the set speeches in the prose passages often assume a formal, balanced, and lyrical spirit.

Only in the last act of his masterpiece does Bhavabhūti desert, to any notable degree, his formula in favor of the skeletal type of writing so often encountered in Bhāsa. Here the action is accelerated by the crisper idiom of the play-within-the-play. Obviously a generous display of spectacle, stage business, and pantomime is demanded. Even the musical instruments, say the stage direction, are removed to make way for elaborate transactions on a crowded stage. The music itself may have been almost as conspicuous as the words, though heard in part, one presumes, from behind the rear curtain. Sensational visual features must also have rivalled the poetry in importance and acted to the discouragement of the richly developed lyrical manner of the six preceding acts. A faster tempo of the action clearly reduces the more leisurely movement demanded by a style in which essentially lyrical speeches follow in stately sequence.

Remarkably lyrical as Bhavabhūti's manner may be, *The Little Clay Cart* provides by far the most instructive source for study of the lyrical feeling in Indian drama. Incidentally, this affords an appropriate moment to voice regret that criticism in India itself has given less acclaim to this great drama than to the more serious or at least more romantic plays, as the masterpieces of Kālidāsa, Bhavabhūti, and Visākhadatta. The motive of this prejudice is clear enough : the mythological subject matter of the *nātaka* commanded in the traditional view a higher respect than the invented stories of the *prakarana*, where characters of less than divine stature are represented. Yet from the aspects of comparative literature and drama the most elaborate and consummate art of Sūdraka's play in balanced conjunction with its relative naturalism and superlative humanity should win it at least as much or even greater attention. Above all, in any consideration of the lyrical infusion it ranks supreme.

Although surviving plays hardly allow confident generalizations, it is highly probable that in the lighter form of play, the *prakarana*, virtually tragi-comedy or dramatic romance, the musical and choreographic elements come more conspicuously to the surface. This would seem a tendency throughout the world. The most serious or pretentious drama instructs its audience through its text, the lighter forms of theatre amuse their spectators with music and dance. And wherever music and dance gain in prominence, lyrical sentiment is almost sure to gain also. There is nothing trivial in Sūdraka's play, yet it contains the most conspicuous or one may even say inspired examples of choreography and pantomime. Vasantasēnā's appearances in her two most striking scenes in the first half of the play, her flight through the darkened streets from Samsthānaka's violence and her later journey on a stormy night through the same streets in quest of Chārudatta, are both essentially dance scenes. In the last act the pageant of Chārudatta's passionate pilgrimage to the place of execution at the Southern Cemetery is a stately dance-ritual. In all cases Sūdraka's speeches accompanying such actions are, as would be supposed, superlatively lyrical in inspiration. Moreover, they constitute in many respects what is possibly the finest lyric style ever developed in a theatre of literary distinction. Here great spectacle and great poetry meet. Sūdraka's technique repays virtually endless study.

An essentially stanzaic structure is clear. The speeches are of roughly similar length, neither excessively short nor long, and meticulously balance one another. There are no formulas of almost mathematical precision, as in Greek strophe, antistrophe, and epode, but fresh proportions appear in each instance while symmetry is always present in clearly perceptible degree. In Act One, each speaking a different idiom, we have the outbursts of Smasthānaka, his Vita, and his slave. Vasantasēnā is actually the chief figure here but acts largely in pantomime. In Act Five a duet form succeeds the trio. The ball of speech is tossed rhythmically between Vasantasēnā and her own Vita. The mute figure, of the utmost importance, is a slave carrying the umbrella, violently tossed by the tempest. From a spectacular point of view the passage is an umbrella dance, so important is this stage property in conveying the playwright's thought and imagery. Vasantasēnā, while reciting poetry on the storm, may switch her garments in as wind-blown a manner as possible and still fall short of the spectacular potentialities of the umbrella overhead. The action is by no means irrelevant so far as the lyric spirit is concerned. On the contrary, the dance beats out and accentuates the lyric form. To a certain point the technique is roughly that of the Greek chorus, equally a dance and a lyric. But there is a vital distinction between the Sanskrit and the Greek. The former is the more synthetic and possible the more artful, for whereas the Greek ode is more or less an interlude in the play, during whose course the action is arrested and the play's major characters may well be absent from the stage, Sūdraka's scenes stand among the most animated action of his play ; they are enacted by the chief figures of the play, not by choral accompanyists. The scenes are thus completely built into the play's fabric. Its three most memorable actions are its three most lyrical passages, Vasantasēnā's flight and pursuit and her lover's death march to his execution. Which is the superior manner cannot with assurance be determined. But it can definitely be asserted that here the Sanskrit drama proves to be much more essentially lyrical and choreographic than the Greek. Lyric and dance are incidental to the one, fundamental to the other.

There are further distinctions. The Greek chorus is cast in the form of the ode. Despite the customary division into its constituent parts, presumably occasioned by demands of the dance, the ode is a single poem, embracing its entire episode. Its strophes have far less independent value than the chief verse speeches in the Sanskrit scenes. In construction, to repeat, the Sanskrit manner suggests less the Greek ode than a sequence of Greek epigrams. Nor is it in the least irrelevant historically that Oriental literatures are singularly devoted to the conception of a sequence of short poems which may equally be regarded as a collection of epigrams or a single organism divided into segments. Long before Omar's *Rubaiyat* the Oriental literatures and Sanskrit in particular abounded in these works wherein each unit might stand by itself yet all be regarded as a larger unity. The image from jewelry seems inevitable. The items are pearls upon a string. Such was essentially what Sūdraka intended.

That this was his view is further indicated, or better, confirmed, by the repetition of "stanzas," or semi-lyrical speeches. This technique is seen built into the fabric of many Sanskrit plays, in none of the *nātaka* more brilliantly than in *Rāma's Later History*. The plot's progress is itself marked by the repetition of stanzas never understood twice in quite the same spirit. Dramatic irony is strongly enforced by this practice. Thus Act Three of *Rāma's Later History* repeats with radically different meanings several passages first encountered in Act One and the last act recapitulates other passages always with a fresh connotation. Bhavabhūti is the most inspired in the use of this technique but Sūdraka is still more insistent and exercises fully as firm a hand. Only a minor proportion of the words spoken by the hero in the last act of *The Little Clay Cart* are spoken for the first time. Chārudatta repeats many speeches, some even three or four times. The official proclamation for his death is ceremoniously entoned on four occasions, at each of the four gates of the town, each time with the emphasis of an accompanying drum-roll. Such repetitions are encountered, though less spectacularly, in all parts of the play. In Act One, for example, Samasthānaka's defiance of the hero is heard first from his own lips and later as repeated by Maitreya. (One recalls the similar repetition of messages in The *Iliad*.) This technique fixes the precise wording in mind. It assists the strong impression of cells within the framework of the play as a whole. It both contributes to the firm form of the play, and creates a firm form within the play. Its most obvious analogy is repetition in music. It provides a measure which will at least to some degree bear abstraction from its parent work, as fruit is plucked from trees. Similarly some of the self-contained stanzas in *The Fairie Queene, Orlando Furioso*, and *Jerusalem Delivered* were extracted as texts for English and Italian madrigals. Such technique provides additional demonstration of the lyrical element within the Sanskrit play.

The relation of dramatic poetry to established forms and qualities of the short poem in Sanskrit becomes especially clear in Sūdraka's play. Despite its urban setting, there are many passages descriptive of nature, of the sky and its storms, torrid noon, peaceful evening, night's magic. This is wholly in keeping with Sanskrit lyric practice. Similarly, many brief erotic poems of considerable beauty are embeded in the dialogue. The insatiable appetite of Sanskrit readers for short poems of a didactic character is represented almost to excess. Yet there is artistic calculation even here. A large number of these aphoristic pieces deal with the play's outstanding didactic theme : that poverty is the worst of ills, above all not because of the physical privations entailed but because friendships and social relationships of all sorts deteriorate under its chilling spell. Passages in which all these ideas are expressed are repeated much as themes or passages in music. Chārudatta, himself the prime exemplar of noble poverty and the ironic refutation of his own creed, is the most repetitious of the speakers and here it may be thought no accident that he is himself also depicted as a musical connoisseur and amateur of considerable skill. The robber on entering his house finds it so crowded with musical instruments that he assumes it the home of a professional musician—and therefore a man of no wealth. Among the play's unseen but significant characters is "the accomplished Rebhila," chief of the musicians, who delights Chārudatta with his music, protects Madanikā when honor thrusts her newly wedded husband from her arms, and informs Maitreya of the trial of Chārudatta. With music repeatedly in the play-wright's thought, the groundwork for a lyrical style is so much the better prepared.

As already noted on examination of *Rāma's Later History*, a lyrical sensibility belongs even to certain prose passages in only a lesser degree than to the more substantial among the verse speeches. Maitreya in Act Four on his visit to Vasantasēnā's palace passes through its eight courts delivering balanced harangues in each. Each is itself even divided into two parts as, according to stage directions, the brahmana looks in turn to right and left. His speeches are in prose. They fall between the remarkable series of ironic stanzas in pompous Sanskrit delivered by the brahmanical thief, Sarvilaka, in Act Three, and the incantations during the evening storm recited by Chārudatta, Vasantasēnā, and her Vita. The *Vidūsaka* is not entitled to speak in verse and contrast and emphasis call for this distinction between his own utterances and those of the more dignified characters. But it is clear that a similar aesthetics reigns in all. If the prose and the descriptive and objective aspect prevent these prose passages from conveying an impression of lyri-cism, it still remains true that they have much the same independence as the lyric passages and in many ways continue the pattern of the unmistakably lyric speeches. Each speech by Maitreya is a vignette so calculated and artificially balanced both in language and gesture as to accord with several leading qualities of the lyric form. The accounts of the successive courtyards depict in turn a dazzling display of decorated architecture, an accommodation for prize work-animals, an elegant rendezvous for young gentlemen and their mistresses, a foyer for music, a luxurious restaurant, a treasury for jewelry and other decorative objects, an aviary, and a reception court. In front of all stands a magnificent portal ; still further within lies a resplendent garden. All these are painted according to a formal pattern of rhetoric, each picture exclusive of its neighbors and in its own terms sufficient yet all comprising a pageant of opulent magnificence. Even a considerable movement and stage business are provided. By some criteria these passages are prose poems. And even if in terms of severer criteria they themselves are not poems, they illustrate many of the devices by which short poems of lyrical flavor provide constituent parts of Indian dramas.

This investigation leads to several conclusions. Since it shows the plays to be both sharply segmented into small particles and to be also eminently organic, it behoves the reader or spectator to acknowledge both the divisible and indivisible features. The latter may be assumed. The former repay and demand special effort and attention. All true works of art are reputed to have unity but few possess the eclectic character of these plays. The individual passages have great charm in themselves. When experienced from this point of view, they yield surprising pleasure, becoming additional jewels in the already large collection of distinguished Indian short poems. More harmoniously and more fully than any other school of drama, the Indian school unites the attractions of both essential lyricism and pure dramatic art. This style constitutes a virtually unique achievement yet one of much potential significance for the future development of musical or poetic drama in any part of the world. Reading Sanskrit plays resembles walking along a spacious ocean beach. The panorama in its whole extent is noble. Exquisite shells are deposited in its sands, entirely natural in their setting and yet each in itself an entity to be cherished and enjoyed. Even acknowledging a great expense of ingenuity and sophistication, these results are a normal growth of Indian cultural values. Nothing strictly of the sort exists elsewhere in the entire annals of poetry or the stage. Should imaginative writers today in India or elsewhere penetrate into the secrets of this remarkable artistry, there is no telling what new features dramatic poetry might acquire. The world today stands in a period of transition for the musical, the choreographic, and the poetic stage. The plays of ancient India offer us a wealth of suggestion.

time promises to please its audience and to reward either amateurs or the most experienced actors, who through its production will presumably be learning new potentialities in their art. Sūdraka's work is the very apotheosis of theatrical style.

Perhaps only a philistine will ask what *The Little Clay Cart* means. In a word, it means life. Shrewd observations and perceptions abound in its presentation of all manner of themes, including politics, religion, society, psychology, art. It is not a "problem play" for the sufficient reason that its discursive thoughts impinge on most of the chief matters that vitally concern mankind. Seldom does a work of art possess such fullness. One is even reminded of the amplitude of perception and imagination in the masterpieces of Shakespeare, Tolstoy, or Balzac. We shall return to these considerations of meaning later. But at least it should be recognized from the first that the play should be produced with a maximum fidelity to its original style and meaning and with a firm confidence that these need not and should not be sacrificed to any supposed need for compromise with the modern theatre. The longer the play has been produced in the Western World, the closer, on the whole, the productions have come to the spirit of the original. To be sure, it is virtually essential, if it is to be seen under any but the most extraordinary circumstances today, that it should be reduced in length by some thirty per cent. Even so, the length of the original presents a serious obstacle, for though considerably longer than most Sanskrit plays, it contains remarkably little that under any terms can be regarded as dead wood. Historically speaking, it comes extremely close to being two plays. As read today, it is described in our translations as in ten acts. There are certainly ten major divisions ; as we shall later see, the word "act" may really be more misleading than helpful. A version of the four earlier acts, at a few points identical with Sūdraka's play and never far removed from it, is attributed to Bhāsa, almost certainly an earlier writer than the author of *The Little Clay Cart*. Bhāsa's work is known as *Chārudatta in Poverty*. Very likely it was itself the first part of a play wholly composed at the same time, the second part of which might—if conjecture be allowed—have been called *Chārudatta Restored to Prosperity*, and have been not greatly different from the second part of Sūdraka's work. In Act Five the lovers are brought together and though the heroine, Vasantasēnā, declares that, in the dark, she has not gratified herself with the unimpeded sight of her lover and moreover that she has not as yet established the ideal relation with him, at least the physical consummation of their passion may be assumed and an important step forward in their emotional relationship has been won. Though many threads remain, to use the Sanskrit metaphor, "untied," the play does come with Act Five to a plausible resting place and may possibly have been produced with this gratifying result. It can be so produced today. Since acts one to five are much the less ambitious in stage pageantry and elaboration, this part of the work may conceivably be given to good advantage by amateurs, on a relatively small stage, and with comparatively slight expense. The imaginative style is quite as brilliantly achieved here as in the .later section. If half the work is shorter than the average play today, the whole is longer. But unquestionably the full value of any act or part whatsoever depends on the production of the work in its entirety. In more serious and professional productions this should always be given intact. The whole is very much of a piece and far more than the sum of its constituent parts. Although Part One, then, may conceivably be given without Part Two, the latter cannot be given without Part One. Effects are to a remarkable degree accumulative. The relation is not that of a pedestal to its statue ; it is that of a growing organism : from the trunk spring the many branches with their surprisingly abundant foliage.

The performance should be given in an unadulterated form, without scenery, though an appropriate background is, of course, desirable as a screen. There should be, according to Indian usage, two entrances, with curtains, to the rear, precisely as in the famous drawing of the Elizabethan theatre by De Witt. Frequently two or more groups of characters occupy the stage imagined as invisible to each other but in clear sight of the audience. Such being the case, possibly very short screens or artificial shrubbery may be used extending toward the audience at right angles from the rear wall, thus emphasizing the separateness, though these are by no means essential. The familiar variant of this situation, whereby one group is aware of the other but the second group is unaware of the first, argues against any considerable obstruction. The background should remain background, relatively inconspicuous, a neutral foil against which the actors themselves will be accentuated. Most modern productions of Sanskrit plays have been embarrassed by a far too developed scenic picture. The slighter the

machinery, the better. Musicians, about a dozen in number, originally filled the back wall, and this should be the disposition wherever
practicable. Instances of the danger of using excessive machinery
are numerous. To cite a typical problem : there are scenes in
The Little Clay Cart that imagine an actor in an elevated position.
Samsthānaka, from a window or balcony in the palace, observes
his slave, Sthāvaraka, at the window of a cell in the tower opposite.
Samsthānaka may also be imagined as present on the same balcony
overhearing his defiant declaration read to Chārudatta in Act One.
Such episodes would on the Elizabethan stage have requisitioned
the use of the balcony behind the stage itself. But the Indian theatre
was almost certainly without such a balcony. All such scenes could
have been performed with no mechanical aid whatsoever, as, in
Shakespeare, when King Lear leaps off an imaginary Dover Cliff ;
but a small movable platform might possibly have been used, from
which Sthāvaraka makes his desperate jump.

Assume, then, a stage bare of any elaborate construction or
representational effects and no curtain between stage and audience
—the only curtains cover the two doors and are brushed aside as
the actors enter. This simplicity, of course, eliminates any time-
problem for change of scene. In modern production there should
be pauses between the acts, marked by some very brief musical
interlude ; the theatre lights should not go on. These musical
interludes are of some importance, for the act divisions are, in fact,
more important and less arbitrary than in Western drama. Each
act exhibits a distinct "sentiment," which, in turn, is expressed
by an appropriate mode in music. It is evident that wind and
percussion instruments are especially prominent in the last acts of
each Part in the play, that is, acts five and ten. In the first instance,
the music must express the storm, with its rush of rain and roar
of thunder, both symbolic of an emotional crisis. In the second
instance, drums are specifically demanded for the ceremonial
procession, and trumpets as well should accompany the repeated
reading of Chārudatta's death sentence. Here the music is of a
fearsome temper and a ponderous tone, announcing death with
torture, the closing-in of fate under the pressure of a ruthless, tyrannical king. Prokofiev might offer suggestions. Music of a satirical
and ironic tone, such as Stravinsky so often composes, is clearly
called for as prelude to Act Two, "The Masseur Who Gambled" ;
finally, notes of pathos, such as Debussy might have supplied, are

demanded for Act Eight, "The Murder of Vasantasēnā" ; Sanskrit plays are commonly provided with titles for the individual acts. Critically considered, these resemble less the acts of modern plays than the movements in classical music itself, as in the symphony and the sonata. These are considerations of major importance for presentation. The director should, accordingly, study each act as though it were not an act but, instead, a one-act play. He must also, of course, ponder the countless threads binding the acts into a comprehensive unity.

Such a play as *The Little Clay Cart*—if, indeed, there be such another—is both long and closely written. It demands an attention almost as close as music and this demand must not result in fatigue for the audience. Given in its ten acts it calls, therefore, for an intermission, rather more generous than brief, between Part One, or *Chārudatta in Poverty*, and Part Two, or *Chārudatta Restored to Prosperity*. Happily, this demand is distinctly to the convenience of modern theatrical practice.

To any student of theatrical history, *The Little Clay Cart* must seem almost encyclopedic, so remarkably does it summarize what is known of the theatre throughout the world. In short, it is much more unusual in its scope than in its parts, for its parts represent much of the best that has been thought and heard on the stage, though seldom, if ever, gathered together so inclusively. Incident after incident reminds the informed reader of outstanding passages in Aristophanes, Plautus, Lope de Vega, Shakespeare, Jonson, Molière, Goldoni, Strindberg, Pirandello, Shaw, Brecht, or Tennessee Williams. Turn, for example, to half-a-dozen lines in the Third Act. Sarvilaka releases a moth to extinguish a nightlamp (the imagined flame is evidently small, like that of a candle). One may well think today of one of Marcel Marceau's most inspired acts, that depicting the clown and the imaginary butterfly. No sooner is the light extinguished than Sarvilaka reflects that the offense which he is committing is notorious much less for extinguishing the light of the lamp than for overwhelming the life of his honor by his crime. The extinction of the flame instantly takes on a deep, symbolical meaning. "Put out the light, and then put out the light". Shakespeare seldom wrote a more remarkable line. Yet essentially the same line is to be read in the Sanskrit of a thousand years earlier. To an attentive reader of *The Little Clay Cart* such parallels are virtually endless. Poetry and the theatre shift and change far less than those ingenious gentlemen, the professional historical scholars, would sometimes lead us to suppose. Western playwrights have quite unwittingly been traversing the same grounds as Sūdraka for over a thousand years. His play, which presents these innumerable analogues, is thus equally compendious and prophetic.

The allied question, how "original" his characters are, is, strictly speaking, somewhat difficult to answer, to begin with, because closely analogous plays from the Sanskrit are few in number, if indeed, there can be said to be any. But it may safely be concluded that, much as might be expected and desired, the chief characters are both fresh and typical, since they are given features peculiar to the present play and yet preserve many of the aspects of well-established stage personages.

In terms of Indian dramatic practice one at once observes the usual hero and heroine, for Sanskrit drama is even more committed to the presence of these two leading figures than is European. Both are invariably idealized, partly because the Indian aesthetics regards all art as by rights idealistic. This idealism is not so much intellectual or moral as spiritual. A play is intended to leave its audience spiritually edified, uplifted, and serene, though not, perhaps, the wiser through the presentation of any particular moral or ethical problem. The purgation of tragedy is not demanded, nor the satirical wit of an intellectual comedy. The hero need not be conspicuously active. But he must be spiritually admirable, even though he need not be humorlessly perfect and must not be a prude. The pious Chārudatta and the pleasure-loving Vasantasēnā are typical variations on this basic theme of idealization. His poverty, for example, symbolical of a more general conception of privation, gives him a distinguishing feature, as, in compensation, does Vasantasēnā's opulence. She is in many respects more aggressive and enterprising than her melancholy lover. The other characters follow suit. The reckless and acquisitive gambler, the *Vidūsaka*, or clown, attendant on the hero, being a Brahmana who loves good eating and all physical pleasures, except, perhaps, those of sex, the witty maid, the subservient courtier, the princely buffoon, the corpulent bawd, mother of the resplendent and generous courtesan—all these are familiar figures on the Indian stage. Sūdraka contributes fresh developments to all of them on the basis of well established themes. Such are the familiar ways of the theatre.

Somewhat surprising, however, is the existence of much the same types in the European drama both before and after the composition of *The Little Clay Cart*, which may well have been as early as the fourth century, A.D. The development of the plot, or plots, in this play has similarly led to speculation on possible European influence on the Indian theatre, much as scholarship has clearly established such influence on Indian sculpture through the Gandhara school, of Alexandrian origin. The historical problem clearly need not detain us here ; but the basic facts, regardless of their origins, are of much importance.

Samsthānaka is by no means unfamiliar compound of villain and buffoon as he appears in Western drama, well known to the *commedia dell'arte* and sufficiently exemplified as recently as the monstrous braggart in Samuel Backett's *Waiting for Godot*. Hero and heroine, Chārudatta and Vasantasēnā, the generous young man prodigal of his wealth, and the noble-minded hetaera, are essentially the same figures as those in works of Plautus and Terence. But there are, of course, distinctions and also parallels within parallels. Thus the pietistic and the melancholy strains in Chāru-datta remind us respectively of Everyman and of Hamlet, and Vasantasēnā's elegance and sophistication suggest heroines in Calderón or Racine. The conversion of Samsthānaka's *vita*, or gentleman-attendant, from easy compliance to outraged honor is familiar in innumerable Western plays, exemplifying the moral education of a man of no more than average courage provoked at length by flagrant injustice to a courageous act. The stout mother of the courtesan, essentially a procuress, is as old as Greek farce and as recent as Tennessee Williams' strongest play, *Camino Real*. Maitreya, the priestly Brahmana, attendant in the household of Chārudatta, is in peculiarly interesting ways compounded of various familiar attributes in theatrical creations. He is the rough but faithful servant attending in complete confidence on the fortunes of the hero. He is also the parody of the man of religion, who, though no impiety is intended, loves food, drink, and physical well-being quite as truly as he loves the gods. He is no hypocrite and irreligion is not suggested, yet, despite his religious station in life he is both less religious and less idealistic than the hero. Gruff and lovable, he suggests a hero in a comedy or a novel by Henry Fielding. He is also the hopelessly ineffectual clown.

The weak and melancholy gambler who turns to religion, becoming a mendicant "friar," presents another type clearly defined here, quite as familiar to us, to be sure, in real life as on the stage. He is an Expressionist character who would be at home in a play by George Kaiser. Sarvilaka is astonishingly like a fantastic figure in Shaw, following a strictly logical path to the defiance of conventional morality, violating a social code in the interests of a generous emotional impulse. Madanikā is to all intents and purposes the witty and enterprising servant-girl of European comedy, appearing as Maria in *Twelfth Night*, a score of times in Molière, and countless times in *opera comique*. There are at least ten such universally meaningful roles of much importance in *The Little Clay Cart*, and an equal number of minor roles that are still of such types as are of considerable attraction for actor and audience. The servants are by no means dwarfed by their masters or reduced to indignity. Sthāvaraka, the most valiant and honest of all, is given two important scenes, highly congruous with each other, in which he speaks some of the most moving lines in the play. In each case he is thwarted and beaten ; the first time on making his exit he declares that he has done all he can to save Vasantasēnā, but without success ; the second time, on making his exit, he declares that he has done all in his power to save Chārudatta, but to no avail. He exhibits the impotence of a good and even a brave man overpowered by the brutal rulers of man's destiny. This is both a moving and an all-too-familiar conception, executed with great delicacy and with an art, but not a pathos, that all but conceals itself.

From the foregoing two conclusions are to be drawn. The play is brutally damaged if any considerable feature of it is removed, and its many actors are rewarded with remarkably good roles, which enable them to use much of their experience in other plays and further prepare them for plays in which they will appear later. Most emphatically, *The Little Clay Cart* stands in the main line of theatrical discipline. It might well be in the program for the early years in any drama school in any land or period.

Prologues may often be safely omitted, but neither prologue nor epilogue can reasonably be omitted here. The prologue may be described as Brecht translated out of the robustious into the adroitly refined. The forescene of a Sanskrit play in general repays close attention. That in *Shakuntalā*, for example, is rightly the most famous, a miracle of succinctness and grace. In all cases a leading aesthetic motive is to facilitate a transition between two aspects of consciousness, the mundane world and the stage-world. The Manager of the Theatre appears, usually with his leading actress, cast as his wife. Naturally and casually, a highly contrived scene within the green-room merges into the fully developed fiction of the play. Perhaps Pirandello no less than Brecht would applaud, but then, from the former Brecht largely derived his ideas in this regard, translating Italian charm into German violence. Neither, one presumes, had studied the Sanskrit, yet how truly is the theatre the theatre, for-ever-and-a-day !

The Sanskrit forescenes, then, have much suavity and wit. It will be recalled that the Manager in *Shakuntalā* announces the play that is to be given, summons the actress to perform a song, which is a celebration of spring, and then wholly forgets that he has announced a play because he—as he explains it—no less than the audience has been wholly entranced by the singing. The spell of one art is invoked to enhance the spell of another. The prologue is an *hors d'oeuvre* to improve appetite. One would be hard put to find a neater trick in the theatre. This Manager further describes himself as lured by the song just as the king is lured by the deer which, in a matter of seconds, will be pursued by the monarch across the stage. Such is the almost uncanny tact of the highly professional Sanskrit playwrights.

Even Kālidāsa himself, however, must not completely lure us from our proper theme, which is Sūdraka. The prologue of the play now before us has similar if rather less brilliant and perspicuous virtues. Like Shakuntalā, Vasantasēnā, is symbolical of the spring. This is the root meaning in her name, the word *vasanta* meaning "spring," and the actress should be costumed in a manner to suggest that season. The Manager in Sūdraka's play begins with the usual prayers. The first prayer is here clearly ascetic ; the second, as befits a comedy, to all appearances sensuous. "May the throat of the Indigo-Throated protect you—the throat that is like a dark cloud and about which gleam like lightning-flashes the vine-like arms of Gaurī." Commentary on these vivid words might profitably extend to a matter of pages but it suffices here to remark that the allusions are to Siva, patron of the stage, and his wife, Gaurī, that the allusion to his throat befits the prayer of the poet-playwright for the gift of his eloquence, and that the image of the cloud and the lightning is artfully repeated in the play's climax, when Vasantasēnā comes to Chārudatta battling her way through a rain storm. This poetic imagery firmly establishes the woman as the lightning and the cloud as the man. Chārudatta himself repeats the image which Vasantasēnā instantaneously enacts by rushing into his arms. He borrows her lightning, catching fire from her energy. The basic image is that of *Shakuntalā*, and, indeed, of all three of Kālidāsa's dramas, not to mention masterpieces by Bhavabhūti and other important Sanskrit dramatists. Man and nature become merged.

But, as previously indicated, *Shakuntalā* and *The Little Clay Cart* cannot follow precisely the same pattern, for one is a superlatively idealized and largely mythological drama, prevailingly sober, the other, a more synthetic work, a story of city life and manners, with political features, and a strong, persistent current of humor. Its most remarkable role is that of a braggart, half villain and half clown. It is important to note that Sanskrit drama at no time takes itself quite as seriously as Western "drama," for the philosophy of the East distrusts the validity of any philosophy wholly committed to the tragic or the heroic. Hindu thought, which created Krishna, can hardly comprehend an unsmiling Savior. Thus *The Little Clay Cart* both is and is not religious. More religious thought is strongly felt than superficially apparent. A deeply religious community is reflected more or less by indirection. The hero is pious, a Brahmana. He is first seen offering a sacrifice ; in the last act he himself is virtually the sacrifice. The gods are at least outwardly revered, though there is, I think, a suspicion that the more rigid orthodoxies in both Indian religion and politics may be called to some account and readjustment. Mythical symbolism exists and the characters mean far more than appears on the surface. The predominant outlook is thus in many ways idealistic. But this idealism is abundantly seasoned with the comic spirit. The play combines the virtues of *Everyman* and the *commedia dell'arte*.

"Enough of this verbiage, which tires the patience of the audience." These are the words abruptly spoken by the Manager immediately after the "Benediction" with which, according to tradition, the play begins. Neither the prayer nor the raillery epitomizes the play's spirit, which is, of course, a conjunction of the two, a harmonizing of their opposing moods. So the Manager himself, after speaking with much earnestness and eloquence, declares himself done with his declamation and demands food and drink to refresh himself and supply much needed relaxation. Religion and art are not to be equated. The play, in short, not only has many characters but many facets.

Its sophistication in this respect is still further foreshadowed in the conclusion of the forescene, where the Manager invites one of the characters in the play, Maitreya, to dine with him and his wife. Maitreya declines, his chief reason being that he has an immediate duty to perform, to deliver a cloak which he carries on his arm to his friend and master, Chārudatta. This is not merely to say that the action of the play itself is preferred to that of the prologue. The dinner was to have been a feast of a religious nature, with a petition to the gods relative to the fate of the Manager and his wife in their future incarnations. Maitreya is a man of priestly functions. But he is also a prominent figure in a comedy and earnestly given, like the Manager himself, to the joys of eating and drinking. At this moment the secular takes precedence over the priestly function. Yet each is viewed as ultimately important, as the prologue itself is important, though promptly merging into the main stream of the action.

It would, accordingly, be a serious misinterpretation to underplay either the earnestness or the mirth, as consideration of all parts and persons in the play shows. Consider the characters. Samsthā-naka is both monstrous and burlesque ; Chārudatta, both heroic and, happily, a little ridiculous, especially in competition with Vasanta-sēnā. The remarkable Fifth Act is conceived on both planes. In an intensely lyric passage Vasantasēnā rushes through a storm to meet her lover. For a few minutes, however, on their meeting in the garden, the tension notably relaxes, exactly as the *vita* has suggested, who prescribes that the true strategy of lovers is alternation between vehemence and reserve. So in her spirit of humorous reserve, Vasantasēnā greets her lover by striking him lightly with a bouquet and inquiring for the health of "the gambler." The reference here, so archly witty, is to her knowledge of the generous deception which in his gallantry he has played upon her. The act is heavily charged with passion and yet this episode is full of delicate raillery. The play is thus a study in poise to be maintained between rapidly shifting incidents, which reflects, indeed, the ironic Hindu conception of the universe as a conjunction of comple-mentary forces. The title of the play is ironic. Its first words are ironic. All is ironic. It is a course that makes for delightful theatre. It may also make for the highest wisdom.

A bit more in illustration of so important a feature may be helpful. Sarvilaka is both a knavish wit and a romantic hero ; Vasantasēnā, both a coquette and a romantic heroine ; Chārudatta, both a god led to religious sacrifice and the dupe of his own generous folly ; the Masseur, both a witty gambler and a sincere Buddhist "friar ;" Maitreya, perhaps the most life-like figure in the play, both ridiculous in his futility and sincere in his friendship and his willingness to sacrifice his life for his master ; Rohasena, both a petulant child and a highly emotional symbol for the family, the cornerstone of Hindu morality. Any director enjoys a rare opportunity in balancing the moods of this infinitely rich drama that is neither purgative as tragedy nor hilarious as farce but suspended in the purest element of art, which, according to Indian aesthetics, is a means to establish the illusion of happiness, harmoniousness, and well-being, without sentimentality or the falsification of a morally invalid optimistic illusionism—in other words, to attain the condition most clearly experienced in music.

This aesthetics is a highly convincing body of thought, based, as it is, to so great a degree on music and the dance, of which Siva is the ultimate patron. Drama thus becomes a translation of music into words and action. Poetry is, of course, words without action ; the dance action without words ; only drama is words—action— music in one, to which is added an imagined spectacle that embraces the quintessence of painting, sculpture, architecture, and decoration. Thus the Indian theatre, unquestionably one of the highest achievements of Indian art, is the legitimate flower of a refined aesthetic theory and practice. Anyone who participates in it and shares its disciplines should gain an experience of no inconsiderable value. The more mature and sophisticated our own aesthetic ideals become, the closer they must lie to the Sanskrit stage. The chief reservation to this proposition lies primarily in the singular lack of specialization in that stage. In ancient India the arts tend to be synthetic ; each shares much with all others. Western theatre and literature are more specialized but on that account not obviously either the better or the worse. The adjudication of that vexed case lies, happily, beyond the province of this introduction. All insisted upon here by way of comparison is that the best products of East or West are of vital importance in both sections of the world.

The demands of production for *The Little Clay Cart*, as for almost all Sanskrit drama, require extreme attention to both choreography and poetry, the two most disparate elements in the theatre. Our actors are as a rule too little trained in the conjunction of these fields, even presuming that they have mastered one or both. Remarkably enough, the most powerful and important scenes in Sūdraka's play, those on which its action and conduct chiefly depend, mark its highest development in both respects. The more dramatic the scene, the more lyrical the language and the more formal and stylized the action. That these features pose important problems for the play's interpretation and production is sufficiently obvious but only some close inspection shows the extent of the challenge. Few plays give as great opportunities for the performers in both regards. Some outstanding passages may be examined.

There are three major scenes in the ceremonial or ritualistic manner, located at the three most strategic points, namely, acts one, five, and ten. The chief incident in the First Act is a ceremonious pursuit of Vasantasēnā by night through the streets of the city, ending only when she escapes through the open side-door of Chārudatta's house. This scene resembles a piano quartet, with Vasantasēnā as the outstanding instrument. Yet even if she is the composition's focus, she by no means speaks the most voluminous role. There are in all, three pursuers and their victim. She has, incidentally, in the course of the chase, lost three servants, to whom she calls in vain, so that all odds for an even contest stand against her. Prince Samsthānaka is the leader in the attack, supported by the *vita*, who is his attendant, counsellor and friend, and by a slave. Each of the three men literally talks a different dialect. Together they chase the courtesan through the streets, symbolized by repeated rotation about the stage. As they do so, they recite balanced stanzas, each in the pursuit reflecting his distinct role or attitude. Thus as the chase accelerates, the *vita*, increasingly disgusted by his hateful lord, as he will be again and ultimately in Act Eight, plays traitor and shrewdly enables the girl to escape under the very nose of her false lover and fated enemy. The stanzas are introduced by phrases repeated virtually as a refrain. The men exclaim, "Stop, Vasantasēnā, stop !" Samsthānaka prefixes several of his harangues with his exhortation to his preceptor, "Mentor, mentor !" The set speeches are very striking, just as the action, if properly achieved, must also be. An elaborate pantomime is greatly aided by the assumption of a

143

dark night. Though Samsthānaka is often almost touching the girl, he either sees her dimly or not at all. Three times is he baffled by mistaking another for her, the first time grasping a man, then two women. The scene is a burlesque of crude passion, a ridicule of ungovernable and unregenerate lust. The rudest violence is translated into the suavest art. The speeches, some in verse, some in prose, are for the most part highly eloquent. The episode becomes a masterpiece in both choreography and lyrical expression.

The second of these episodes, the central incident in Act Five, a closely studied parallel to the First Act, is enacted by four figures, with no less vigorous poetry and no less animated gesture. Vasantasēnā hastens through a spring storm to the house of her beloved. She is followed by a *vita*, also addressed at times as "Mentor", a slave-girl and a slave with an umbrella. In this scene both slaves are mute. Further on in the Act, the slave-girl speaks a few lines. Probably the umbrella holder was an exceptionally accomplished dancer. The scene's pantomime consists largely in simulating the progress of the group through two storms, one in general nature, the other, symbolically, in human passion. Vasantasēnā, however sophisticated she may be and however much her protrait is painted as that of a warm-blooded courtesan, is, like Shakuntalā goddess of spring. In this episode she appears in her richest trysting costume. These flowing and flowery garments she must swirl about her as though tossed by the storm. At the same time she must appear to shelter herself from the deluge and express her delight in it. Unquestionably she is the leading lady in the dance, but not impossibly the slave is the leading dancer, as her umbrella is certainly the outstanding stage-property. In what may be called an umbrella dance the slave must give the utmost dimensions to the conception of the episode. Alternating stanzas of courtesan and *vita*, strophe and antistrophe, express the divergent aspects of the scene, which is equally poetic and choreographic.

The third and final passage conspicuously combining pageant movement with poetical afflatus is much more complex. The proclamation announcing Chārudatta's execution is declaimed four times by the executioners and imagined as heard in the four chief sections of the city. At the South Gate the execution itself is to take place. In addition to the proclamation, there are several stanzas spoken at repeated intervals by Chārudatta, keeping pace with the relentless march to the Southern Cemetery. As a result, the entire act constitutes a prolonged and carefully contrived montage, far exceeding the earlier passages in length and elaboration though by no means different from them in aesthetic principle. Action is more leisurely or long drawn out because the force and momentum is actually the greater and many more figures crowd the stage. The whole act is a study of the most elaborate balances in both speech and action. In the interstices between the proclamation occur impressive episodes, calculated intrusions or interruptions caused in turn by the appearances of Rohasena, Chārudatta's son, and by Sthāvaraka, with his plea for Chārudatta's liberation, thwarted so surprisingly by Samsthānaka. Thus two attempts to halt the ceremonial march are frustrated. The third effort, after the final recitation of the proclamation, the appearance of Vasantasēnā, who has been supposed dead at her lover's hands, alone cancels the horrible proceeding. The act is a gigantic death-march, ending in a complete reversal. The red robe worn to execution becomes the marriage robe worn by Chārudatta when Vasantasēnā is elevated by the new prince to the position of wife. The same ironic and ceremonial symbolism of the red robe, it may be noted, occurs in the last scene of Harsa's remarkable play, *Nāgānanda*.

The studiously calculated tempo of Sūdraka's act is solemn and slow ; the recitation demanded is heavy and lugubrious ; the gestures are ponderous and tragic. An appropriate music must accompany the action. Chārudatta is led as a reluctant sacrifice to the apparent tyranny of fate. There can be no question of the essentially religious aspect of the imagery thus far. He is the god led to death, Dionysus destined to be reborn. For fate, it seems, has been wrongly interpreted. The denouement is to the contrary of appearances—a condition, one recalls, recommended by Aristotle. A miracle deflects the sword of the executioner as he strikes the first blow, which he has promised to be fatal. A religious mendicant abruptly presents the redeeming deity, Vasantasēnā, the goddess of spring, as salvation to a world threatened by the extinction of winter. Sterility is overcome. The prodigious pageant ends happily. The meaning is not that human affairs present this aspect to the sober and literal eye of history. No interpretation of life in either optimistic or naturalistic terms is offered. That life contains extreme pain is neither sentimentally nor rationally denied. But in the eyes of the poet the end of art itself, as of wisdom and of religion, is to create a condition of harmony and peace within man's imagination. Evil is shown as ultimately transcended by contemplative, not by moral, power.

Two symbols, or dramatic metaphors, each with the force of sexual allusion, accent the conclusion of the two parts of this play. The First Part, as already indicated, reaches its resolution, or tying together of the knot, when the lightning and the cloud, Vasantasēnā and Chārudatta, become one. As Chārudatta speaks the lines descriptive of nature, Vasantasēnā, who has already anticipated them in her great lyric dance-ode, enacts them by living out the terms of Chārudatta's metaphor and throwing herself into his arms. Similarly, on the reunion of the lovers in Act Ten, Chārudatta exclaims that love brings the dead to life. Vasantasēnā has been supposed dead and Chārudatta's death has been decreed and in thought already has occurred—for who in reason can believe that the executioner's sword has not killed him? But they live, far more ardently than ever before! The funeral meats have truly served the marriage table. Production requires special emphasis on these ceremonious actions, so that they may be unmistakably symbolical. Sūdraka develops his metaphors as musical themes. The full music inherent in the speeches and the ritualistic action must be realized in production.

The truly colossal proportions of the montage in this final act may well impress the Western reader as baroque. Even the macabre humor of the Executioners has its parallels in baroque art and theatre. The English reader will perhaps be reminded of Ben Jonson, whose *Bartholomew Fair* offers by far the closest analogue in English to the Sanskrit play. As usual, the Sanskrit combines where the West distinguishes. To say that Sūdraka is as heavy as Seneca and as light as Plautus would constitute an understatement. The last act of *The Little Clay Cart* is presumably weightier in aesthetic, or moral, terms than any passage in Seneca, and Act Two, with the pantomime of the gambler impersonating a statue, is presumably lighter, more deft, and more sophisticated than any scene in Plautus. Yet Sūdraka's work is very much of a unity. The diversity of its materials is successfully cultivated in part because of the Hindu convention of acts, each of which possesses a prevailing tenure or mood, based in turn upon the musical theory of modes.

The text ranges artfully through verse and prose and through several dialects, or Prakrits, this popular speech being side by side with the aristocratic or liturgical Sanskrit. These distinctions clearly constitute a vital feature of the work. Hence in most translations, the verse passages, frequently in Sanskrit, are distinguished by an indented margin on the left of the page. These are the passages most weighted with poetic imagination and should be declaimed with at least a suggestion of recitative.

Such a play, then, achieves a triumph of plasticity, speech ranging from the most exalted verse to the most colloquial prose idiom and acting styles evidently no less varied. The actors must comprehend this eminently complex manner, rendering the diverse parts in such a way that smoothness and unity in the over-all effect be maintained. Passages originally in Sanskrit or in verse must never seem forced or wanting in spontaneity ; those originally in Prakrit, or in prose, must never lack grace or fall into a completely naturalistic style. A similar problem occurs in Shakespeare, but the Indian dramatists worked with more ironically contrasted elements than Shakespeare and, it seems, with a correspondingly more self-conscious technique. Their plays are, accordingly, unsurpassed exercises for mastering the universal principles involved. Still another way of examining these conditions is to observe that the lyrical, or choral elements treated, as a rule, in Greek drama in dramatic odes, are treated in Sanskrit drama in such passages as those recently examined, with both poetic and choreographic elements woven more subtly into the general context of the action. What the Greeks logically divided into dramatic action and poetic chorus the Hindus combine both by strength of intuition and by philosophical theory. Similarly, Greek drama in its conclusion presents a "denouement," or untying of the knot, Sanskrit drama, a tying together of the diverse threads. The Sanskrit word itself for the finale of a play employs precisely this image of unification, or binding together. More of this will be considered later, under the heading of plot.

In a stage bare of scenery, a special emphasis falls upon the stage properties, almost always more intimate to the characters than a painted scene. With this emphasis the Western actor may not be at first fully acquainted. What he or his director may mistake for a minor incident may thus prove a major one. A ready instance is the cloak, brought in on the arm of the first character to appear in the play, Maitreya. This, as we have already seen, is being faithfully delivered to his master, Chārudatta, beset with poverty, as a gift from one of his still faithful and wealthy friends and a promise of more good fortune in time to come. Maitreya, the glutton, is offered a free meal and gifts, which he declines out of his friendship and loyalty. Later in the act Vasantasēnā sees the cloak and views it with pleasure, for it is scented with jasmine, which to her discerning mind supplies convincing proof that Chārudatta is not averse to the pleasures of youth. Chārudatta shows his affection for his young son by ordering his slave-girl to take the cloak to the boy as protection against the chill night air. By mistake, in the darkness, she hands it to Vasantasēnā, who embraces it and inhales its perfume.

In Act Two, the episode of the escaped elephant, which at first seems wildly extraneous, is at length firmly tied to the main strand of the play by an ingenious series of incidents in which the cloak has a major part. The gallant who curbs the elephant is admired by the impoverished but generous Chārudatta, who, having no alms to give, sighs and in gratitude throws the public benefactor the cloak. This the gallant boastfully shows to Vasantasēnā, in whose service he is employed. She recognizes it, takes it from him, with the gift of a jewel in return, and, in an ecstacy, throws it about her own shoulders. Wearing it, she mounts to the roof of her house to see the noble Chārudatta pass by, this being the last and most heavily accented incident of Act Two. The incident may seem in itself slight and might easily be omitted in an arrangement of the play, as, indeed, has been done frequently. A few modern critics have deplored it. They are possibly more concerned with philology than with the theatre. In fact, the episode is of high poetic moment for the emotional progress of the work and of much aesthetic value, though its worth proves more conspicuous in the eloquence of the action than in the eloquence of the simple words themselves. This is essential theatre. The actors must learn every device for focussing attention on the garment.

Indeed to present the play without full emphasis at all times on the sensuous allusions and especially on allusions to reflections of the arts in general would be to defeat its poetical intention and to dilute it almost beyond recognition. Or perhaps it would better be said that it would be like serving naked a dish which demands a carefully prepared sauce. Consider first the art closest to drama, viz., pantomime. Sarvilaka's pantomime in Act Three, "The House-breaking," must on no account be underplayed. The deliciously and

eminently Shavian paradox of his pride in efficiency and scorn
of popular morality must on no account be overlooked nor the
further irony that the housebreaker himself is a sentimentalist, a
romanticist, equally tender in heart and conscience. The pages of
dramatic literature offer few more glowing tributes to architecture
and decoration than the stage peregrination of Maitreya as he
traverses the eight courtyards of Vasantasēnā's gorgeous palace.
Verbal refrains and ceremonious action both insure a poetic sentiment and keep the description firmly in its ligitimate place in
theatrical procedure. Again, the Masseur's attempt to be mistaken
for a statue, turns the theatrical imagination in the direction of
sculpture. The witty talk on Vasantasēnā's painting of Chārudatta,
which is displayed, borrows the brilliance of that art for the stage.
Of the pervasiveness of music and its sister art, the dance, we have
already spoken. It is notable that the hero is represented as an
accomplished musician. These features of Sūdraka's play are all
thoroughly conventional on the Indian stage, though seldom, if
ever, more successfully presented. To Western eyes they may
seem at first to pad out the performance and smother it in over-
coloring, without serving the play's more intrinsic purposes. But
in every case a closer inspection reveals not only that the Indian
idiom is not ours but that it is essential in the true interests of
the Indian work itself. Further evidence of this is to be found in
the relation of the extended episode of Maitreya's inspection of
Vasantasēnā's palace to the act immediately following, where he
guides the fabulously wealthy courtesan through the delapidated
courts and ruinous gardens of Chārudatta's crumbling mansion.
Verbal echoes assist in the ironic inter-relations of the two
scenes.

Similar evidence of the need to preserve as much of the stylistic
texture of the play's language as possible appears in the abundant
but never diffuse imagery. Characters, as often in Shakespeare,
are painted by their imagery which is elevated by poetic imagination into symbolism. Maitreya, for example, employs many coarse,
homely, earthy images, in keeping with his earthy character.
Rob him of his flow of metaphors, and he will scarcely be recogniz-
able. Vasantasēnā is encompassed in symbols of the spring. Samsthānaka uses both imagery and diction peculiar to himself. He
talks virtually a language of his own, considerable parts of which,
however, are discernible in the vivid and faithful translation by

Revilo Pendleton Oliver. From the Hindu standpoint, he commits the unpardonable sin of referring to animals disrespectfully, seeing all creatures in a comprehensive degradation, reducing the dog to the ignominy of the jackal. His Asiatic fustian out-Tamburlaines Tamburlaine. Thus one may generalize by applying to the language of the play Ben Jonson's laconicisms : "Language best showeth the man ; speak that I may know thee." This is the very essence of drama. With eyes shut, we hear Sūdraka's characters and at once distinguish each. The value of this manner of composition has, of course, recently been demonstrated by brilliant reading performances of plays by Dylan Thomas, Sean O'Casey, and Bernard Shaw, not to mention Emlyn Williams' recitations of Charles Dickens, and further by the best radio productions. One instantly recognizes that Act Eight, "The Murder of Vasantasēnā", would be highly effective merely as a voiced play. It would be no less effective as pantomime. How much more effective, then, as a work in its own rightful medium !

The Little Clay Cart is a long play singularly lacking in longeurs. This is partially accounted for by the fully developed theatrical idiom whereby action is concentrated and brisk and few lines are without implied movement of one sort or another. It is, perhaps, notable that Sanskrit writers delighted in stage directions. Playwriting from this eminently pragmatic point of view consists in fitting the word to the action and the action to the word. The eye does not accompany the ear, nor the ear, the eye. The fusion of equal parts is complete. This holds conspicuously true throughout all the great Sanskrit drama, from Bhāsa's masterpiece, *The Vision of Vāsavadattā*, to Bhavabhūti's masterpiece, *Rāma's Later History*. These are facts which no attentive reader can miss. In no play is this more evident than in Sūdraka's. This each page shows but three striking episodes may be mentioned as not untypical. These are : "The Housebreaking," where Sarvilaka's pantomime, cutting his way through a house-wall and rifling a chamber, is attended —not merely accompanied—by a continuous flow of grandiloquent words to the same effect as the action, and the brisk episodes of the exchange of *gharris* and the loading of the clay cart with jewels. Here is simply sound playwriting, yielding delight for the actor to realize and the public to attend. The world has, of course, many plays that stand this test but few more conspicuously than *The Little Clay Cart*. A possible method in rehearsing would be to

require several readings merely for eloqution and several pantomimic renditions.

As repeatedly observed, this is a play in two parts and ten acts.
More is implied in this statement than might at first be supposed.
Just as the acts are sharply distinguished from one another, so are
the parts and this distinction should be noted both by readers and
actors. To use Western terms, the First Part tends to be high
comedy, the Second, poetic melodrama. Yet their relation is
organic and well known in the theory of playwriting. It is even
at times asserted that in musical composition, as in the symphony
or the sonata, the first movement is generally the more "intellectual," the last, the more emotional. Also, the tempo of events
in the play tends to increase. This signifies that the movement
of the plot is concentrated and accelerated. The further the play
advances, the more attention comes to a conscious focus on the
main characters and their precarious destiny. Part One should
thus be performed in a comparatively intimate manner, Part Two,
in a broad, public manner. The same contrast may be seen in the
next to the last and the last scene in *Die Meistersinger*. The early
section of *The Little Clay Cart* establishes characters and ideas; the
later drives home the thoughts already defined. One is not superior
to the other, though one impresses us as the more thoughtful, the
other as the more theatrical. There is actually much action in the
first half and much thought in the second. A change occurs in
the ratio, not in the basic qualities themselves. On returning after
the intermission following Act Five, the audience should comfor-
tably recognize that it is witnessing the same play but a new section
in a distinctly different phase or key. In fact, even each act is
keyed separately.

The peculiar nature and ingenuity of Sūdraka's plot requires
careful pointing to bring out clearly its sophisticated organization,
which rests quite often more on implication than on persistent
statement. The production, accordingly, requires imagination and
nuance to establish the unity that is actually realized in playwriting, both in its conception and execution. To use an arboreal
metaphor, the eye of the audience is led to realize the construction
of the tree not by proceeding from the stem outwards but by proceeding from the tips of the branches inwards. It is the sophisticated
manner of indirection. All leads to the fundamental theme, the
relation between Chārudatta and Vasantasēnā but the full force

of their own relation is seen by the drawing inwards of relationships to figures at first surprisingly remote and by including in the large, ensemble picture full-length portraits of their friends and servants. Thus various admirable qualities are depicted in both hero and heroine and made the convincing explanation of their attraction for one another, an attraction insistently regarded not only as physical and aesthetic but as moral and spiritual. For the basic conception of the play, its satire and burlesque notwithstanding, is idealistic. The negative elements are designed in a proportion that saves this idealism from either sentimentality or insipidity, preserving it, at least in its own terms, on a convincing and substantial basis. Faith is not shaken by disturbing doubts where the critical intelligence itself is so actively engaged. These complex structural features just described are naturally the most conspicuous in the first half of the play. As the firmly held strands of the plot wind themselves more and more closely together, approaching the peak of the spiral, the play presents, from orthodox Western standards, a more readily apprehensible form. A contrast is invited between Sūdraka's work and one of the most classically constructed of English comedies, Ben Jonson's *The Alchemist*. The first act of Jonson's work fully states all the propositions on which it is founded. The rest is elaboration upon a given theme. The knot is unravelled. Such is the meaning of the term, "denouement." In the Sanskrit play the threads are picked up one by one and gradually brought together, so that, in the revealing terminology of Sanskrit dramatic criticism, only by the end of the play is the knot tied. Especially with stage performance before an audience unfamiliar with Oriental indirection, a production carefully accenting each successive linking in the progress and development of the story becomes essential. Possibly Chārudatta's name should never be spoken without a drum-roll or flourish of trumpets.

A few instances of Sūdraka's practice suffice to clarify the sufficiently conspicuous manner of Sanskrit play-design. In Act Two, three gamblers are seen quarreling in a street. Their dispute at first appears utterly extraneous to the story. Presently one of them rushes through the side-door of Vasantasēnā's house. Thereupon we discover that he has been a devoted servant to Chārudatta, whose generosity he has enjoyed and whose poverty has plunged him into his present desperate manner of living. The mere mention of Chārudatta's name reacts as magic upon Vasantasēnā, who on hearing it ceremoniously rises from her chair and even seems reluctant to reseat herself as long as the discussion concerns her beloved. Chārudatta's poverty corrupts the Masseur, as her generosity, impelled by her love, saves him and leads him to reject his gambling life and to become a Buddhist ascetic, or wandering mendicant. While on his wanderings, he encounters the half-strangled Vasantasēnā, his patroness, and becomes responsible for saving both her life and Chārudatta's.

Again, the braggart, Karṇapūraka, bursts abruptly into Vasantasēnā's presence with the sole purpose of boasting in the utmost egoism and arrogance of his service in curbing a mad elephant who has escaped from his post and terrified the entire city. This is the episode previously discussed in relation to the importance of stage properties but it should be further considered from a new angle. No interruption could be more complete so far as the apparent conduct of the story goes. But presently we hear—a minor though no insignificant point—that Karṇapūraka has rescued a Buddhist mendicant who has been tossed upon the elephant's tusks. The thread is drawn into the main strand of the story only as we learn of the incident immediately following the capture of the escaped beast. In gratitude, a spectator has thrown to Karṇapūraka the one possession available on his person, a magnificent jasmine scented cloak. This is, of course, the cloak presented to Chārudatta and which Maitreya carries on his arm in the play's first moments. Incidentally, the play's vivid and realistic sensuous imagery is well disclosed in this episode. Not at first identifying the cloak, but suspecting it to be Chārudatta's, Vasantasēnā asks whether it is scented with jasmine. Karṇapūraka replies that he is so far permeated with the crude odor of the elephant that he cannot say and hands the garment to her. As she casts it on her shoulders, her body and soul thrill with ecstatic joy. Chārudatta himself does not appear in this act, yet, as we have seen, the act concludes with Vasantasēnā's announcement that, clad in this cloak, she is about to ascend the tower of her palace to watch her hero as he passes in the street below. The thread has been drawn inward. Nothing has been incongruous.

The basic principle of this plotting is irony. From the very scaffold of execution Chārudatta steps to the fulfillment of all his wishes, his marriage with Vasantasēnā, his new life of wealth and prosperity, and ample rewards for all his friends. The road to felicity has led through misery. In the Sanskrit play this signifies not merely a theatrical convenience, a mere formula for melodrama, but a religious convinction. The Sanskrit critics themselves recognized almost innumerable types of plays but pure tragedy or the pure comedy of wit are not among them. In the broader outlook, *The Little Clay Cart* belongs to the same category—their highest category—as *Shakuntalā*, *Vikramorvacī*, *Rāma's Later History*, *The Vision of Vāsavadattā*, and all the most serious and poetic of Indian dramas, the relatively naturalistic setting and ample humor in Sūdraka's work notwithstanding. The simplest and truest statement is that a rough road leads to human felicity.

The vicissitudes attending Vasantasēnā's jewels constitute the main strand of the plot. At no time do the conditions point conclusively to the final result. On the contrary, it is of the essence of the ploting that the incidents appear to lead directly away from the conclusion and not towards it, either by negating the actual conclusion or by complete irrelevance. As an instance, consider the role of the housebreaker. The greater part of Act Three depicts his technically perfect performance of housebreaking. The audience is completely absorbed, as he appears himself to be, in his own perfect work of art. As he explains, his performance is almost as much for the joy of a job well done as for the gain which he expects from it, the ransom for Madanikā, Vasantasēnā's slave girl. In the scene itself Madanikā's name is not mentioned till virtually the close. The audience at first is certainly not encouraged to consider the vital relation which the housebreaking bears to the main action. The only clue has been Maitreya's humorous and petulant remark that he hopes the treasure may be stolen. The actual theft appears to thwart the expected development, not to advance it. Nor is surprise precisely what the playwright desires. The return of the treasure to Vasantasēnā, as Madanikā's ransom, likewise appears as the merest caprice of fortune. So far as a thesis lies behind such incidents, it is that destiny works in the most capricious or humorously ironic ways. By contrast, the plot of *Oedipus Rex*, which indeed unfolds a secret, proceeds by logic along a line as straight as a logical argument by Aristotle, who so warmly admired it. The plot of *The Little Clay Cart* rejoices in bringing indirection to a goal, criss-crossing the incidents with the utmost caprice.

The later accidents attending Vasantasēnā's treasure have the same quality as the first. Jewels which she deposits in a toy cart to please a child fall out of Maitreya's gown before an astonished courtroom and to everyone's surprise. Maitreya's zeal in gesticulating in behalf of his beloved master results in the immediate condemnation of Chārudatta to death. With the jewels about his neck he marches to his execution. The plot is a line on which these jewels are strung, the characters being puppets of this most curious destiny. Only Act Two conspicuously overlooks them. But Act Two exists in large part to give Vasantasēnā's portrait, much as the function of Act One is to depict Chārudatta and his foil, Samsthānaka. She must appear his rival in generosity. Only a weeping woman, ravished of her jewels, who throws herself upon the body of the condemned man at the place of execution, ends a story up to this point tragic, in which human life has been victimized by property abused and misplaced. Every device in the play's production must be used to cast a glittering high-light upon these minute but prodigious stage properties. How much more conspicuous are they, for example, than the miniature worn about her neck by Hamlet's mother, and how much more persistent in their appearances than Desdemona's handkerchief! The same realization of calculated caprice appears, of course, in the dual misadventures of the two *gharris*, Chārudatta's and Samsthānaka's.

One of the firmest themes in the play's development and one of the least contorted by fantasy is the political. With the exception of the antagonist, Samsthānaka, all characters agree in detesting the tyrannical king Pālaka and in admiration of the rightful heir to the throne, the cruelly imprisoned Āryaka. The housebreaker is the logical man to break also into Āryaka's prison and to release him. Disparate characters and episodes are repeatedly held in place by this reassuring factor strengthening the play's order. The importance of the political theme is shrewdly indicated in *Chārudatta in Poverty*, but commences its impressive progress only with the first act of Part Two, that is, Act Six. Āryaka himself plays a conspicuous role only in the brief Act Seven. Here he is seen in debt to Chārudatta's generosity. But even here it is Chārudatta, not Āryaka, who holds the center of the stage and is shown as the more potent figure. Chārudatta befriends Āryaka, whereas Āryaka merely bows in gratitude before him. The faithful friend is seen as mightier than the future prince. Only in a deed imagined offstage, the prince ultimately grants Chārudatta's release, reinstates him in wealth, power, and splendor and enfranchises the hetaera as his wife. This political strand in the action is on the whole clearly secondary yet steadily maintained and without it the entire fabric would collapse. The theme is handled with much adroitness. No aspect can be omitted, if the whole is to achieve the designed effect.

Although Chārudatta's role carries him into only six of the ten acts, the force of his personality pervades the entire play and, as the original title indicated, he is obviously the central figure. The arrangement of his appearances is calculated. Thus he is present in Acts One, Three, Five of the First Part, and in Acts Seven, Nine and Ten of the Second. During the long and important Act Eight he remains absent, though, as Vasantasēnā declares, it is his absence that determines the whole course of affairs. The scene is devoted chiefly to his mistress and to his foil, Samsthānaka. In all the acts where Chārudatta is not seen, she is conspicuously present. The two leading figures actually confront each other only in the three acts of highest importance to the play's conduct, namely, Acts One, Five, and Ten. He proves himself rather a shy lover, who, chiefly because of his poverty, hesitates in making advances. The one decisive move, occurring in Act Five, he is capable of executing. We witness much more of Vasantasēnā's love for him than of his love for her. This is certainly not because her love is assumed to be greater than his. In his final scene his thoughts for her are only surpassed or rivalled by his thoughts for his son. But he is revered and beloved by all the chief persons in the play, the arch-villain, Samsthānaka, alone excepted. The magnetism of his personality dominates scenes in which he is absent. It is the theatrical device of understatement so brilliantly cultivated by Strindberg, who better, perhaps, than any other Western playwright, has known the art of building up a central character without his too-frequent appearance—for Molière's technique in this regard, which caused him to delay the entrace of Tartuffe until half his play was run, seems comparatively elementary and almost naive beside Strindberg's. Here again is evidence of the unity of the Sanskrit play and the importance, in greater or less degree, of all its characters and scenes. Every friend of Chārudatta's is valuable in establishing him as the master of friendship, the generous and out-going hero, and almost all persons are in fact his friends and admirers. He is repeatedly called "the noble Chārudatta." The epithet proves important and its value must on no account be overlooked. The spectator must be made to feel that this is Chārudatta, his play. When, in Act Six, Chandanaka, the civil guard, debates with himself whether or not he will expose Āryaka's escape in Chārudatta's *gharri*, his decision is determined partly, to be sure, by his friend Sarvilaka's association with the pro-Āryaka conspiracy but still more by his desire to free Chārudatta from any embarrassing exposure, such as actually occurs later in the trial scene. When, in Act Eight, Vasantasēnā is threatened with death at Samsthānaka's hands, it is on his name that she calls and her call upon him incites the scoundrel to his crime. In acts where Chārudatta does not appear, he still remains the decisive figure. The construction is firm and imaginative. The performance must tie its most disparate threads about Chārudatta's heart.

Any superficial view to the contrary, *The Little Clay Cart* is neither a meretricious melodrama nor a typical banal love story. There are, in fact, three major elements in its meaning, or content; these may be described in terms of love, friendship, and religion. The love-factor is the most evident and least in need of critical exposition. Vasantasēnā is a true courtesan and the role should be played with full, Indian voluptuousness. The secondary love-scene, depicting the relation between Vasantasēnā's favorite servant, Madanikā, and that pivotal figure in the progress of the plot, the housebreaker, Sarvilaka, contributes a useful underplot, well joined to the major actions. It is eminently fitting that the two wittiest persons should come together. But the morality of the play is chivalrous and friendship is scarcely less idealized than passion. Vasantasēnā befriends her servant by freeing her and assisting in her marriage with Sarvilaka. Madanikā precedes her mistress in the achievement of what Hindu morality regards as a woman's highest honor, the title of wife. Vasantasēnā is not meanly jealous of her servant's sexual success but nobly jealous of her success in attaining matrimony. The mistress is indeed a true friend and, in turn, Madanikā is in tears as she leaves the service of so loving a lady. Even Vasantasēnā and Chārudatta's wife vie with each other in an exchange of favors. Through thick and thin Chārudatta and Maitreya are devoted to each other, though, ironically, the clumsy Maitreya in court drops the jewels that are the final evidence for Chārudatta's conviction. The Masseur is a friend of Sarvilaka and the latter, a valiant friend of Āryaka. In an outburst of chivalrous sentiment, Sarvilaka, on hearing of Āryaka's fate, immediately sends his newly won bride to a protector (the chief of the musicians) and declares that the claims of a friend must always take precedence over those of a mistress or wife. Chārudatta is apparently devoted to his wife, as his wife is certainly devoted to him; but he is still more devoted to his son. And everywhere his most insistent cry is his devotion to his friends. Poverty is misery to him, he declares, not because possessions in themselves are lost but because he cannot give as he wishes to his friends and because his friends fall off. The rationally plausible and cynical observation here concerning his friends is singularly absent. The importance of the secondary roles is largely in the circumstance that through them the warmth of friendship as a sentiment is powerfully engendered. The performance must express this. There are really no minor roles, for on inspection it is found that all speaking parts of consequence—and there is indeed a considerable number—contribute to the development of this generous sentiment. Politics itself is viewed largely in a personal light. The personal claim of any individual placing himself under the protection of another is the most binding of social ties. Chārudatta himself is preeminently both a lover and a friend.

He is also depicted as a pious man. As already observed, on his first appearance he is engaged in religious observances, and on his last he appears as a victim brought in sacrifice to the altar of destiny. *The Little Clay Cart* may superficially be related to the Western conception of comedy as a theatrical genre but is even more closely related to the patterns of mythological and religious thought. This can hardly be clear to a Western reader altogether uninformed on the general patterns of Eastern thought or ignorant of the larger part of Sanskrit drama. Almost all the major Sanskrit plays are love stories of separation, divorcement, and final union. This describes, for example, the four masterpieces already mentioned, *Shakuntalā, Vikramorvacī, Rāma's Later History,* and *The Vision of Vāsavadattā*. At the conclusion of these plays Dushyanta rejoins Shakuntalā, Purūravas rejoins Urvasī, Rāma rejoins Sītā, and Udayana rejoins Vāsavadattā. The evil is division but, ultimately, what is divided is remade and becomes whole. Each play has behind it the mystical philosophies of the East, the conception of an ultimate reconciliation of flesh and spirit, cruelty and mercy, earth and heaven. Each has behind it also, and at times virtually pushed into the foreground, the seasonal myth, the absence of fertility in winter and its return with the spring. The women are conceived as spring godesses; the heroes suffer for a protracted period in the winter of their discontent. We cannot think of Shakuntalā apart from spring flowers. Purūravas embraces a plant which turns by metamorphosis into his beloved. As previously observed, the name "Vasantasēnā" signifies spring. When Vasantasēnā is first embraced by Chārudatta, the image in their dialogue describes a union of the lightning and the cloud, from which issues the spring rain. This rain is clearly made symbol of both vegetative fertility and the sexual fertility of mankind. Again, in their reunion and at the moment of their embrace Chārudatta declares that love is the power turning death itself into life. No episode in drama can well be more ritualistic or ceremonial than the procession of this hero to his apparent doom. The religious significance is consistently stressed in metaphor and imagery, though not in the plot. Yet few serious readers today will doubt either its presence or importance and any production failing to convey the religious sentiment and gravity must sadly vitiate the play's intended force. There is here a largeness of conception and spirit which, of course, has nothing whatsoever to do with the play's spacious length, though the spell of the ceremony requires a certain leisurely development.

Even the name of Sūdraka's play points to religious connotations. The "toy cart" is presumably a reference to the celebrated Buddhistic parable of the burning house. In this parable the house signifies the material world and the worldly life of man. The most effective means that the gods have found to lure man out of his predicament is a subterfuge. Reason is of small avail. But on being told that toy carts are just outside his door, the wise man, at least, leaves his fatal dwelling to play with these deceptive trifles. They are no trifles but lures to catch the soul. Furthermore, the clay cart is preferred by the playwright as symbolic of Chārudatta's poverty and enforced asceticism; the gold cart, so much preferred by his son, is symbolic of Vasantasēnā's magnificence. In terms familiar to European aesthetics, the playwright rubs his cup of instruction with honey. His lightness of touch is a sophisticated assumption. Behind the mask of human comedy is the grave face of religious idealism.

Although the play's emotional and spiritual values may well come first in appraising it and in defining its ultimate purpose, problems of theatrical style must assume the foreground in any consideration by the director or the actors. And in any adequate modern production it is only too true that an audience will be even more conscious of a foreign style than of a universal message. Yet it should first of all be realized that differences in style between theatres of East and West are more the matters of degree than of essential qualities. The Eastern manner is not radically unlike styles well-known in the West but simply more developed stylistically, more poetic, more imaginative, and less naturalistic. As much is seen upon the stage in the East as in the West but more is implied by the style of the former. In general these conditions are well known, though perhaps in no play can they be more readily observed and studied than in *The Little Clay Cart*. The basic conventions here are made conspicuous by the dialogue itself and by the stage directions in the Sanskrit original. In fact, so clear are these conditions that relatively little need be said of them. There remains only the long and possibly painful experience of perfecting and smoothing the style in actual production. Any successfully stylized acting in the West at least gives its initial aid. Among the most suggestive productions in this regard, for example, are Sir John Gielgud's presentations of *The Importance of Being Earnest*, and *Love's Labour's Lost*. But in this respect the Sanskrit stage goes far beyond any familiar Western style.

The closest tradition in the West to one phase, at least, of the Hindu acting, miming, is afforded by pantomime, especially in the *commedia dell'arte* tradition and in the consummate art today of Marcel Marceau. Silence is a leading character in all Sanskrit plays. Thus the most important lines in the first and third acts of *Rāma's Later History* are unheard. They are whispered in the ear of one of the figures. The audience knows only too well what these unspeakable and harrowing words are. Similarly, "This is what happened," says Maitreya to the Slave Girl in the Fifth Act, and "This is what happened," she says to him. Their further words are not spoken but are all the better understood. So in the preceding act Madanikā whispers her dangerous secret into the ear of her lover.

Pantomime is extended in many directions, casting its shadow over the whole. In Act Two, for example, the Masseur talks to persons imagined to be on the stage but not actually there and reports their replies which are merely imagined as spoken. Similarly, in the episode of the escaped elephant the Masseur engages in a conversation of which only his own voice is heard, as of a speaker over the telephone. He conveniently repeats the words that are only imagined as spoken off stage.

An enormous amount of "business" is conducted where the objects that would be stage properties in a contemporary Western performance are merely imaginary. No wall and no door is to be seen during Sarvilaka's long-drawn-out housebreaking. They are imagined. The same is also true, of course, of the moth which he releases to extinguish the lamp. His brahmanical cord, on the contrary, is real, but it remains arbitrary, I presume, whether this is true of his mannikin. The presumption, however, is that the figure is imaginary. The numerous stage journeys are all in imagined space. No streets, doors, courtyards are actually represented. Actors cross thresholds with symbolical gestures. When convenient for the story, they become invisible to each other, though they are wholly visible to the audience. To increase the degree of imaginative stimulus, their words are often heard from off stage before entrance, and it is conventional for them to enter repeating the phrase already heard from off stage, giving a new spatial dimension to the illusion. Whole scenes are incorporated in what may be called a theatrical parenthesis with the same words spoken before and after by a different group of characters.

This economy of presentation places special emphasis upon the relatively few stage properties actually introduced. There are two kinds of wagons, the toy cart and the *gharries*, both of which are undoubtedly real. But the oxen are, of course, stage constructions with men inside them and no close realism is aspired to. The *gharris* appear very conspicuously in three acts, from Act Six to Act Eight. Probably to understand their full meaning as originally presented we should think of them as in part parodies or at least analogues of one of the most beloved effects on the Sanskrit stage. The heroes of *Shakuntalā*, *Vikramorvaçī*, and the two celebrated plays on Rāma by Bhavabhūti, for example, appear in many of their most impressive scenes in chariots, driven by charioteers. The charioteer himself becomes a familiar figure in this heroic theatre, as he is in Indian mythology. We cannot be completely sure whether any mechanism was employed in these scenes or not or whether techniques changed through the centuries, but the strong presumption is that the whole elaborate business was conducted in pantomime. Thus the chariots of Dushyanta, Pururavas, and Rāma were wholly mental and their aerial journeys all the more resplendent and poetic on that account. The comic spirit in *The Little Clay Cart* aided a qualified compromise with mundane reality. The original audience probably enjoyed an implicit contrast with the heroic treatment. The earthy journeys of Āryaka and Vasantasēnā were accomplished in practicable wagons with simulated animals.

Chārudatta's garden is painted entirely by words, not by scenery. The elaborate court-room scene is merely sketched; so far as properties are concerned, half-a-dozen stools must largely suffice. Stools were frequently moved on and off stage. When Durduraka, the "dear friend" of Sarvilaka, stoops down and throws dust into the gambling-master's eyes, the dust is imaginary, the gesture real. When the Masseur enters the temple and takes the attitude of a statue, the temple is built by imagination only, no Constructivist machinery being in demand.

Small comment is required on the Sanskrit use of soliloquies and asides except to note that both conventions are employed more profusely and with greater variations of effect than on any European stages. Westerners have the devices but have not used them so persistently. They add materially to the artifice of production. More distinctive and also more imaginative is the convention, already alluded to, of off-stage voices, which are peculiarly challenging to the audience, demanding its active cooperation, the imagination being especially stimulated by sounds that are heard from sources unseen.

Certain further details in structural practice and convention have much importance and should be closely observed. One of these is an uninhibited emphasis upon the uncoming character or scene. In a naturalistic theatre, positive offence may arise from the introduction of a character on the stage itself immediately on reference to him. But such scruples may well be regarded as themselves obstructions to the proper flow of the performance. If the subject of the scene calls aloud for such close sequence, why should objections on the ground of naturalism intrude? Repeatedly thought is inforced and action sharpened by such practices. What a character thinks, the audience sees, almost as in a shift of scene in a film. The Masseur turned Friar thinks of his benefactress and a moment thereafter sees her pleading hand raised out of a pile of leaves beneath which she has been buried by her would-be murderer, Samsthānaka. This filmic aspect of *The Little Clay Cart* proves one of its distinguishing features and one of the most agreeable to modern taste. Several Western critics, to be sure, inflexibly naturalistic in prejudice, describe the technique employed more than once in the trial scene, or Act Nine, as primitive and clumsy. But is not their own standard of naturalism itself primitive and clumsy? The judge sends an attendant at the court to the royal gardens to discover if a body or the traces of a body of a murdered woman may be found. The attendant goes and returns in a matter of seconds. A similarly expeditious manner is employed in providing for the important entrances of Vasantasēnā's mother, Chārudatta himself, and Maitrēya in the trial scene, the effectiveness of which is much enhanced by this convention. Chārudatta's prayer, twice repeated at the very threshold of his execution, to the effect that at some time, in this or in a future life, Vasantasēnā may vindicate his honor, is at long last dramatically answered by her miraculous appearance. For several minutes the audience has witnessed her approach on her desperately hastening mission of rescue. Nothing could be more artificial than the conduct of this climax yet little in the repertoire of theatrical devices can be more effective. A successful production on a twentieth-century stage need not and should not bypass these inspired features of the original, for the oriental technique is perfectly clear in meaning and has of late, partly through the film, partly through an advance in poetic and Expressionistic drama, become familiar and acceptable. The artificial features of Südraka's play should not be self-consciously over-scored but should be fully and spontaneously accepted.

Something should be said here regarding the imagined time of the scenes. Although a few conspicuously mythological scenes in Sanskrit drama may appear pinnacled in a dim timelessness, the playwrights on the whole show especially close attention to time. To begin with, it constitutes, philosophically considered, one of their major themes, for in most of their famous, mythological, metaphysical and clearly religious dramas the scenes are singularly rich in retrospection and prophecy and the characters live even more in past and future than in the present. *The Vision of Vāsavadattā* is a recollection of time past, mistaken for "actuality." Rāma similarly dreams images of Sītā, which he thinks are reality and on meeting her in reality mistakes her for a vision; he is further confused by seeing her in a play-within-a-play. Dushyanta consoles himself by dreaming of the absent Shakuntalā and virtually brings her portrait to life. Such metaphysical features are less prominent in *The Little Clay Cart*, though present, as when Chārudatta at first thinks Vasantasēnā, as she hastens to rescue him from execution, to be an apparition. (He, of course, imagines her to be dead.)

Time in this play is most significant in the emphasis upon the timing of the individual acts. Thus Act One is a night-piece, Act Three is from midnight to dawn, Act Five is in the late afternoon and evening, Act Six, in the morning, Act Seven, shortly before noon of the same day, Act Eight, close to noon, or the hottest hour of the day, Act Nine, the following morning, and the final act, about noon of the same day. Morning, evening, noon and night are deliberately and most effectively portrayed. The descriptive poetry with great eloquence depicts the very atmosphere of the hour.

In comparison with the great Sanskrit romantic plays this city eclogue seems weak in natural scenery; there are no aerial travels, no mountains, forests or streams; but the park, the streets, the air, and the hourly passage of time are feelingly portrayed. The men and women stumble in the dark, grow tense and even madden in the heat of noon, are refreshed by dawn, or stimulated by evening and its atmospheric splendor. The poet studies the blazing sun, the terrifying cloud carrying lightning, thunder and rain. He explores atmospheric pressure to define the moods of his characters and the special qualities of the successive acts. Possibly the poetic descriptions and allusions suffice in themselves and actor or director need give them no peculiar attention on presentation. The author's poetry speaks directly. One recalls that it is unnecessary to use electrical displays in the storm scenes of *King Lear*. There is a suspicion of vulgarity there, as when colored lights are cast on Niagara. How many times Shakespeare's poetry and his play alike have been destroyed by monstrosities and banalities of stage lightning, thunder and rain! Macbeth's witches in Act One are possibly the most harrowing with absolutely nothing of these meretricious aids. The Elizabethan public liked them, but Ben Jonson did not. Shakespeare himself is, of course, as inscrutable as "the taciturnity of nature." One hesitates to conclude what is the wisest strategy in presenting *The Little Clay Cart*. Certainly the sound of the storm should be entirely reserved for the orchestra, with no extraneous racket. But a highly restrained shifting in lighting may at times be desirable, dimming the nocturnal first act, though never to anything remotely like the darkness of night, and casting a golden glow over the tragic scene of Vasantasēnā's noon-time "murder" in the garden. If Laurence Olivier were producing the play, the changes in lighting would probably be conspicuous; if Bertolt Brecht had produced it towards the close of his career, no lighting effects would have been used. These effects at most should probably be felt by the audience but not observed.

Although for actual performance the play's authorship is clearly of small importance, there is a possible aesthetic significance in the readiest answer to this question. My answer is simply and in all seriousness that which Lord Byron gave facetiously to the mystery of "Junius," namely, that the person in question "was nobody at all"! It will be recalled that the king Sūdraka is described as having "the dignity of an elephant, the eye of a *chakora*, a face like the full moon, and a body harmoniously proportioned. The profundity of his wisdom was unfathomable. He knew the *Rig Veda*, the *Sāma-Veda*, mathematics, the science of erotics, and the art of training elephants. By the grace of Siva, the veil of ignorance was lifted from Sūdraka's eyes, so that, after he had witnessed the coronation of his son and had performed the incomparable Horse-Sacrifice, he, having attained the incomparable age of one hundred years and ten days, cast himself into the flames." There is much more to the same effect. The Manager, who utters these words, speaks humorously of his own harangue. Scholarship has failed to fix upon any king who can with any degree of confidence answer this description. Have we here the flattery of an ancestor of a patron? Or is "Sūdraka", perhaps, as much a fiction as any character in the play, a dream-idealization, a humorous wish-fulfillment, of the author's own psyche? A writer capable of creating as many convincing characters as appear in this play could assuredly create an imaginary author with the greatest ease. The superlatives, even for Sanskrit literature, read very like parody, and the play itself is singularly well stocked with parody. Until better evidence than now available is procured, the present writer prefers to regard "Sūdraka" himself as a charming fictional creation and a cypher as mystifying as Byron's interpretation of "Junius". Bhāsa may or may not be author of the early work, *Chārudatta in Poverty*. which laid firm foundations for the first part of the present play. In any case, his authorship is very generally assumed. He is believed to have flourished before 200 A. D. *The Little Clay Cart* itself is of a most indeterminate date. It is thought that it may have received its present form at any time within the following four or five centuries. The date should probably be nearer the beginning than the conclusion of this spacious period. No precise answers to the questions of authorship or date, then, can be given, It is possible that the political sub-plot reflects some actual change of dynasty. Nevertheless in the end, the play is left where it so happily belongs, in the domain of pure imagination, with a meaning relevant to any time or society and a philosophy of insinuating charm for any heart or mind.

13 / A Nātaka: Rama's Later History

DRAMATIC THEORY in India recognizes many types of drama, two of the chief being the *Nātaka,* and the *Prakarana.* The first is the more exalted; its story is mythological; its spirit, notably religious; its characters are legendary or superhuman. The second is less exalted; its story is invented; its characters are not far from the social position of its audience; and at least it impinges on naturalism and the comedy of manners. The chief distinction lies simply in the degree of gravity. In terms that are, to be sure, more of the West than of the East, the first type stands closer to tragedy, the second, to various lighter theatrical forms. One more powerful invokes the emotions, the other, the mind; one lays its emphasis on the heart and soul, the other, on entertainment and humor. To use references to English literature, one impresses us as having much in common with Elizabethan poetic imagination, the other, as sharing at least something with Augustan wit. Both types of drama are highly sophisticated; both are comprised of full-length plays of imposing dimensions and force; and both require a happy ending.

The most cursory view of the Sanskrit stage reveals these two varieties and the most elementary survey must take them into account. The outstanding example of the *Prakarana* is certainly *The Little Clay Cart,* though this extraordinary play lacks a few of the requirements made by Indian critical dogma; this criticism has further concluded that high among the *Nātaka* stands Bhavabhūti's masterpiece, *Rāma's Later History.* Hence this book places the two works side by side. They comment upon each other by their proximity. The dramatic romance stands somewhere between Western tragedy and the representative *Prakarana,* while the *Praka-*

rana stands somewhere between Western high comedy and the *Nātaka*. The most serious Hindu plays are less portentous and more romantic than the typical high tragedy of European origin ; the most accomplished of Hindu "comedies," if the word be admissible here, is less comic and more romantic or even religious in its feeling than its closest parallel in the West.

When these two Sanskrit plays are surveyed together, the reader almost inevitably reflects on the persistent and pervasive significance for the stage of this distinction between grave and light. All cultures acknowledge it, almost as if it reflects biological facts, as tears and laughter. Especially the performing arts respond to these conditions of human nature, as drama, music and the dance. Our art seems incomplete without this duality, paralleling in the mind the great duality of the flesh, sex. The chemistry of the human spirit appears to demand such balance for its sustenance, as the body requires an equilibrium in different elements of diet. Socrates himself maintained that a writer of tragedy should also be a writer of comedy, a view fundamentally in keeping with the traditional wisdom of the Sanskrit playwrights, though they themselves cultivated neither tragedy nor the Western type of comedy. The full and comprehensive outline of our nature cannot, it seems, be reflected in a single species of art and especially is this seen to be true of the stage. Similarly, religious systems as a rule demand a multiplicity of basic texts. Much of the strength of the Bible as literary foundation of Christianity derives from its varied contents, its books revealing the most diverse aspects of the human spirit. In representing both the art and wisdom of the Sanskrit drama no one work even approximates sufficiency. At the very least two are demanded. This accounts for the analysis here of two contrasted plays, thereby charting a line to which most of this considerable body of drama can be referred and from whose base its major qualities of art, thought, and feeling are projected. In the end, which of the two plays, if either, is preferred must derive chiefly from personal predilection. Far from being hostile to each other, they are mutually sustaining. The more normal or desirable our outlook, the more strongly both works will be found compelling.

Emotional sensibility is of the very essence of Bhavabhūti's remarkable play. Its sufficiency, or better, its high distinction, in this respect is no less noteworthy than the absence in its scenes of any truly rational view of experience. This is most readily seen by examination of the plot. Its story springs entirely from Rāma's sacrifice of his wife, Sītā, to the will of "the citizens and country people." Yielding to public opinion, the hero ruthlessly exiles his queen. His decision seems extraordinarily drastic and cold-blooded ; indeed, it would be hard to imagine an act better warranting this description. Sītā is pregnant, innocent of any known fault, and completely devoted to Rāma. He is as deeply in love with her. Yet, in collusion with his brother, Lakshmana, he deposits her in the midst of a forest, or jungle, presumably not only to die but to be killed by wild beasts. No religious rite is being observed. She is no Andromeda tied to a rock as a vowed offering to a monster. Nor can the incident be dismissed as pure allegory. So far as ancient Indian thought can divorce political from religious consideration, Rāma's decision seems purely political. One would suppose it at least subject to debate. An analogous episode in Western drama would almost certainly lead to a pro- longed discussion, with partisans arranged dramatically on two sides. But Rāma's decision is a bland and instantaneous assump- tion, as if predestined and beyond argument or the reach of intel- lectual or moral appraisal. It is neither whole-heartedly endorsed, nor condemned, nor viewed skeptically. The ethical problem is wholly ignored. The playwright proceeds at once to what he deems his proper task, the development of the emotional aspects of the situation.

Rāma's Later History is in this respect the complete antithesis of *A Doll's House.* The Sanskrit play certainly implies moral stan- dards and reponsibilities, or at least standards of social value, but at no time are these standards brought within the level of intellec- tual scrutiny. The play exists first of all through its evocation of emotional values, exhibited in the devotion between man and woman, parent and child, friend and friend. The gods themselves exist primarily as patrons of the forces within the personal life, which in turn are referred back to the forces in nature itself.

There are, to be sure, several notable Sanskrit plays, as Bhāsa's *Minister's Vows*, and Visākhadatta's *Mudrārākshasa*, which deal most specifically with politics and even with diplomacy. But Indian dramatic theory provides for a type of play of quite another description, which is, on the whole, the type more popular and more esteemed. This largely ignores political considerations and focuses upon the personal lives of monarchs, who are also regarded as half-divine. To this type of drama, the purest *Nātaka*, belong the masterpieces of Kālidāsa, Harsa, and Bhavabhūti. To be sure, Rāma longs for an heir to his throne as well as for a son. He is every inch a king as well as a man. His "Horse-Sacrifice" is a political as well as a fertility rite. But there can be no question as to the true focus of *Rāma's Later History*. In short, it celebrates values and emotions that derive from family life.

The impression left by this picture is in Western eyes one of extreme warmth and lushness, not only in contrast with Western thought or drama themselves but in contrast with *The Little Clay Cart*. That play is, indeed, sufficiently warm and colorful in comparison with any drama of the West ; but when placed beside Bhavabhūti's work, Sūdraka's seems positively crisp and cool. *The Little Clay Cart* in its view of life and as a work in itself appears both cosmopolitan and urbane, a creation of the wit and humor of a sophisticated city, with many analogies to Hellenistic and Islamic culture. To our view, its atmosphere, all its profuse allusions to the contrary, does not seem uncompromisingly Indian. But with *Rāma's Later History*, the sophistication of its art notwithstanding, we enter regions of folklore. The atmosphere seems unmistakably both Indian and tropical, a flower blooming in the jungle, moist, warm, intense, exquisite, with an exotic and overpowering perfume. Its characters are frequently depicted as on the verge of swooning from grief, or, especially in the latter part of the play, as raised to ecstatic joy. Emotions are pressed to extremes, without the restraints in various ways and degrees employed in the West, or —to glance still further abroad—without that deliberated, abnormal, artificial super-stoicism typical of repressed Japan. Ancient Greeks, had they encountered such emotionalism, would probably have written it down as barbarous and Asiatic. The poets of *The Song of Roland*, by no means beyond Islamic contamination, might have found themselves more at home.

This orientation as imagined for the stage proves acceptable and enjoyable largely because of the mastery, both in theory and practice, which Indian art attains in terms of aesthetic projection. According to Indian aesthetics, the actor does not feel the emotions which he expresses nor are the emotional impressions made upon the audience designed to be those of real life. The Sanskrit theatre is by long tradition pure illusionism, yet in the instance of any advanced specimen of the *Nātaka* an illusionism almost wholly conjured up in an address to the heart. Such art is a joy in itself yet highly relevant to the basic emotional life, is therapeutic, eminently useful, salutary, producing a sentiment of well being and spiritual equilibrium. Purer art the West has hardly achieved, yet scarcely in the most extreme romanticism of the West is there so intense a fixity of mental vision on emotional experience.

An appraisal of Bhavabhūti's play must lie, then, not alone in terms of itself but in relation to a wide prospect of Indian thought, one which includes also such works as *The Little Clay Cart*. A vital or just view of India or of either of the two types of plays requires a study of the complementary relations which the types imply. Man's spirit in any context would founder if committed to an unremitted diet of Bhavabhūti's romanticism, and the deep-seated classicism of Sūdraka would by itself ultimately leave a sense of spiritual privation. The religious enthusiasm expressed in the one, the urbane wit in the other, are basically complementary, not mutually exclusive.

A similar conclusion is, somewhat unexpectedly, perhaps, advanced by the thought of one of the most eloquent, brilliant and moving poems written within the present century in America, Wallace Stevens' *Sunday Morning*. Much of Stevens' own thinking springs from a dualism distinguishing on the one hand a tropical warmth, with its romantic emotionalism, and on the other hand, a northern coolness, with its classical rationality and reserve. His imagery contrasts two scenes which for him possess compelling fascination and force, the landscape or seascape of the West Indies and the landscape and seascape of New England. A wise intuition instructs him that man is sadly incomplete without the essential features of both the dominions which these regions symbolize for the poet. The Hindus, though largely surrounded by a tropical landscape (the austerities of the Tibetan tundra need not be urged here), likewise came to both a philosophical and a pragmatic realization of the just claims of these two major elements within human nature. Stevens became, not impossibly, more a philosopher in verse than a true poet, but the Indians succeeded in utilizing both the aesthetic and the philosophical vision with equal success.

It is, then, within the experience of the present writer—and such an experience is certainly not eccentric—that admirable and aesthetically gratifying as Bhavabhūti's and Sūdraka's works are, each in itself when pondered continuously leaves the mind conscious of a considerable want. The brittleness and contrivance of the *Prakarana* gratifies aesthetically but fails to suffice spiritually ; the surface glitters but there is insufficient depth. The warmth and depth of this *Nātaka* also leads to gratifying art but the spirit cannot thrive continuously in a region so taxing to the emotions, so negligent in its revelations of the material world and its material problems as viewed by the intellectual and moral consciousness. Yet one play with its particular realm is strongly complementary to the other. Two partial regions constitute one vision that seems remarkably a whole.

Thus far, the Indian view resembles the Greek. From the variety of his parts the whole man is constructed. Much of positive gain is achieved on each extreme. The equilibrium of the mean itself is best established only where the extremes have been thoroughly explored. In Western terms, if the mind does not extend itself in the seemingly contradictory directions of both tragedy and comedy, it suffers from incompletion and disproportion. In Eastern terms, if the mind does not extend itself in the opposed directions of both the *Nātaka* and the *Prakarana*, it suffers similarly. Each civilization has achieved a formula holding the contrasted elements of our ironically composed human nature in equipoise. Accordingly, even the most moving aesthetic experiences spring from essentially biased types of thinking. A limiting aestheticism, regarding only the perfection of individual art works, too often conceals the deeper meanings of artistic or imaginative experience. Our natures crave scope and flourish only in its fulfillment. Art in a sense divides what religion and philosophy combine. But art also embraces possibly an even wider scope than religion or philosophy and hence best expresses a civilization. This breadth is disclosed by the radically disparate qualities of the art types themselves. A successful culture must be described not only as one producing many admirable works of art but as one providing different types of art which support each other and so produce within the architecture of the spirit a harmonious and proportioned life.

That these reflections spring naturally from a contrast between two outstanding Indian plays further suggests some general comments on Indian thought and the fruits of Indian imagination in contrast with art and theory in the West. Speculation on the relation of Western tragedy and comedy has often led to rather surprising conclusions regarding the extensive common ground between these two dramatic modes so deeply significant for the Western World. Molière and Racine are found to share much in common. The world of Shakespearean comedy proves not as different from that of Shakespearean tragedy as first supposed. The song serving as epilogue for *Twelfth Night* is echoed in *King Lear*. Here are not the areas of that extreme specialization so often undeniably characterizing Western thought.

Conversely, the tendency to unity strongly prevalent in the East, as in the synthesis of the various arts themselves under the guidance of both religious and aesthetic controls, might lead to the erroneous presumption that the grave and light in Indian drama would stand closer together than the most nearly comparable forms, as tragedy and comedy, in the West. Religious and often erotic elements, factors assuming in literary terms qualities of the romantic, undeniably override the boundaries or classifications of the types of Indian drama. Yet a gulf as wide as that separating Bhavabhūti's play and Sūdraka's is hard to discover among the dramas of Europe. The possible strangeness of this conclusion may, as already indicated, be relieved by a consideration readily expressed in terms more physical than merely metaphorical. Europe and the West are temperate ; India is tropical. And climate is in nature an analogue to the emotional life in man. The seasons are, perhaps equally contrasted in the two regions, the chief seasonal discrepancies in one instance lying primarily in temperature, in the other, in humidity. But the tropical soul appears to Western eyes violent and uninhibited. In India heart and mind may join in the most extreme intimacy ; they also may draw apart to great distances. There is observable a basic unreserve, a capacity, for example, for the utmost extremes of worldliness and other-worldliness, of flesh and spirit, of sensuality and contemplation. The oracle of the heart is seldom if ever heard with the purity and distinctness in Western drama with which it is heard in Bhavabhūti's masterpiece. Similarly, the dramatic mind as the mind of purely imaginative and intuitive wit or invention is seldom encountered in Western drama as fully as in Sūdraka's play. Tragedy and satirical comedy are certainly better represented in the West. Indeed, the East is often said, and no doubt rightly, to have no tragedy ; and the problem play, the play which is, in Matthew Arnold's words, a criticism of life, the prevailingly intellectual type of serious comedy, is almost equally foreign to the Indian mind, which has produced neither a *Hamlet* nor a *Candida*. Sanskrit drama offers us no *Oedipus Rex* and no *Lysistrata*, no *Andromache* and no *Enemy of the People*. But in their own terms the Sanskrit playwrights draw still further apart from one another. The greatest Western tragedy is commonly austere, philosophical, bitter ; the greatest Western comedy, commonly dry, reflective, tart, and also satirical. Our deepest tragedy is a satire on impersonal fate, our highest comedy, a satire on social man. In all these terms the West combines where the East divides. We are here in a totally different area of discourse from that in the chapter in this book devoted to *The Little Clay Cart*. There the East appeared synthetic and the West analytical. Here the tables are reversed.

Little doubt arises as to the desirability of representing the *Prakarana* by *The Little Clay Cart*. The choice of *Rāma's Later History* to represent the *Nātaka* may be less obviously desirable. Although a few Indian scholars themselves seem actually to prefer this play to any drama whatsoever, in the popular mind of both East and West Kālidāsa's *Shakuntalā* is better loved. It has certainly been more often seen in production and more widely read in translation. Undeniably Kālidāsa is the more suave and polished of the two poets, though possibly not the more powerfully imaginative in his playwriting. Almost beyond question *Shakuntalā* stands a test for formal perfection that *Rāma's Later History* will not withstand. Each line of Kālidāsa's work seems essential. That play, when seriously considered, defies really successful abridgment and one can scarcely conceive any addition or alteration which could improve it on its own terms. But in some respects it resembles the pastoral poetry of the West, as Bhavabhūti's play comes closer to the majesty of high tragedy. One play strikes us as on its surface a romance, the other, as on its surface a courtly epic. One, to be more specific, has many affinities with the Greek pastoral romances, is, in fact, astonishingly Alexandrian ; the other is, of course, itself a dramatization of one of the world's most eloquent epics, the *Rāmāyana*. Where Indian drama is secular, it is likely to have at least a tint of the Hellenistic ; where it is the most religious, it is likely to be the most profoundly indigenous. Seen from quite a different angle, Kālidāsa's profound and exquisite play expresses traditional Indian attitudes toward sex very difficult to reveal clearly in an English translation or to present on a Western stage in a production uncontaminated by Western romantic views of the same subject, diluted by bourgeois sentimentality. It is transported in a highly debauched form with great facility and appalling results. How often has an unlucky Shakuntalā, in a new exile, stepped unto the Western stage not as an Indian woman but as a sentimental, pre-Raphaelite maiden or as a German musical-comedy heroine ! However great may be its own proper merits—and they are assuredly very high—*Shakuntalā* is not the ideal anti-type to *The Little Clay Cart*. That condition is almost perfectly fulfilled by Bhavabhūti's great play.

A few words must be added to this general introduction. The reader should not infer that the two plays examined here are in a really strict sense representative of large groups of plays preserved in Sanskrit. They are, to begin with, quite superior. No *Prakarana* seriously rivals *The Little Clay Cart*. There are relatively few truly eminent *Nātaka*. Closest in spirit to *Rāma's Later History* is, presumably, Kālidāsa's drama in the manner of the courtly epic, his *Vikramorvacī*. Nevertheless, in a broad sense, more philosophical than aesthetic, the two works here examined faithfully represent the best of Indian drama and dramatic poetry. To describe their meaning, some collation with the larger aspects of cultural, literary and dramatic history has been required. But from such broad considerations we must now pass to more specific comments, more clearly pertinent to the requirements of theatrical production.

In a large number of their qualities Bhavabhūti's play and Sūdraka's stand at opposite poles. Plot and theme in Bhavabhūti's work are remarkably simplified. His play strongly suggests Racine's maxim, that dramatic art consists in making the most out of the most severely restricted subject matter. Grandeur is achieved by fidelity to a simple, austerely contained theme. In keeping with such a precept, the play really has no plot and reduces narrative to an absolute minimum. Little occurs and that little is not willed by mortal man. Half-way through the final act Rāma and Sītā stand almost precisely where they stood at the end of the first act. There is only one event, brought about more by the will of fate than by any human will. Sītā is separated from her husband and twelve years later reunited. The first act depicts the episode of their separation. Acts Two and Three exist in large part to depict Rāma's grief, though Sītā's unhappiness is also shown in Act Three. Act Four adds the grief of the parents and, towards its close, introduces one of the twin sons whom Sītā has born to Rāma during their separation. Act Five and the first part of Act Six transfer the center of attention to Rāma's younger son, Lava. In Act Six Rāma himself reappears, now in warlike guise, but still overcome with grief because of the long divorcement. In Act Seven a play-within-a-play is presented which deals with Sītā's adventures for the last twelve years. In this production she plays the role of herself. By this path of indirection the lovers are finally brought together once more. The philosophical inference of Act Seven is that the wise, like the poet and sage Vālmīki, regard life itself as a play. Wisdom, in short, lies in the measure of detachment. Art is midway between reality and *Nirvana*. One recalls that Shakespeare declared "All the world's a stage," and Calderón, "Life Is a Dream".

During almost all Bhavabhūti's own play the two chief figures remain essentially passive, acted upon rather than acting. As a result, the pathetic takes precedence over the heroic—though both modes are certainly present. To be specific, Rāma and Sītā exemplify the pathetic sentiment, Lava and his brother, Kusa, the heroic. Rāma's only action of consequence is a strangely unheroic one as well as essentially subordinate. To lure him into the forest where he lived happily with Sītā during the period of their youthful love, when they shared exile in common, the deities have arranged that Rāma shall perform the ceremonious act of decapitating an ascetic to nullify an offense against the gods occasioned by the death of a young Brahmana. This ascetic resides in the forest of Sītā's exile. The symbolical theme of death and rebirth is present, for the youth is restored to life, as Sītā is reborn after her sojourn in the underworld. The incident is distinctly congruous and pertinent but definitely subordinate, a means to an end. Of no major importance in itself, or at best a commentary on the thought of the play, it is designed to serve the purpose of returning Rāma to the forest with which he has such tender associations and to which the deities also beguile Sītā, so that she may again see her husband. As he is thinking of her, the forest recalling her all the more vividly to mind, he hears her voice. A magic spell is cast over her which tantalizes him, rendering him still more melancholy at his loss and so preparing him emotionally for the joy of their ultimate reunion. Fate is coy and so excites passion. Sītā is made invisible. Clearly, this is psychological drama, not the drama of action. The scene abounds in many eloquent gestures but does not tell a story. Later Rāma's appearance, in Act Six, serves, as if by magic, to pacify the angry and eminently adolescent Lava. His appearance thwarts action ; it does not promote it.

The play, then, is a magnification of the majesty of the family, celebrating the devotion between man and wife, their common cause in their devotion to their children, and, to a less degree, the love and veneration of offspring for their parents. The theme of separation and reunion is somewhat like that in Shakespeare's retelling of a Greek pastoral romance in *The Winter's Tale*. Not only is the action simplified to a phenomenal degree ; the senti-ment is similarly concentrated and distilled. There is but one overmastering sentiment : the longing and the love of a man and a woman for each other and for their offspring. There is really no secondary theme and certainly no secondary plot. The nearest approach to the latter is the brief, curious, and already mentioned episode of the decapitated ascetic. The most impressive variation on the theme of family sanctity lies in the introduction of the elders in the families of both Rāma and Sītā, as seen in Act Four. They repeat the theme, so to speak, on the double bass. The grandparents are as devoted to their offspring as Rāma and Sītā are in turn to theirs. Moreover, the elders exist strictly as choral, not as active, figures. They sorrow with the sorrowful and rejoice with the rejoicing. They contribute also to still another variation of the major theme : the juxtaposition of older and younger gene-rations. The dramatic force of this highly calculated counterpoint appears in the arrangement of the fourth act itself, the first half of which introduces the elders, the second half, the youngsters, an unruly crowd led by Lava. The play presents the ages of man somewhat as the art of William Blake, where graybeards and children, or infants, so often stand side by side.

This concentration upon the prevailing sentiment and thus upon the emotional element in experience further appears in the drastic pushing aside of a factor in the story which the modern, or Western, mind, would presumably find insistent, the political —a feature already mentioned but sufficiently important to be restated and enlarged. Rāma sends Sītā into exile because "the citizens and country-people" insist upon this divorce. They assume that the queen has been corrupted while in captivity under Rāvana and is, therefore, unfit to be the wife of their sovereign. Rāma asserts the principle that he must yield to the popular will. The Western mind is likely, of course, to call the underlying propositions into question. From this point of view the play begins with excellent materials for a problem play. Nothing, however, could be further from Bhavabhūti's mind. True, some hint is thrown out that Rāma's action may not be entirely justified and especially that he might have behaved otherwise if at the crucial moment the elders had been present to advise him and qualify his precipitate decision. Even the deeply devoted Sītā herself shows at least a shadow of dissent. But on the whole the deed is relegated to the status of an assumption ; Rāma is defended as a hero who, if not utterly faultless, is all but faultless ; attention passes with the most remarkable abruptness from the moral or political to the purely emotional realm. Not only is there no struggle between Rāma and Sītā ; save for the radical differences proceeding from sex, there are virtually no distinctions. Sītā's feelings are to a large extent merely the duplicates or reflections of Rāma's, a condition specifically stated by Bhavabhūti in a quotation from the *Rāmāyana*. It is almost as though he stood beside a pool of smooth water, her heart the reflected image of his. Or the converse might be asserted with almost equal justice ; if one prefers to view the play as a celebration of the goddess rather than of the god, it is his heart that reflects hers. Both are, of course, descended from immortals, he from the race of the sun ; she, from that of earth and water. Air and fire meet water and earth. Who will say which elements are the mightier ? As woman and wife, Sītā is subordinate to her husband ; as the feminine principle in the universe she is his equal or even superior. Notably it is on her behalf that the gods seem the most pleased to intervene.

In more then a figurative sense, then, the two lovers are the equivalents of each other. They share the same joys and sorrows, are, in fact, variations on a single idea. The play is in no sense a story of domestic conflict, of ironical contentions between contrasted and opposing forces. It is incomparably spectacular but hardly dramatic in a familiar Western definition of the term. It is at heart as lyrical as a bird's egg. As no opposition exists between man and woman, so no opposition exists between protagonist and antagonist, hero or villain. Consider the distinction here between Bhavabhūti's play and Sūdraka's. In *The Little Clay Cart* Samsthānaka is the foil to Chārudatta. In many respects, for example, as regards poverty and opulence, Chārudatta and his fabulous hetaera, Vasantasēnā, are contrasted. He signifies the very winter of discontent ; her name itself signifies spring. Bhavabhūti's play, *The Adventures of Rāma*, to which *Rāma's Later History* is, in a sense, a equel, is incomparably more epic and less lyric than this. The earlier work has at least an Oriental villain, Rāvana, and many secondary heroes and villains, with plot and counter-plot, brother set against brother, enmeshed in all varieties of internecine strife. The full irony of epic and heroic narrative is transferred from the *Rāmīyana* into its scenes. Complexity is of its essence, as a most sophisticated simplicity is, in turn, the soul of *Rāma's Later History*.

Once more the contrast with *The Little Clay Cart* proves the most striking and instructive. Few plays rival Sūdraka's in drawing apparently disparate themes into a final concord. An uncommonly large number of characters, incidents and their accompanying ideas are at length resolved into a perfect harmony. The spectator —or reader—is kept jumping from moment to moment between widely deployed materials. Moods change not only between the acts but within them and with the utmost abruptness. In all the arts few parallels can be educed for such virtuosity or plasticity, unless it be in the major compositions of Ludwig von Beethoven. Sūdraka's story thus proves highly complicated and contrived. These contrivances further result in a super-melodramatic con-clusion. A piquant discrepancy exists between the realism of image and detail, together with the almost photographic picturing of manners, and the enormously artifical narrative. Sūdraka's play is intensely human, all the more so because humanity is represented as irrational, though fate imposes a strict order upon this irresponsible human world. The extreme diversity in similes and metaphors reflects even in the style this passion for abundance and diversity. Sūdraka is the most Shakespearean of Asian drama-tists. His unreal-realism even suggests the super-contrived natura-lism of Charles Dickens, and Act Nine of *Thé Little Clay Cart* is not as far removed as might be supposed from the great melodram-atic trial scene in *The Pickwick Papers*. There is a paradox here. From a psychologist's point of view, *The Little Clay Cart* is classical and *Rāma's Later History* romantic. The wit of the one is as dry as Molière's *Le Bourgeois Gentilhomme*, the sentiment of the other, as exaggerated as Goethe's *Die Leiden des Jugen Werthers*. From the point of view of the aesthetician, however, the organization of Sūdraka's play, with its passion for paradox, is completely romantic, whereas the organization of Bhavabhūti's play, with its extraordinary economy, is completely classical. One is a moving picture, the other, a still picture ; one a fantasy, the other a fugue. Examined from a slightly different angle : in English translations of Bhavabhūti's masterpiece, the two leading characters are described as repeatedly plunged into a state of "swoon." In actual presentation these incidents were, as we have seen, highly stylized, the action frozen into a tableau. But if the hero or heroine swoons, the playwright emphatically does not. No poet or playwright has walked a straighter line to his goal. His art, aesthetically considered, is undeviating perfection. It is also emotionally gratifying. Both Sūdraka and Bhavabhūti are consumate craftsmen, achieving constructions of the utmost firmness and stability. Each knows precisely what he desires and just what routes to take to his goal. No scheme of values adequately appraises their relative merit, for the ultimate end of art, which both attain, is reached by totally different and completely incomparable paths. One playwright works on the broadest surfaces, as a mural painter, the other, on a limited surface, as a cabinet painter, never too minute to be insignificant yet never sufficiently commodious to be expansive or abundant. One would no more compare Bhavabhūti with Sūdraka than Chardin with Orozco, or Mozart with Wagner.

Being dramatists in a single major tradition, that of the Indian stage at its height, the two Sanskrit masters still share much of significance in common. The differences are finite and specific, the similarities, infinite and various. Among the more instructive likenesses is the division of each play into two parts. *Rāma's Later History*, as already seen, consists of seven acts, with the division, as in the case of *The Little Clay Cart*, approximately half-way through its course, that is, at the conclusion of the relatively long Act Three. Especially underlining this arrangement is the benediction at the end of this act, an unusual feature in Sanskrit playwriting. The first half is distinctly elegiac and retrospective, its ruling sentiment melancholy. Frustration and suffering mark virtually all its scenes. Little exhilaration is obtainable from the episode of the decapitation of the ascetic, where Rāma is as loth to strike the fated blow as he was earlier to exile Sītā. The long review of Rāma's history as witnessed in the murals of his palace, which might have been expected to glow with the pride of life, unexpectedly reveals much more that is painful or embarrassing than invigorating or heroic. The pictures are shown to relieve Sītā's grief at her parents' absence. Like the rest of the play, the episode is a miracle of subtlety, nuance and inuendo. As Sītā and Rāma look on their adventures, two sentiments chiefly stir them : sadness that their joys are so deeply of the past, faded in memory, and grief that their sorrows are so omnipresent, like wounds that smart and refuse to heal. The audience, with a foreseeing eye, detects irony in every turn of the talk. The characters inhabit an impending doom which they themselves do not understand but whose chill reaches them, felt but not seen. Among Sītā's first words are her petition to revisit once more the scenes of their youthful love together in their forest exile. The irony is, of course, that at the end of the scene she will start, riding in her smooth carriage, to this very scene, with death and not life hovering over her. The lovers seem to live in a dream world ; all is unreal and all symbolical of evil ; the orchestration is superb.

In this play, as in *The Little Clay Cart*, there are three scenes of supreme counterpoint, and they fall in the corresponding places in the two works. In *Rāma's Later History* they are Acts One, Three, and Seven, in *The Little Clay Cart*, Acts One, Five, and Ten. In Bhavabhūti's earlier play, *The Adventures of Rāma*, there is absolutely nothing of the severe structure or the metaphysical poetry found in the poet's masterpiece. There events are insistently in the present tense, imminent, excitingly new from day to day and hour to hour. In the sequel even from the first lines melancholy broodings over past events or forebodings for the future predominate. The melancholy rules Acts One, Two and Three, and continues through those parts of Acts Four, Six and Seven where Rāma's fate remains in the shadow. With Act Four, however, we meet the confluence of another stream of sentiment, or mood.

The play's action occurs largely, or even wholly, on two days, separated by twelve years. The first day is the First Act, ending with Sītā's banishment. The second day is determined by the initiation ceremony of the children of Rāma and Sītā into manhood. Although in point of time Acts Two and Three belong with the later period, in the all-important matter of sentiment they adhere to the first half of Bhavabhūti's design. In Act One, or "The Picture Gallery", the spirit is retrospective and virtually un-relieved in its gloom. In Acts Two and Three this gloom deepens, reaching its extreme in the finale. As figures in their own right the hero and heroine thus far seem capable of little or no joy. Destiny has left their lives in ruin. Their tragedy is, if anything, even dark-ened by the intense melancholy and frozen retrospection of the early episode in Act Four, where the lovers do not appear. This episode depicts the older members of both their families. Grief settles down more grimly with the prolongation of life itself. Then, with the utmost abruptness, the sky clears. The heroic, or epic, spirit invades the pathetic. One of the grandparents knows the secret : that Sītā and her children live and are destined in time to reunion with Rāma. Which of the twins stands before her, however, on her seeing Lava she does not know. But on beholding this beautiful and ardent boy all the elders experience a sudden burst of joy. Lava is the very soul of activity, the pride of life, the faith in it, the spontaneous delight in generous deeds. He is described as Rāma before Rāma's agony overtook him. The play, accordingly, changes from the most bleak introspection to the most animated action. Attention focuses on a defiant, restive, arro-gant adolescent. Presently the stage also holds his older brother, Kusa, and Lava's chivalrous rival, young Chandrakētu, who, though the relationship is as yet unknown, is their cousin. Chand-rakētu is son of Lakshmana, Rāma's devoted friend and younger brother. The style and the entire spirit of the play is immediately revolutionized. The spirited description of the horse sets the new key by way of metaphor. A brilliant battle takes place, with much heroic—or operatic—display of war's splendor and nothing of its agony or physical and moral deformities. The struggle is actually more a display of magic than of arms : the weapons of stupefaction petrify the warriors into inaction ; those of fire and water more resemble a brilliant display of the aurora borealis than any missiles of actual warfare. The youthful champions confront each other with the most generous sentiments and fiery courage. They even speak in consort. No one whom we know or see is hurt. Although Rāma is still pressed down with grief at his loss of Sītā, his grief is partly assuaged by his instantaneous and spontaneous affection for his sons, whose identity remains as yet unknown to him. Even his sorrow for his lost wife becomes partially eclipsed by this delight, on the one hand, in the sight of the boys, and, on the other hand, by a flattering hope that they may actually be his sons. Or rather, that they might have been his sons—this further thought in turn rendering him once more aware of his loss of Sītā and of his own childless state. With each fluctuation of faith and doubt, the tension heightens between hope and despair. Rāma's deepest despair, his final swoon on witnessing Sītā's sufferings in the play-within-the-play, marks his deepest misery ; his recovery, a moment afterwards, of both Sītā and his lost children is his final and ultimate joy. The frozen melancholy of the first half of the play has been left behind in the greater portion of the second part. The play thus presents a simple transition between midnight and sunrise. The first half is midnight, the second, a dramatic sunrise, beginning in a dim twilight, advancing through alternating moments of the lustre of hope and the clouds of doubt, and concluding with the dispersal of the clouds and the triumph of Rāma, who belongs himself to the family of the Sun, the Sun being his majestic ancestor. The entire play is a long, almost incredibly sophisticated montage. "Three Travellers Watch a Sunrise," is the title of a short play in the oriental manner by Wallace Stevens. "An Audience Watches a Sunrise" might be at least a descriptive title for Bhava-bhūti's drama. Before sunrise is the midnight storm in the forested mountains. The play may also be likened to a musical composition in seven movements, the third, a prolonged adagio, the finale, a brilliant allegro symbolizing the glorification of Rāma's kingly race and more especially his family, constituting himself, Sītā, and their two offspring. Or Act One is a trio, Act Three, a quartet, Act Seven, a score for the full orchestra. The entire closely wrought work may even be regarded as a gigantic lyric turned drama, or, in historical perspective, as a Renaissance mask in honor of a Sun Monarch. In the last case, the meaningful distinction must be that the Sanskrit play expresses a vital religion and a living mytho-logy, an interpretation of essential and universal man, whereas the Renaissance mask too seldom rises above the flattery of a prince, couched in imagery from a mythology at the time of compo-sition merely literary and spiritually outlived. In such an instance there is small occasion for India to bow its head before an arrogant Bacchus marching in triumph out of the West. Rather, it is for the West to drink at a deeper and clearer fountain.

The style of acting in such a play must be more than merely

stylized ; it must clearly be dream-like, visionary, liturgical. The first principle to be considered is that little occurs that is occurring as a simple, imminent and direct action. By far the greater part of the play, as we have seen, deals not with the present—as most plays do—but with past and future, with memory and prophecy. Act One is a trance of recollection. The characters examine the paintings that are, theatrically considered, wholly imaginary. Woe to a director who should hang pictorial curtains on the stage ! The speakers actually survey their past not on painted cloth or wall but in the mind's eye. There is a complete analogy between Acts One and Seven. In the one, the past of the characters is seen in paintings ; in the other, in the play-within-the-play. In each case the art proves so potent that they forget that it is art and instead fancy themselves transported, as it were, into themselves. So strong is Sītā's conviction, that she expresses her desire to return to the magical forest of her first year of married life. The scene in Act One is further laden with incidents prophetic for several later acts. Sītā is, of course, herself pregnant. From her husband she extracts the promise that their sons shall inherit the miraculous weapons which Lava employs later against his father's army. The scene is weighted on every side with thoughts significant for the imagination.

The action must furthermore be stylized because so many of the characters are superhuman and, indeed, the entire play lives within the element of myth. The choral figures are divine or, at the very least, demi-gods. These include the forest goddess, Vāsantī, protectress of the Forest of Janasthāna to which Rāma and Sītā resort, the principal choral figure in Act Two ; the two river goddesses, Tamasā and Murala, the choral figures in Act Three ; and the male and female spirits of the air, who in Act Six describe, with such ecstatic joy, the miraculous warfare between Lava and the young Chandrakētu, the latter supported by his multitudinous army. The play-within-the-play in Act Seven is presented by *Apsaras*, or angels, and itself represents divine beings. Foremost of these are Sītā's two protectresses, Prithvī, goddess of the earth, and Ganga, or Bhāgīrathī, goddess of the River Ganges. In this episode Sītā herself appears primarily in her divine aspect. While immersed in the waters of the Ganges she gives birth to twins ; she has herself been on a protracted visit to the underworld. Such figures are as far removed from any possible naturalistic representation as the deities in romantic compositions by Southey or Shelley, as, for example, those in *Prometheus Unbound*, which were in their turn largely suggested on the basis of the new discoveries of Hindu mythology, poetry and drama just made in the West. When one recalls the figure, Asia, in Shelley's remarkable play, it seems hardly excessive to remark that for Shelley it was Asia who undid Prometheus' chains. Incidentally, the early translations of *Shakuntalā* played a perceptible role in the unfolding of the romantic movements in both England and Germany. For such supernatural scenes and personages as these Indian plays contain, naturalistic acting becomes virtually impossible. The mirror that is held to nature here is the mirror of imagination, not the lesser lense of mimicry. Much of the speech is in lyrical stanzas and most of it in Sanskrit. The actors require movements heavily indebted to dancing. Instrumental music must have played a considerable part in the scenes and the stanzas themselves were no doubt intoned though not actually sung.

All the passages just referred to as choral are worked with high skill into the texture of Bhavabhūti's play. As Rāma mistakes pictures for actuality in the first act, he mistakes actors for real persons in the last. The *Rāmāyana* and the play, equally indebted to mythology, are thrown into fascinating and highly unusual relations. Characters in the play are imagined as having read the poem and thus become, as it were, preacquainted with each other. It is truly a Pirandellesque world! Emotionally moving and delicate in perception is the passage at the conclusion of Act Six in which Lava and Kusa recite to Rāma passages from the epic dealing with the mutual affection between Rāma and Sītā, the boys themselves being unaware that it is their parents of whom they speak. The divinities of the rivers and the earth join in the general action and converse with human beings. The two aerial spirits in Act Six are less social but no less intimately involved in human affairs. The heat of human warfare becomes so intense that the male spirit is forced to shield the female spirit, his mistress, from its ardent blaze. The passage is, of course, descriptive but also demands vigorous and sharply controlled action. It is almost as choreographic as poetic. Such descriptive poetry nowhere brings action to a halt. Rather, it impells it over bridges, as the spirits of the other world transport Dante in vision from one to another circle of Paradise, Purgatory, or Hell.

Act Two, like Act One, divides the claims of retrospection and of prophecy. There is barely the hint of an action. Rāma appears in his magic chariot, his sword drawn, having, it seems, just decapitated the ascetic who enters in his celestial state, with his head returned to his shoulders and considerable volubility on his tongue. They discuss events past and to come, especially the miraculous resurrection of a slain Brahman youth which Rāma has achieved by his act of violence against the ascetic. The death offstage complies with the theory of Sanskrit drama no less than with that of Greek. Incidentally, the infatuation that decapitation held for Yeats as a playwright is oddly suggested by this episode. The ascetic has lived in the woods that were the scene of Rāma's original exile with Sītā. It is with this landscape that the talk between Rāma and the celestial spirit of the ascetic is now concerned, not for the sake of the forest as seen in itself but for what it signified for human beings years before' and for what it will signify in succeeding scenes of the play when Rāma first partially and at last completely recovers Sītā.

The remarkable Act Three is retrospective with further mysterious accretions. It is a quartet, mimed, spoken, embodied, heard, the instruments being two heroic mortals and two demi-gods. Rāma relives his past. The audience—and the major gods—know of his complete reunion with Sītā that is still to come through the mediation of their children, who hold the key to all the play's action and morality. But for the time being we see nothing of the children. Sītā, of course, knows their existence. Rāma knows nothing. Sītā is under her spell of invisibility. Neither Rāma nor his friend, the woodland goddess, Vāsantī, can see her. He only hears her, causing him to imagine her presence which, however, he holds to be impossible as reality. She both sees and hears him but obviously cannot consort with him openly. Thrice they touch ; on each occasion Rāma is recovered from his swoon but on each occasion he concludes that their physical contact has been a dream. This is the metaphysical theme first powerfully injected into Sanskrit drama, so far as we are cognizant of its history, by Bhāsa's *Vision of Vāsavadattā*. The entire act must obviously be played with trance-like movements. Its unity of conception is exquisitely and with much sophistication explained in concluding remarks by Sītā's confidante, the River Goddess, Tamasā : "Oh wonderful is the arrangement of incidents ! The pathetic sentiment, though

one in itself, being modified by various occasions, seems to assume
different forms, as water assumes the various modifications of
eddies, bubbles, and waves and it is all, nevertheless, only water."
Bhavabhūti was well justified in throwing himself this bouquet
at the end of a scene of such incomparable virtuosity. The final
benediction of the act is spoken simultaneously by the two goddesses, one of the forest, the other of the stream.

This essentially ritualistic character of the play is further evinced
by the discussion of the rituals of hospitality with which Act
Four opens. The early scene here, presenting the grief of the elder
members of the families of Rāma and Sīta, is a choral *planctus*, or
lament, varied with some undercurrent of anger at Rāma's precipitate action of twelve years past. We have reached the middle of
Act Four, precisely the play's center. Then, in rapid succession,
follow the scene with Lava and his young playmates and Act Five,
or the contention between Lava and Chandrakētu, which is the
simplest of the acts in its conception and is pure military splendor,
morally heightened by a strong note of chivalry. All its action
remains ceremonious and basically choreographic, calling for
theatrical magnificence and display at its highest and best. Vast
multitudes are imagined as engaged. Something may well be
thrown to indicate the fall of flowers, missiles, fire and water. The
English reader may be reminded of the barrage of red roses symbolizing the wounds of Christ which good spirits throw at attacking
demons in the ballet-like scene of the medieval mystery play, *The
Castle of Perseverance*. Personification is also evident in the Sanskrit drama. Several small groups of dancers, as in the case of the
missiles, are required. Pantomime depicting mounting and dis-
mounting from imaginary chariots contributes considerably to the
ceremonious effect. But the production even here must keep lavish-
ness under strict control. The Indian stage welcomes splendor
but still more ardently demands imagination and moreover requires
that much more shall always be felt than seen. Opulence and
frugality must meet, as Vasantasēnā, the mistress of abundance,
embraces Chārudatta, a master even in poverty.

Few plays demand so much from the imagination of all concerned,
as the reader, the actor, the producer, and the stage designer.
The first words of the final act sufficiently indicate the almost
unprecedented scope of these demands. Lakshmana, Rāma's
brother, declares : "The revered Vālmīki having summoned to-

187

gether with us the people including Brahmaṇas, Kshatrīyas, citizens and country people, by his power has placed here the whole world of creatures movable and immovable, consisting of the host of the chiefs of the gods, demons, animals, and serpents." This astonishing assembly is to witness a play performed by the *Apsaras*, or angelic beings. Further on in the act occur lines presenting still graver problems for production. A Voice behind the scenes exclaims : "Remove the musical instruments ! O creatures, including both animate and inanimate ones, mortals and immortals, behold now a holy miracle ordained by the great sage, the venerable Vālmikī." Lakshmaṇa's words explain the event : "The water of the Ganges is agitated as if churned, and the sky is crowded with divine sages. Wonderful ! the noble queen together with the goddesses Ganga and Earth rises from the water." It is to be noted that Sītā does not descend from the sky, as the typical *deus ex machina ;* she rises from the waves, supported by the goddesses of earth and water, each bearing a child in her arms.

All this obviously indicates a highly elaborate spectacle, though failing to reveal its precise theatrical character. The musical instruments are removed apparently to make room for an exceptionally large assemblage on the stage. Whether the musicians left as well is open to question. Vocal music might have been heard, though it seems more likely that the instruments were to be played behind the stage, which is itself evidently crowded with as many figures of as many types as possible. All beings are supposed present by proxy, the outstanding groups represented by their leaders. Children and the aged, beasts, birds, serpents, demons, and angelic spirits, are at hand, together with the gods and men and women, both secular and divine. Possibly the leading characters in the play crowd into the sides to make way for the play-within-the-play. The stage must be ablaze with symbolical colors. Trap doors were probably not used to depict Sītā's emergence from the river or her travel to the underworld. The style of the acting should unquestionably be strongly choreographic, especially in the inner play.

Almost continually from the beginning of Act Four to the play's end, or, in other words, throughout the second part, the stage is crowded, This is, of course, in sharp and deliberate contrast with the first part. The longest scene in that section is the quartet in Act Three, with Rāma and Vāsantī on one side of the stage and

Sītā and Tamasā on the other. The scene most nearly approaching its length and importance is the visit to the picture gallery, which presents a trio consisting of Rāma, Sītā, and Lakshmana. Throughout this half of the work a comparatively intimate style of acting is in request.

Most passages in this play are rythmical in more respects than one. An exceptional quantity of heroic verse occurs. From time to time characters speak the same words simultaneously, as the two goddesses at the conclusion of Act Three, or Lava and Chandraketu just before their engagement in Act Six. Stanzas are repeated at calculated intervals, much as in the procession scene in *The Little Clay Cart*. Episodes are meticulously balanced, as the passages of reminiscence in the astonishing Third Act. Regardless of the amount of music actually heard, this is obviously a strongly lyric theatre, a condition of prime importance for the production to express.

The First and Third Acts in particular faithfully indicate still another of the play's outstanding characteristics. As in such Shakespearean plays as *A Midsummer-Night's Dream, The Tempest, Macbeth*, and *Antony and Cleopatra*, but to a far greater degree, a considerable proportion of the speeches is descriptive poetry. A landscape is evoked in a manner that nevertheless proves highly dramatic. Like the three heroines in Kālidāsa's three extant dramas, Sītā embodies natural forces ; she is born, like rice or grain, from the earth, and herself gives birth while immersed in a great river. Kālidāsa's figures, who are brighter, more cheerful, more youthful, and more a pure pleasure to contemplate, have a firmer association with the spring. Sītā seems rather a harvest image ; the burning hues of autumn, at times fierce, at times inclining to the sombre, befit her. Shadows fall thickly about her. She loves dense forests, the dark, rapidly flowing streams, the high mountains with their strong shadows. Acts Two and Three are in large proportion a descriptive poetry deftly merged into the development of the human situation. The human figures perform but few violent actions. They imagine that they see the past in the present, or better, that a double exposure in time takes place. The birds, beasts and trees are those known to them a dozen years ago and are now inevitably changed with the course of years. All have grown older in this pathetic tale of knowledge won by suffering. The scenery lies in the mind's eye of the audience yet on this account is all the more powerful than were it depicted on a series of painted cloths or pictures on a moving film. To Indian audiences this highly demanding technique constituted a favorite and familiar course whereas to Western audiences it must at first appear strange. Yet the idea is executed so powerfully that keen enjoyment is still possible. After all, as previously urged, these are matters of degree. Most drama of the romantic period from Goethe to Ibsen, or, one may prefer to say, all the way from *Faust* to *Uncle Tom's Cabin*, abounds in landscape effects. The romantics relied heavily on scenery, Shakespeare, like the Hindus, on descriptive poetry. Our Western culture knows this method though has by no means utilized it in such tropical abundance nor with such sophisticated nuances as the Sanskrit stage.

Rāma's Later History, it should further be noted, clings closer to earth than many celebrated Sanskrit plays; it contains fewer passages with scenes laid in the sky and amidst the clouds than other works. The famous aerial view of earth in the scene with the airborne chariot in *Shakuntalā*, or, for that matter, the long air journey of Rāma's chariot from Ceylon to Ayodhyā in *The Adventures of Rāma*, has no close parallel in *Rāma's Later History*. Yet Rāma himself abruptly enters from the clouds in his chariot in Act Six, and the prologue to that act is a dialogue between two winged spirits swirling through the air to mark and describe a battle-scene below them, much as aerial spirits and celestial messengers describe analogous scenes in Thomas Hardy's *The Dynasts*. Still, there is more of the earthy Hardy than of the etherial Shelley, more of the mole than of the skylark. Scenes in the later acts of Bhavabhūti's play are on a sublime scale. Although air remains a vital element, on the whole the work is distinguished for its forest scenes, its terrestrial images; rich colors suggesting earth or water in a sunset light may invest it best.

The time-scheme, with its scenes occurring principally on two days twelve years apart, poses questions of costume and make-up. Sītā grows from a young woman to a mature matron, exactly as do so many of the most impressive of Sanskrit dramatic heroines, as Shakuntalā and Urvacī. During her exile Sītā, divorced from common mortals, has consorted with gods and sages. She has herself grown increasingly into her role as a divinity and a divinity more in sadness than in joy. In Act One she should, then, appear as a young and gaily clad girl. In that act Rāma should have the outward form of a serene and youthful hero. Both are in reality suffering ; but innocence and youth are at their side. In Act Three this is much changed. Both facial make-up and costume in the forest scene must show marks of suffering and bereavement. In his triumphal entry in Act Six Rāma must, on the contrary, appear as the glittering and conquering hero. So he remains until the thought comes to him that he is without an heir and until the desperate hope that the youths who shine before him may in bare possibility be his sons reminds him once more of his unnatural, childless condition and of his crime against Sītā. Sītā in the play-within-the-play is of an ambiguous age but in any case must appear there as the desperately suffering woman in exile, not as the all-favored queen. Lava and Kusa must be imagined as dressed and made up with definite reminiscences of their father in Act One. Youth is of the essence of these warrior-twins ; they hold a highly important and indeed a crucial position in the play, which is even more a study of the recognition of father and sons than of the recovery of the lost wife and mother. Only striplings can play these roles adequately and their costume as soldiers must not conceal their boyish bodies. They are students and ascetics, educated in the holy texts, with a supplementary training in the arts of war to render them in the end wise rulers of the state and skilled leaders of armies. As previously observed, there is no villain in the play, unless it is the unseen "citizens and country people" who force Sītā into exile. Divinity is crucified by the mob, as in the Christian story. Rāma's nearest counterpart is Lava and Kusa, whose brilliance and faith in life reflect his own splendor before he became afflicted by his melancholy and sense of guilt. He fully recovers himself and secures his kingdom only on recovering them. It is as though he had recovered his own youth. Sītā, too, rejoices more warmly and spontaneously in her reunion with her children than with her lord. The roles of the boys must be played to the hilt.

Like Kālidāsa, Bhavabhūti is emphatically a poet as well as master of the theatre and, like the Kālidāsa of his own non-dramatic poems in particular, he possesses a strongly religious nature. Both art and religion are leading themes in his play and apparently occupied his thoughts as a man no less than his thoughts as a playwright. Almost in one breath Bhavabhūti invokes art and divinity, though he never equates or confuses them. Much of the

INDEX

193

INDEX

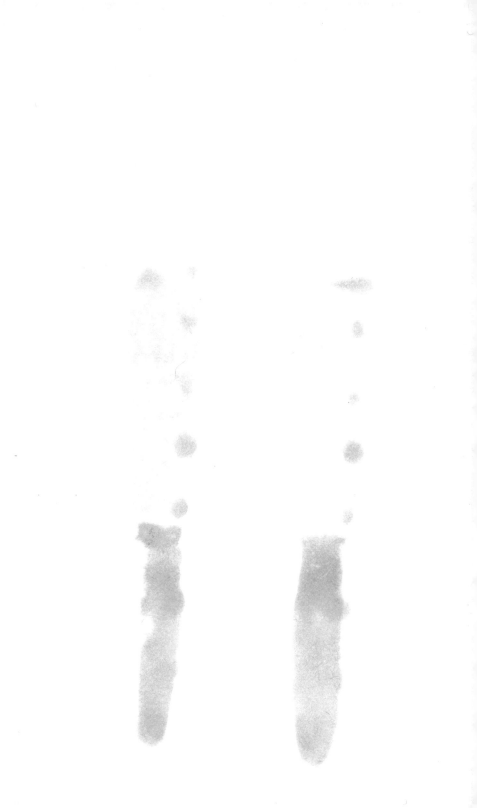

DATE DUE